little ◄ ·······
free 📖
······· ► library

NORTHERN LIGHTS LIBRARY SYSTEM

Scan me

D0955870

A BAD WOMAN FEELING GOOD

A BAD WOMAN FEELING GOOD

Blues and the Women Who Sing Them

BUZZY JACKSON

W. W. NORTON & COMPANY
NEW YORK   LONDON

Copyright © 2005 by Buzzy Jackson

For information about permission to reproduce selections from this book,
write to Permissions, W. W. Norton & Company, Inc., 500 Fifth Avenue,
New York, NY 10110

Manufacturing by Quebecor World Fairfield
Book design by Lovedog Studio
Production manager: Anna Oler

Library of Congress Cataloging-in-Publication Data

Jackson, Buzzy.
A bad woman feeling good : blues and the women who sing them / Buzzy Jackson.—
1st ed.
p. cm.
Includes bibliographical references and index.
ISBN 0-393-05936-7 (hardcover)
1. Women blues musicians—United States—Biography. 2. Blues (Music)—
History and criticism. I. Title.
ML400.J24 2005
782.421643'092'273—dc22
2004026996

W. W. Norton & Company, Inc.
500 Fifth Avenue, New York, N.Y. 10110
www.wwnorton.com

W. W. Norton & Company Ltd.
Castle House, 75/76 Wells Street, London W1T 3QT

1 2 3 4 5 6 7 8 9 0

This book is dedicated

to my parents
Ruth Baum Jackson Hall and Jon A. Jackson

to my mentor
Leon F. Litwack

and to

Ben
my sweetheart.

CONTENTS

Acknowledgments   *ix*

Introduction   *xi*

Chapter One
Bad Women—The Early Years:
Mamie Desdoumes, Sophie Tucker,
Mamie Smith, and Ma Rainey   *1*

Chapter Two
The Air and How to Fill It:
Bessie Smith, Blues Singer   *37*

Chapter Three
Jazz Noir: Billie Holiday   *85*

Chapter Four
The Devil and the Deep Blue Sea:
Etta James and Aretha Franklin   *135*

Chapter Five
The Great Saturday Night Swindle:
Tina Turner and Janis Joplin   179

Chapter Six
Blues Attitude   239

Notes   277

Credits   297

Index   299

ACKNOWLEDGMENTS

This book was originally conceived as a doctoral dissertation at the University of California, Berkeley, and the support of many people there made its completion possible. Thanks to Mabel Lee, Sandy Richmond, Heather McCarty, Laura Mihailof, and Justin Suran of the History Department; Cheryl Griffith-Peel at the Music Library; Elissa Mondschein at Interlibrary Borrowing Services; and my always supportive and inspiring doctoral dissertation committee: Leon F. Litwack, Waldo E. Martin, and Olly W. Wilson.

To Gary Morris, my friend and agent: your vision and your enthusiasm made this book possible. Thank you.

To Amy Cherry, my wonderful editor—thank you for your enthusiasm and your brilliant suggestions and for all the work you put into this book.

Thank you, Lucinda Williams and Laura Joplin, for the time you contributed to this book, and for helping me better understand the blues.

For spiritual and intellectual inspiration way back in the beginning, thanks go to my family, Ben Kirshner, the Meschery family, and Greil Marcus.

And finally, it is with deep gratitude that I acknowledge the blueswomen whose music has been such a huge part of my life these past several years. To Ma Rainey, Bessie Smith, Billie Holiday, Etta James, Aretha Franklin, Tina Turner, Janis Joplin, Joni Mitchell, Patti Smith, Courtney Love, and Lucinda Williams: You showed me the air, I tried to fill it.

INTRODUCTION

Throughout the twentieth century, a powerful tradition of American women singers has helped women everywhere find their own voices. The lives and art of these women singers set new examples, challenging the limits society had placed on women's personal achievements and expectations. These singers discovered truer versions of themselves when they broke society's rules about how women should act, look, sound, and feel. They refused to follow the rules of good behavior, and in the process earned some scandalous reputations. Bad women? Perhaps. But being good had never gotten them anywhere.

The chapters that follow are a chronicle of the influence and a testament to the very real power wielded by these women artists, a power that has often been overlooked, just as these artists have been overlooked in traditional stories about important people in American music and notable figures in American history. *A Bad Woman Feeling Good* tells a different story—one in which the names, faces, and voices are familiar, but their roles are not. The stories of these singers' lives shed light upon the changing historical context of women in the twentieth century, and their art is a window onto the inner lives of women at that time. Each generation of women found its own Bessie

Smith, Billie Holiday, or Janis Joplin, a woman willing to testify to her inner pain and pleasure.

One hundred years ago, American women singers first began cultivating their own style of music, using the blues as a medium for deep truth-telling about what it meant to be a woman. *A Bad Woman Feeling Good* starts with these first blueswomen—Mamie Desdoumes, Gertrude "Ma" Rainey, and the immortal Bessie Smith—exploring their work and phenomenal success in the early days of recording. These artistic pioneers staked out territory for women artists that provided a safe haven for strong women in the century that followed. The success of the early blueswomen was crucial to the survival of many early recording companies, and thus women laid claim to an important role in the industry from the earliest days of this new form of mass media. This role has made popular music a cultural vehicle for representations of female strength in a way that film and television have never matched. The early blueswomen were strong, sexy, aggressive, emotional, spiritual, and absolutely unashamed of their desires and demands, and so were the singers who followed them.

Singers such as Billie Holiday arrived in their wake, with an air of dark mystery that brought a sense of danger to jazz. Etta James consciously crafted a "bad girl" persona that gave new energy to 1950s rhythm and blues, and likewise Tina Turner, whose gutsy, scorching voice catapulted her husband Ike's group from dive bars in the Deep South to world tours with the Rolling Stones. Then there was Aretha Franklin, a "good girl" among bad women whose turn from gospel to rock 'n' roll created its own revolution, with a voice that spanned heaven and hell. And Janis Joplin, whose reinterpretation of the early blueswomen brought new depth to 1960s rock, and whose influence upon subsequent generations of female and male singers has yet to be fully acknowledged. From Joplin's day to the present, the blueswomen's legacy has survived in musical form but, more important, as an attitude toward life, and it can be found in the work of singers as musically diverse as Patti Smith, Lauryn Hill, Courtney Love, and

Lucinda Williams. None are traditional blues singers, but all are living examples of the heritage passed down by the early blueswomen.

While the singers profiled here have much in common, they are different, too. In a century when the realities of women's lives experienced radical change, the lives and work of each one of these singers responded to and reflected the historical context of her own time. From Ma Rainey's "Traveling Blues" (1928), which gave voice to Southern black women yearning to move north, to Janis Joplin, whose explosive 1960s concerts drew thousands of women who were, in Joplin's own words, "lookin' for liberation," this legacy of women in music identified the issues central to women's lives and insisted that the world take notice. It was Ma Rainey's piano player, Thomas Dorsey, who said, "The blues is a good woman feeling bad." The greatest American women singers wouldn't have denied it, but they took the blues and reworked it according to their own gifts, proving that there were other, equally significant contributions to be made by a bad woman feeling good.[1]

A BAD WOMAN FEELING GOOD

BAD WOMEN— THE EARLY YEARS: MAMIE DESDOUMES, SOPHIE TUCKER, MAMIE SMITH, AND MA RAINEY

1902

In some little dancehall . . . one can often hear a Negro girl singing the same melody for an hour at a time, a melody which is often shrill, but quite as perfect as any of the beautiful classic recitatives. . . . Here we are at the first sources of this music, with its deep human content which is about to create as complete a revolution as any of the masterpieces now universally recognized.

—Darius Milhaud, 1924[1]

In Some Little Dance Hall

This is the demimonde. All the way against the back wall, far from the streets outside and its throngs, a lone woman stands on a bare wooden stage, a piano player beside her as she counts off the time, two, three, four, and *I've been downhearted, baby*. . . . The demimonde, this is where the half of the world that works on being respectable loses its cool and drifts into the world's other half, which doesn't care what anyone else thinks at all. The singer, a woman (never a girl, her voice tells that much) with Africa and the New World in her blood and on her skin, smiles and sweats in the crowded, noisy room where drinking has been going on for days and weeks without stop, fearing a crackdown. There is always the specter of the Law and its foibles, even in Storyville, where prostitution is legal, drinking is legal, gambling is, well, overlooked. Storyville is a free ticket where people work for their money, not least the woman in the back of the saloon, singing the blues over the laughter and shouts of a roomful of happy men. The women in Storyville are there to work, not play. They sing, play piano, dance, fetch food and drinks, and take men to bed to pay their bills, and their music reflects it, these songs of happiness, sadness, and death.

It's dark here at the back of the bar, the stage crammed into the shadowy corners of a low-ceilinged room. Nothing amplifies the music but her lungs and her charm as she competes for attention against the noise of conversation and the omnipresence of Storyville's music, "like a phenomenon, like the Aurora Borealis," flowing down the streets from the barrooms, brothels, and sidewalk bands, mixing together in a funk of melody and rhythm. Her sound is deep, sexy, knowing, moving up and down a simple blues scale like she could do it in her sleep. She looks good with her Mississippi-River-water skin, long hair and shiny dress, lips and cheeks blushed red and eyes closing when she mentions love. *I've been downhearted, baby* . . . something we can all relate to, which after all is the point. The demimonde is a reminder: we're all in this together, we've all got our needs, our wants. Rich and poor, men and women, respectable and not-quite-so. She keeps singing, the music goes on, and the men listen and so do the other women around Storyville, learning the rules of song, work, and love from each other in the smoke and the sounds of the demimonde.[2]

Mamie Desdoumes

The blues grew out of a rich Southern, African-American culture in which music accompanied nearly every aspect of African-American life: sweet lullabies, work songs, field hollers, chain-gang chants, Baptist spirituals, funeral tunes, and the evocative nonverbal calls, hollers, and moans that had always been central to African musical expression.[3]

African-American music retained not only its traditional sounds but also its cultural position as an integrated part of everyday life. Post-Renaissance Europeans generally understood art (including music) as creations that were valuable but nonutilitarian—apart from their ability to provide aesthetic enjoyment—and they accordingly relegated art to its own separate social spheres: museums, private salons, and concert halls. Africans, in contrast, recognized no such distinctions. In virtually every African culture, creative expressions in the form of music, sculpture, and dance were forces in their own right, and they were combined with religion, politics, and personal relationships as part of a seamless cultural fabric. Music was not merely entertainment but also a bridge between man and the gods, and a form of public address within a community. Likewise, singing was a natural extension of speech, one stop on a continuum of vocal expression that also included shouting, humming, and moaning. For the peoples of the African diaspora, music was an important part of daily life, and its pleasures and its power were accessible to all.[4]

While it is true that the experience of slavery produced a music that was a mixture of traditional West African rhythms and scales with European harmonies, using instruments from both cultures (European horns with African banjos, for example), the combination was deeper than simply the mingling of two types of music. African-Americans introduced new sounds to the New World as well as a radically different attitude toward music. The ability of the blues to communicate lived emotion is a product of those African traditions.

The moment in which blues became its own identifiable genre will probably never be known, but the earliest references to this new music arise in the late 1890s and early 1900s, and women figure prominently in many of the earliest memories. In 1898, the folklorist John Jacob Niles reported seeing a young black woman named Ophelia Simpson at a medicine show singing a song called "Black Alfalfa's Jailhouse Shouting Blues," and he categorized her style as that of a "shouter and moaner," a description that was still being applied to women blues singers in the 1920s. But one of the most memorable of the early blueswomen was New Orleans's Mamie Desdoumes.[5]

Jelly Roll Morton, one of jazz's most important early composers and performers, remembered Mamie Desdoumes well. "The one blues I can never forget," said Morton, remembering the New Orleans of 1902, "happened to be played by a woman. . . . The name of this musician was Mamie Desdoumes. Two middle fingers of her right hand had been cut off, so she played the blues with only three fingers on her right hand." Pianist Bunk Johnson, Morton's contemporary, recalled Desdoumes. "I knew Mamie Desdoumes real well," he said. "Played many a concert with her singing those same blues. . . . She was a hustlin' woman. A blues singing poor gal. Used to play pretty passable piano around them dance halls on Perdido Street."[6]

This was Mamie Desdoumes's New Orleans: a port city that had long served as a cultural crossroads. In slavery times, New Orleans was one of the only cities in the New World that allowed the playing of African drums, and from then on, the music of the African diaspora filled its squares and back alleys, bringing West African rhythms, early versions of the guitar and banjo, and the distinctive patterns of call-and-response singing. In the post-Emancipation years, the city hosted an ever-changing population of sailors, itinerant laborers, and country folk with their own regional musical traditions. Geographically speaking, New Orleans was practically Caribbean, and the influence of the islands and their Spanish, French, and African rhythms influenced the city's sounds, too. This was the heritage of blues and jazz, and the basis for nearly all homegrown American music.

New Orleans was famous for its unrestrained nightlife, and Story-ville, the city's red-light district, was the epicenter of all things bad and beautiful. The original "Sin City," Storyville was an experiment in creative urban planning: from 1898 to 1917, the nearly forty-square-block neighborhood of stately Victorian buildings (formerly resi-dences), with their balconies and ballrooms, was set aside as an adult playground. While prostitution was never legalized in Storyville, it was officially prohibited only outside its boundaries, a form of tacit decrim-inalization. It was well known to all—residents, tourists, sailors on leave—that Storyville was the place to go for a good time, and early blues and jazz provided the soundtrack. "Hundreds of men were pass-ing through the streets day and night," said Jelly Roll Morton. "The chippies in their little-girl dresses were standing in the crib doors singing the blues."[7]

Although Storyville offered freedom from moral censure, it was not free from racism. The creation of Storyville coincided with the early stages of Jim Crow—the system of racial segregation that would come to define the limits of African-American freedom in the American South. Before this time, New Orleans had a relatively liberal—if extremely complicated—attitude toward race and racial integration, recognizing a range of racial types (Creoles, quadroons, octoroons, etc.) as citizens with varying degrees of privilege. All this changed after Reconstruction. Suddenly, New Orleans was no longer seen as a city of mixed races, but simply as a city of blacks and whites. In some ways, the creation of Storyville as a distinct business zone was just another example of this drive toward segregation—in this case, a desire to isolate vice from virtue.

Nonetheless, Storyville itself was a racially segregated place, with blacks allowed in Storyville proper solely as entertainers or prostitutes. The black section of Storyville became known as the Back O'Town district, and this is where Morton and Johnson recall seeing Des-doumes play her blues, on Perdido Street, the street on which Louis Armstrong grew up. The Back O'Town was a crucial site for the devel-opment of African-American music, home not only to Desdoumes and

Armstrong but also to the legendary cornet player Buddy Bolden. It was a vibrant, funky neighborhood, where as-yet-unrecorded and -unclassified strains of music vibrated through the bars and parlors of New Orleans's Tenderloin.

It is significant that in the figure of one of the earliest known blueswomen, Mamie Desdoumes, there is already an association between the music and its underworld environment of prostitution, gambling, and drugs. To hear those who were present in the early days of jazz and blues describe it, the extreme characters and excitement of Storyville were an essential part of the music's development. Far from the revival meetings and sermons of the Baptist church, a new, secular music developed through night after long night of practice in the bars, dance halls, and brothels. Bunk Johnson learned to play in one of these. "That was the Crescent City in them days," he said, "full of bars, honky-tonks, and barrel houses. A barrel house was just a piano in a hall. There was always a piano player working. When I was a kid, I'd go into a barrel house and play 'long with them piano players 'til early in the mornin'. We used to play nuthin' but the blues."[8]

This was the domain of Mamie Desdoumes, and it was in these brothels, or "sporting houses," that many of the early blues and jazz (the terms were virtually interchangeable through the 1920s) musicians first learned their craft, playing for the prostitutes and their customers in the brothel lounges. "Talk about those jam sessions you have today!" said Clarence Williams, the piano player, songwriter, and Bessie Smith collaborator, remembering Storyville in the 1900s:

Why you should have seen the sessions we had then. 'Round about four A.M., the girls would get through work and would meet their P.I.'s (that's what we called pimps) at the wine rooms. . . . Most of the P.I.'s were gamblers and pianists. The reason many of them were pianists was because whenever they were down on their luck, they could always get a job and be close to their girls—

play while the girls worked. . . . [E]verybody would gather every night and there'd be singin' and playin' all night long. The piano players from all over the South would be there, in for the races, and everybody would take a turn until daylight.[9]

The music pouring out of New Orleans's red-light district was made by the vibrant mix of people who congregated there: prostitutes, pimps, madams, country folk new to the city, sailors, black people, white people, and the many shades in between in New Orleans, a city with a colored caste system and a tolerance for vice. "New Orleans, until the twenties," the jazz guitarist Danny Barker recalled wryly, "was the safest haven in the Americas for the world's most vicious characters." "Talking 'bout wild and wooly!" said pioneering jazz clarinetist Alphonse Picou. "There were two thousand registered girls and must been ten thousand unregistered. And all crazy about clarinet-blowers!" The terms *registered* and *unregistered* referred to the Blue Books, directories of prostitutes working in Storyville. The Blue Books featured advertisements for brothels, describing prostitutes and madams by name and appearance; music was featured as an attraction, too. One advertisement for "Countess Willie Piazza" proclaimed, "If you have the 'blues,' the Countess and her girls can cure them . . . [and] if there is anything new in the singing and dancing line that you would like to see while in Storyville, Piazza's is the place to visit."[10]

Connections between illegal (or at least "sinful") activities and the blues persisted and continued to influence the perception of later blueswomen (and men), marking them as dangerous types. A bad reputation was often good for drawing crowds, but being controversial had its downside, too. Later, as the blues became more widespread, many women who sang (or simply listened to) the blues felt the need to hide the fact from their churchgoing friends and families. Once recorded and published as sheet music, blues earned a certain degree of respectability, but only if performed in a respectable concert setting and sung in a controlled, almost operatic style.

~

As is evident from the early memories of Mamie Desdoumes's performances and the many recollections of the blues-singing prostitutes of
New Orleans, women were among the first blues singers. A parallel
blues tradition was developing outside the city limits, though. In the
early days of so-called country blues, men were more often the featured
performers at parties, while women generally sang at home with their
families. Although relegated to amateur status, in this role women
blues singers fulfilled another essential cultural function as they passed
on a musical heritage to their children. "I think the first thing I can
remember was my mother singing the blues as she would sit alone in
the evenings in our place in Dallas, Texas," recalled 1940s blues star
T-Bone Walker. "I used to listen to her singing there at night, and I
knew then that the blues was in me, too."[11]

The blues resists definition—that is to say, there are many ways to
define the blues. One of the most common is that of the twelve-bar
blues, made up of three sets of four bars, or measures, with a lyrical
rhyme scheme of AAB (the first verse is usually repeated in the second
line). Variations abound; from eight- to ten- to sixteen-bar blues, yet
they remain recognizable as blues. The three standard blues chords, I,
IV, and V, are relatively simple, and these three elements—structure,
lyrics, and chords—combine in a form that lends itself to a sense of the
song cycling through itself, the end echoing its beginning in a way
that can feel either reassuring or ominous, depending on the mood of
the song.

African-American work songs—as well as the hollers, calls, and
moans of African song—were the roots of the blues. These musical
expressions were sung to accompany hard labor and featured strong,
repetitive rhythms that echoed the swing of an axe, the chopping of
cotton, or, as in the case of the most famous work song of all, the
pounding of John Henry's hammer as he outworked a steam engine
building the railroad.

As with religion and all other forms of African culture, labor was integrally linked with music—not just as a way of easing one's effort, but in a symbiotic expression; work made the music possible. As LeRoi Jones explained, the experience of sharecropping produced "a form of song or shout that did not necessarily have to be concerned with, or inspired by, labor. Each man had his own voice and his own way of shouting—his own life to sing about." Each shouting style was unique: " 'That's George Jones, down in Hartsville, shoutin' like that.' " Individuality was not only valued but expected in African music. Even in a group setting, each singer or player contributed his or her own particular sound. This emphasis on cultivating a personal performance style had a huge impact on the blues and on American music in general— where would Billie Holiday or Charlie Parker have been without it?[12]

Many work-song lamentations survived into the blues form: complaints about hard work and mistreatment by the boss. But transferred from the field to the barroom or brothel lounge, and accompanied by piano or guitar, the blues took on the subject of the human heart. Blues lyrics reflected the reality of life, both the sour and the sweet.

Apart from its musical structure, most performers and fans of the music have always emphasized that, above all, the blues is about a feeling. "The blues is a thing deeper than what you'd call a mood today," explained composer W. C. Handy, self-proclaimed "Father of the Blues." "The blues came from the man farthest down. The blues came from nothingness, from want, from desire. And when a man sang or played the blues, a small part of the want was satisfied from the music." The 1920s blueswoman Sippie Wallace agreed: "I sing the blues to comfort me on. . . . Most all my blues is about myself."[13]

The comfort derived from blues music came not only from hearing, singing, and playing it, but also from dancing to it. As with virtually all African music, a physical response was expected—from the listener as well as the performer. In marked contrast to European musical traditions, blues performances blurred the line between stage and audience. Dancing was central to blues music's dual nature, for these were songs of sorrow that left the listener overjoyed. Blues music "induces dance movement that is the direct opposite of resignation, retreat, or defeat," explained Albert Murray, and "the more lowdown, dirty, and mean the music, the more instantaneously and pervasively sensual the dance gestures it engenders." Blues music was meant to engage its listener on multiple levels—the sensual, the physical, and the emotional.[14]

Blues lyrics were an important element in conveying those feelings to an audience, and the blues drew upon a strong heritage of African-American verbal creativity as its source. Music had always been a foundational aspect of African culture. Relocated in the New World, the slaves' music mixed African and Christian imagery with West African rhythms and melodies. The American antebellum period was marked by religious revivals, and these so-called Great Awakenings brought many African-Americans into the fold of Christianity. The evangelical fervor of revivalist camp meetings in the late eighteenth and early nineteenth centuries offered African-Americans a space in which to adapt their own, expressive spirituality without censure, adapting biblical stories to conform to their own traditional beliefs, through prayer, shouting, and song.[15]

These new religious compositions often disguised revolutionary messages within the lines of white-sanctioned music. Frederick Douglass remembered how lyrics such as "O Canaan, sweet Canaan/I am bound for the land of Canaan" were interpreted by slaves to mean "something more than a hope of reaching heaven. We meant to reach the *north*, and the north was our Canaan." Songs like this remained important even after Emancipation and Reconstruction, when it became clear that blacks were still expected to accept a diminished role in American society. As spirituals evolved into the gospel music of the twentieth century, songs such as "We Shall Overcome" performed the same function, using the Christian metaphor of heavenly deliverance to describe the twentieth-century struggle to secure civil rights.[16]

The dual meanings often found in African-American culture— what W. E. B. Du Bois called "double consciousness"—the struggle to

reconcile the contradiction of being both African and American—
made blues music all the more important, as its performance became
an exorcism of repressed emotion shared between performer and audience. So when Ma Rainey, one of the first great blues stars, sang her
"Chain Gang Blues," this was one of the few chances to acknowledge
publicly the harsh racist treatment of blacks by an all-white judicial
system in the American South. As one black educator said at the time,
"The fact is that lynching has gone on so long in many parts of our
country that it is somewhat difficult to draw at this time a sharp line
marking off distinctly the point where the lynching spirit stops and the
spirit of legal procedure commences. You cannot tell what the most
peaceable community will do at any moment under certain conditions." Although Rainey's song might appear mild on the surface,
against a context of unpredictable violence toward blacks, hers was a
potent expression of pain felt by many in her audience. The African-
American tradition of creating intensely personal music that spoke to
the heart of each individual persisted in women's blues, allowing
women to express viewpoints often silenced in other areas of the
broader American culture.[17]

As a musical venue for personal expression, the blues has no equal.
It encompasses the broadest range of human experience, from love and
death to "homey things," as T-Bone Walker described his mother's
blues, "things that were troubling her. She might sing about the dinner
burning up or anything like that." "The blues?" responded the legendary blues singer Alberta Hunter, when asked for a definition,
"[W]hy, the blues are a part of me. . . . When we sing blues, we're
singin' out our hearts, we're singin' out our feelings. Maybe we're hurt
and we just can't answer back, then we sing or maybe even hum the
blues. Yes, to us the blues are sacred. When I sing, 'I walk the floor,
wring my hands and cry,' what I'm doing is letting my soul out."[18]

Wherever they performed, the early blueswomen let their souls out,
bringing with them a new style of singing and playing that would radically change American music, allowing it to become emotionally

deeper, more individually expressive, and more open to improvisational changes than its European dance-based songs (waltzes, quadrilles), traditional minstrel tunes (e.g., "Swanee River"), and marching band songs had ever been before. Koko Taylor, one of the late twentieth century's most renowned blueswomen, said, "What these womens [sic] did, like Ma Rainey, was the foundation of the blues, you know what I'm saying? They brought the blues from slavery up to today."[19]

Godmother of the Blues

Ma Rainey (1886–1939), who would later be known as the "Godmother of the Blues," first began singing the blues in 1902, the same year that Jelly Roll Morton first heard Mamie Desdoumes in New Orleans. Though little is known of her earliest years, the young Gertrude Pridgett was the child of minstrel-show performers and must have been raised on the minstrel circuit, traveling from town to town in the post-Reconstruction South. Rainey first heard the blues in Missouri, a "strange and poignant" song sung by a local girl who had come to see Rainey perform with the Rabbit Foot Minstrels traveling tent show. Rainey asked the girl to teach it to her and immediately added it to her repertoire. Though the name of the song is lost, its influence remains. The song provoked such a strong reaction that it "won a special place in her act" and Rainey sang the blues from then on.[20]

Ma Rainey's performances were legendary. Beginning at age fourteen in her native Columbus, Georgia, Gertrude traveled throughout the South, singing, dancing, and acting in traveling vaudeville tent shows. She married fellow performer William "Pa" Rainey in 1904 and became known as "Ma" Rainey, sharing the headline with her husband in the Rabbit Foot Minstrels. The "Foots," as they were called by their fans, were one of the most popular black minstrel shows in the South in the second decade of the twentieth century. First created by whites

The great Ma Rainey (1886–1939) in full regalia in the 1920s.
THE SHOWTIME MUSIC ARCHIVE

in blackface, performing exaggerated caricatures of African-Americans in the antebellum period, minstrelsy was so popular that after the Civil War blacks eventually formed their own troupes and performed for mixed audiences (though blacks and whites sat on opposite sides of the tent aisles). Black minstrel shows like those of the Foots were the variety shows of their day, featuring comedians, singers, short comic plays, and novelty acts such as jugglers in the course of their hours-long performances. Traveling from town to town, they would announce their arrival by marching through town with a brass band, gathering audience members as the parade traveled through.[21]

Ma and Pa Rainey were billed as the "Assassinators of the Blues," a phrase that evoked her influential style as a blueswoman: tough, aggressive, and powerful. As a young man, the jazz guitarist Danny Barker saw Rainey perform. He elaborated on the meaning of her stage name:

> Ma, when you say "Ma" that means "mother," that means the tops. She takes charge—Ma Rainey's coming to town; the boss blues singer. You respect Ma. Grand-Ma, Ma-Ma, and "Ma" Ma: "Ma," that's something they respect when they say "Mother." That's the boss of the shack, eh? Not Papa—Mama.[22]

"Mama" was also a term used in the black community to describe a sexy woman, just as "Papa" often referred to a sexual partner and not just a father figure. Rainey embodied all these things: "the boss" and a "hot mama." Her presence meant power.

And what a presence. Everything about her contrived to make her seem larger than life: a round, full figure; lush lips; wide-set and heavy-lidded eyes made larger with an outline of kohl; and a sweet smile of big, irregular teeth, many of which were gold and shone against her dark skin, which distinguished her from the fashionably lighter-skinned women with whom she shared the vaudeville stage. Her sense of style was equally striking; Rainey adorned herself in sumptuous embroidered satin gowns, headdresses, beads, bracelets, and ropes of pearls around her neck, or her famous necklace of gold coins. No one ever called her pretty, but no one forgot her face, either. "She looked too ugly for me," recalled one musician. "Boy, she was the horrible-lookingest thing I ever see." "Yes, she was ugly," recalled another, "but I'll tell you one thing about it: she had such a lovely disposition, you know, and personality, you forget all about it. She commence to lookin' good to you." Indeed, Paramount Records made a point of including reasonably accurate portraits of a large, laughing Rainey in their advertisements. "Stylish, neat, good-looking, lots of pep, 'n everything!" read one ad, ending with a phrase used to describe a sexy person of either gender: "Real pig-meat!"[23]

Pig-meat notwithstanding, it was her voice—deep and slightly rough—that truly established her authority. She drew the lyrics out to the edge of her breath with just a touch of vibrato, conveying an emotional intensity that transformed even mediocre songs into powerful performances. She used her voice in different ways, depending on the song: sometimes slow and sad with a sob in her throat, as in "Chain Gang Blues" and "Cell Bound Blues," and sometimes lighter. She was funny; a frequent onstage persona she adopted was that of a righteous, demanding lover, as in "Hear Me Talkin' to You" (which, as with many of the aforementioned songs, was her own composition), in which she informed her man as to "what it takes to get into these hips of mine."[24]

Many of the songs that were written for her picked up on the theme of the sexually aggressive woman. One of her frequent collaborators, Thomas "Georgia Tom" Dorsey, made his career with Ma Rainey as a pianist, arranger, band director, and songwriter before moving on in the 1930s to become a major figure in gospel music. Later in life, after leaving the realm of secular music, Dorsey described the blues as "a good woman feeling bad." Yet many of the songs he wrote for Rainey suggest a corollary to his definition: the blues could be a bad woman feeling good. His "Memphis Bound Blues" is but one example; as Ma Rainey sings it: "I talk because I'm stubborn, I sing because I'm free."[25]

Stubborn and *free:* These words are essential to understanding the power of the early blueswomen. Through them, their audience vicariously experienced many freedoms: freedom to express anger without fear of white retribution; freedom to travel, just as the blueswomen traveled from town to town; freedom to testify publicly to the black experience of the world; freedom to love whomever they wanted and to reject those they didn't. Rainey's life of constant touring was never luxurious, but it was exciting; joining a traveling minstrel show was akin to joining the circus. It was an escapist fantasy of reinvention, the opportunity to leave behind normal life with all its established problems and relationships. Like the circus, the Rabbit Foot Minstrels carried their theater with them, performing in tents erected in a field, creating a temporary respite from the realities of daily life outside. The Foots sought their audience throughout the South, following the cotton harvest throughout the summer and fall and sometimes stopping for a winter break in New Orleans, where they could share their music with other pioneers of blues and jazz, such as trumpeter Louis Armstrong and clarinetist Sidney Bechet.

This life—full of travel, performance, and collaborative creativity—was only a dream for most African-Americans in the early twentieth century, male or female. Rainey's position as the undisputed star of the Rabbit Foot Minstrels made her an icon among her people. She seemed to embody freedom, and in this embodiment established an archetype for the women in music who followed her: the "stubborn woman"; the "bad woman"; the "wild woman" of the blues. When she began making records, Rainey's record company billed her as "The Paramount Wildcat." The blues queens who came after her—Bessie Smith, Victoria Spivey, Sippie Wallace, and others—took her lead and further developed the persona.

The poet Sterling Brown (1901–1989) met Rainey and was a great fan of her live performances. He captured the affection of her fans in his 1932 poem "Ma Rainey," in which he depicted a rush of excited, happy people pouring into a country dance hall—"from blackbottom cornrows and from lumber camps"—to hear the great singer. These were hardworking rural folk, for whom the arrival of Rainey and her show was a major event. To them, Ma Rainey was a star, but also someone to whom they could relate. Her songs sang of their pain, her jokes laughed at the same problems they faced. Like them, Rainey was a black Southerner, and black Southerners in that era lived in a strange world, one that had seen many changes in the fifty years since Emancipation. What were once dreams of a happier life, free of racism and backbreaking work, had evolved into the system known as Jim Crow. These segregationist policies had redefined the limits of black lives in the South, relegating them to the worst jobs, the worst neighborhoods, and the worst prospects for future happiness. Much of the sadness in blues music reflected the shattered hopes of a people who had escaped slavery only to find a world in which freedom was still just a mirage.[26]

In this environment, Ma Rainey represented a vision of a different kind of life, one unencumbered by fear of white reprisal, social mores, or barred opportunity. She was a folk hero whose private life was a topic of conversation among her fans, and Rainey's onstage personality was enhanced only by her wild performances offstage. In the pre-radio days, gossip was the greatest mass medium, and Rainey's exploits were a regular feature. Rainey's fans knew of her love of parties, dancing, and extramarital activities, including her taste in young men—and women. Despite her married status, she chose not to disguise her polyamorous tastes. Rainey's renegade moral style merely added to her appeal. The great jazz pianist and composer Mary Lou Williams recalled going to downtown Pittsburgh as a young girl to see "the fabulous" Ma Rainey, "the woman who had made blues history":

> Ma was loaded with real diamonds—in her ears, around her neck, in a tiara around her head. Both hands were full of rocks, too; her hair was wild and she had gold teeth. What a sight! To me, as a kid, the whole thing looked and sounded weird.
>
> When the engagement ended, and Ma had quit the scene, rumor had it that the jewelry was bought hot and that Ma was

picked up and made to disgorge—losing all the loot she had paid for the stuff.[27]

In another incident, Rainey was arrested by the Chicago police in 1925 for "running an indecent party." The neighbors complained about the noise and arrived to find Rainey and several naked young women *in flagrante delicto*. Rainey spent the night in jail and was bailed out the next morning by her onetime protégée, Bessie Smith.[28]

Rainey met Smith in 1912, early in her career, when the fourteen-year-old Smith was hired as a dancer in Moses Stokes's traveling minstrel show. According to one contemporary, Rainey was "like a mother" to Smith. (Indeed, Rainey was known for her generosity toward younger performers, male and female, and she and Pa Rainey adopted a boy who worked as a dancer in their show.) It's quite possible that Rainey and Smith were lovers, though neither admitted to it outright. Sam Chatmon, a guitar player in Rainey's tent show, believed that they had been more than just friends. "I believe she was courtin' Bessie," he told an interviewer years later. "She [Bessie] said, 'Me and Ma Rainey had plenty of big times together.' . . . I believe Ma Rainey was the one, was cuttin' up like the man. . . . If Bessie'd be 'round, if she'd get to talkin' to another man, she'd [Rainey] run up. She didn't want no man to talk with her." Rainey's bisexuality was a well-established element of her persona. She wrote and performed several songs on the subject, including her "Prove It on Me Blues," in which she sings of carousing with a group of friends: "They must've been women, 'cause I don't like no men." Rainey dealt with homosexuality in several other songs, including "Sissy Blues," in which she sings of losing her husband to another man.[29]

Homosexuality was a taboo in mainstream American society that applied to men and women, black and white alike. From the turn of the twentieth century onward, physicians, sociologists, anthropologists, and moralists increasingly warned young men and women against the dangers of homosexuality, which was considered a perversion.

Nevertheless, the 1920s saw a rise in "lesbian chic," and representations of boyish girls, mannish women, and doomed lesbian love affairs became common in the upper-class entertainment of the post–World War I period. Lesbian chic never quite extended to the mainstream, yet it flourished within certain subcultures, two of which were located in New York City and cross-pollinated each other: Greenwich Village and Harlem.[30]

The Greenwich Village crowd accepted bisexuality as just one among many thrillingly "free" lifestyle choices by which one could be distinguished from the bourgeoisie. While it had been known as a site for political activism in the prewar era, by the mid-1920s Greenwich Village's "long-haired men and short-haired women" became a tourist attraction unto themselves. When the gay men and women of "the Village" grew tired of sightseers, they in turn traveled uptown to Harlem.[31]

Though separated by race, class, and geography, Harlem and Greenwich Village were twin outposts of the homosexual subculture of New York City. Harlem tolerated its sexually adventurous denizens, too, and for the most part welcomed whites such as writer and socialite Carl Van Vechten, who championed the Harlem scene. Like the white, downtown bohemians, Harlem residents reveled in exercising their freedom of expression, whether through literature, music, or sexual posturing. In Harlem, newly relocated African-Americans strove to create an all-black utopia in which the descendants of slavery could forge lives free of the white man's judgments. This common dream contributed to the general acceptance of homosexuality in Harlem, a place where freedom was the highest value of all.

White homosexuals of the time recognized Harlem's homosexual culture as more open than that of the Village and more exciting. Harlem offered a variety of venues in which gay men and women could express themselves without fear of reprisal. Drag balls, rent parties, gay bars, and artistic salons attracted blacks and whites alike. In this atmosphere, the lesbian antics of Bessie Smith and Ma Rainey were part of the broader social context. As in Greenwich Village,

Harlem's "free love" was in vogue, and Rainey's and Smith's ribald songs of sexual escapades with women—and men—were fodder for their reputation as women who were so sexy they didn't bother with gender distinctions. Although not all Harlemites approved of bisexuality, the artistic and nightlife subcultures in which Smith and Rainey circulated were quite tolerant. Rainey felt free to perform and record her sexually explicit songs without fear; in fact, they provided the soundtracks for the era's innumerable homosexual parties, dances, and drag balls.[32]

While it is clear that Rainey herself was intimate with both men and women, she sang about more than just sex. From alcoholism to crop failure to faded love in all its forms, Ma Rainey broadened the scope of available subject matter for women performers, moving from the shuck-and-jive of the minstrel stage to the recording studio and the mass media of the twentieth century. Through her personality, she also set a key example for Bessie Smith and the others who followed. Flamboyant, self-dramatizing, hard-partying, and unimpressed by conservative mores, Ma Rainey was an icon of strength.

Rainey's influence on other singers was significant not only because of her strong persona but also in musical terms, as her style bridged the gap between traditional, rural, country blues (with its raw vocal style and simple accompaniment of guitar and one or two other instruments) and the vaudeville blues style, which featured a bigger orchestra and a touch of "hokum," humorous material added to the song in the form of skits and sound effects, both embellishments left over from the minstrelsy tradition. Rainey's plaintive, sometimes harsh voice recalled the rusticity of country life, something that appealed to her working-class fans. Yet her appearance was that of a professional stage performer—and then some. Her pearls, silk dresses, and famous necklace of gold coins (not to mention the flash of her gold teeth) showed her audience that she had graduated to another level—but she was taking her down-home sound with her. For all her finery, Rainey was always recognizable as an earthy, country woman, and her fans loved her for it.

While today she is generally remembered as a singer, in her own time she was known as an all-around performer—actress, singer, dancer, comedian—as demanded by the traveling tent show form. This breadth of performance style offered Rainey the opportunity to craft a multidimensional onstage persona, expanding upon her musical repertoire with jokes and onstage banter. Clyde Bernhardt, who played trombone in Rainey's band, remembered her performances well:

> Oh, yeah, she would tell jokes to the audience. . . . You know, back in those days, they used to call young men, you know, "pig meat." . . . So she used to come out there and crack—"Yeah, I like my pig meat men. I like 'em young and tender . . . I ain't got nothin' for an old man to do. . . . If they be nice, I take care of 'em." . . . And she'd get up there and say, "I'm gonna tell you about my man." And then probably she'd start to singin' "A Good Man Is Hard to Find."[33]

In this way, Rainey constructed a consistent onstage character whose personality reverberated through all her jokes, dances, and songs.

Many who bought Rainey's records had seen her live performances. Rainey and the various traveling troupes with which she toured were part of an entertainment network formally called the Theater Owners' Booking Association, or T.O.B.A., but colloquially referred to either as "Toby Time" or "Tough On Black Asses." (Though the majority of any audience for a T.O.B.A. show was black, the organization was owned by whites, a business model that would continuously repeat itself in the entertainment industry, with notable exceptions such as Motown Records, owned by Berry Gordy.) The early 1900s were a time of great change in the entertainment industry as a whole, and theaters around the country were consolidating and standardizing their offerings, establishing soon-to-be well-worn trade routes between major theaters on the circuit.

Founded in 1909, the T.O.B.A. itself was an immensely important institution in terms of its impact on the black community and American culture at large, for it brought the best black performers from the traveling minstrel shows, at the peripheries of the entertainment world, into the concert halls of the biggest cities in the South, the Midwest, and the eastern seaboard. Its derogatory nickname arose from its infamous reputation for low pay, poor backstage accommodations, and grueling schedules, but the T.O.B.A. was tolerated by performers because it was the only show in town open to black entertainers. Charles "Marse" Bailey, the owner and manager of the 81 Theater in Atlanta, a linchpin in the T.O.B.A. circuit, liked to remind his black employees that it was only through his muscle that they were allowed to stay out past the citywide midnight curfew for blacks—he issued them official permits to pacify the police patrols waiting when they left the theater.[34]

Depressing as these limitations were, the T.O.B.A. was immensely successful and offered one of the few opportunities for talented black performers to achieve fame and even a degree of wealth for the lucky few, such as Ma Rainey, Bill "Bojangles" Robinson, Bert Williams, and Bessie Smith. The T.O.B.A. also exposed these artists to white audiences, for many of the theaters (in the South and North) provided "white only" nights at which the biggest vaudeville and minstrel stars appeared. Black vaudeville and minstrelsy were no longer relegated to tents or cotton fields, and neither was the blues. Ma Rainey's career charted the many new developments in the entertainment industry, and her success in each subsequent form testifies to her talent as a performer able to communicate in many different formats.

A T.O.B.A. performance by Rainey circa 1925 at the Frolic Theatre in Birmingham, Alabama, where she performed her standard repertoire, brilliantly dramatized the evolution of popular performance in the twentieth century's first two decades, and it survives today as a vital live performance through the memories of those who witnessed it firsthand.

Bessie Smith and her niece, Ruby Walker, sat down in the darkness between acts just as the stage curtain rose to reveal a giant replica of a Victrola record player, softly lit on an otherwise-darkened stage. Thomas Dorsey described the rest:

> Ma was hidden [inside it]. A girl would come out and put a big record on it. Then the band picked up the "Moonshine Blues." Ma would sing a few bars inside the Victrola. Then she would open the door and step out into the spotlight with her glittering gown that weighed twenty pounds and wearing a necklace of five, ten and twenty dollar gold-pieces. The house went wild. It was as if the show had started all over again. Ma had the audience in the palm of her hand. . . . When Ma had sung her last number and the grand finale, we took seven [curtain] calls.[35]

In this enthralling and strange sequence, Rainey's entrance onstage united old and new forms of performance: the old world of the traditional stage and the new world of sound recordings. Although Rainey was the last in a series of acts, as Dorsey said, "It was as if the show had started all over again."

Many in the theater business worried about the rise in popularity of records, by this time heard not only on Victrolas but also on the radio, a virtually free entertainment medium. How could the live theater compete? Rainey's entrance showed them how. Performing her own composition, "Moonshine Blues," Rainey sang, "You'll find me wrigglin' and a-rockin', howlin' like a hound/Catch the first train that's runnin' South bound," and as one reviewer put it bluntly: "She brought the house down." From Rainey's time on, the strongest and "baddest" women singers have worked the same proving ground, delivering live performances that made their recordings, however popular, pale supplements to the real thing. It is one of the distinguishing qualities of a "bad woman feeling good."[36]

1917–1920
The First Recordings

Ma Rainey was one of the few early blueswomen to make the transi-
tion successfully from rural minstrelsy to the recording studio. One of
the major obstacles facing black women singers was, to put it plainly,
the racism of the recording industry. Perry Bradford, an African-
American musical composer and producer active in the Harlem
Renaissance period, recounted his struggle to get black artists recorded
by recording companies, all of which were white-owned. Bradford
recalled that in his first attempt, in 1918, they replied, "Columbia
wouldn't think of recording a colored girl at this time." Companies
such as Columbia and Victor (the two major labels at the time) occasionally recorded black musicians (usually men), but for the most part
they relegated them to genres such as spirituals, ragtime, and minstrel
songs—music traditionally associated with African-Americans. The
major labels also recorded jazz and blues before 1920, but almost
always with white musicians. Victor had a banner year in 1917 when it
released two of the biggest-selling records of the era, "Livery Stable
Blues," by the all-white Original Dixieland Jazz Band, and W. C.
Handy's "St. Louis Blues," recorded by Sophie Tucker, an immigrant
from Eastern Europe.[37]

Sophie Tucker was not a blues singer per se, but she was savvy
enough to recognize a good thing when she saw it, which explains how
a white comic actress became the first person to record a million-
selling blues record. By the time she did so in 1917, the practice of
white artists "covering" black songs was already well established, with
such artists as Hoagy Carmichael and jazz bandleader Paul Whiteman
among the most famous practitioners, in addition to white artists such
as Al Jolson, who not only covered black songs but did so in blackface.

Sophie Tucker (1884–1966) appropriated black culture in her act
and made a point of crossing and recrossing ethnic and gender-based

lines of traditional American performance throughout her career. Tucker was a Russian Jew who had immigrated to the United States in early childhood and began her stage career at age sixteen. As she told it, she was persuaded to perform in blackface by vaudeville managers in New York who apparently felt that, because she was a large woman, the audience would warm to her more easily if she took on the "Mammy" role so familiar from the minstrelsy tradition. Billed for a time as a "Refined Coon Shouter," Tucker enjoyed pulling off a glove at the end of a performance "to show I was a white girl" to a presumably shocked audience. As soon as she had mustered enough personal career momentum, however, Tucker abandoned the burnt-cork routine and began proclaiming herself "The Last of the Red-Hot Mamas"—a proudly sensual and empowered white woman. It was, ironically, in this post-blackface phase in the mid-teens that Tucker began to show the specific influence of black women blues performers in her own act.[38]

"Sophie Tucker sent her maid, Belle," the legendary black blues and cabaret singer Alberta Hunter recalled, "for me to come to her dressing room and teach her songs, but I never would so her piano player would come over and listen and get everything down." Indeed, Alberta Hunter had been the first singer, black or white, to approach composer W. C. Handy about performing his "St. Louis Blues," and it was Hunter who first popularized it onstage. Yet Hunter herself always credited Sophie Tucker as an influence, and as blues scholar Daphne Duval Harrison puts it, "They influenced each other—Tucker sought the rhythms, emotional expressiveness, and black dialectic inflections and Hunter learned stage presence and the use of sexy innuendoes from Tucker." Hunter's first recording would not come until four years after Tucker's hit, while Tucker went on to score many more hits written and/or influenced by African-Americans and their blues, including "You've Got to See Your Mama Ev'ry Night," "Never Let the Same Dog Bite You Twice," and her theme song, "Some of These Days," written by the African-American composer Shelton Brooks.[39]

Tucker's and Hunter's interaction demonstrates that even though during this period the American stage was by and large a racially segregated one, a mutual fascination, admiration, and circle of influence existed between performers and audiences of different races. In some respects, the performances of Tucker and Hunter had much in common, as both women performed outside the boundaries of refined female behavior. Sophie Tucker exploited her voluptuousness and raw sexuality, while Alberta Hunter embodied the assertive, sophisticated, no-nonsense black woman of the modern city with a taut confidence that might have earned her bodily threats had she performed in the South.

The story of the song "St. Louis Blues" itself tells its own story of black and white influence, as the popular song continued to be performed and heard by audiences of both races. From Hunter it traveled to Tucker's vaudeville stage and record and then back to the black blueswomen's concert halls of 1920s Harlem, eventually inspiring an eponymous black-produced motion picture in 1929, featuring the only on-screen performance of Bessie Smith, who sang the song and played the protagonist in the short film. Many of the boldest women performers in the second and third decades of the twentieth century followed a similar career trajectory from live stage to recording studio to film, with most ultimately finding the greatest opportunity for artistic expression as stage singers, free from the stereotypes imposed by American theatrical traditions and Hollywood's production codes.

~

The success of Sophie Tucker's recording of "St. Louis Blues" in 1917 did not immediately create opportunities for other blues singers, and certainly not for black women. In these early days of recording, the industry was still in flux. The biggest recording companies, such as Columbia and Victor, started their businesses in the late nineteenth and early twentieth centuries with the production of phonographs that used cylinders and, later, 78 rpm discs, or records. The decision of what to record onto the discs was, at first, an arbitrary one made by trial-

and-error. If a particular recording sold well, such as Tucker's "St. Louis Blues," the decision would be made to record Tucker again, but not necessarily the blues. As was demonstrated by the enormous success of a few artists—Sophie Tucker, opera singer Enrico Caruso, minstrel star Bert Williams, and others—the recording industry solidified its pattern of backing a few key "stars" at a very early stage; for businesses operating with large capital investments, it did not make financial sense to take too many risks. As one Columbia executive said at the time (it remains the recording industry's party line), "Why slow down your sales by experimenting?" While the conservative attitude of the industry limited the scope of recorded music, in some respects, this proved to be a good thing for American music's "bad women," who proved their drawing power in the early days of recording and thus earned a niche in the industry that persists to the present day.[40]

In the early 1900s, Columbia and Victor cornered all aspects of the music business: they produced original music and sold the record players (companies used different brand names to distinguish their own record players: Columbia had the Graphophone and later the Grafonola; Victor had the Victrola, which soon became a generic term), and each company merchandised the records through their own stores, which stocked only their own recordings. This model worked for a time, and it encouraged consumers to identify with a particular label and its roster of artists.

The aforementioned recording impresario Perry Bradford finally convinced a producer at Victor in 1918 to give the black blues singer Mamie Smith a test recording. Originally a dancer and singer in vaudeville, Mamie Smith was not a blues singer in the classic sense, though she was happy to sing the blues if that paid the bills. (Nor was she related to any of the other blueswomen named "Smith" of the 1920s and 1930s: Bessie, Clara, and Trixie.) Although Victor chose not to go forward with "That Thing Called Love," Mamie Smith tried again, recording it for Okeh Records, who released it with little publicity in July 1920. "That Thing Called Love" became a runaway hit once the black community was alerted to its existence by the *Chicago Defender*, which was always on the lookout for news about black success stories.[41]

A crucial factor in its success was the recent experiment made by record companies in selling their machines on the installment plan. By lessening the initial investment, many thousands of poor people suddenly were able to take home their own phonographs and, in turn, begin buying records to play on them. The black audience for records was finally becoming a reality.

Okeh Records was struggling to compete with the bigger labels and thus was relatively willing to take a risk in the hopes of a big payoff. "There's fourteen million Negroes in our great country and they will buy records if recorded by one of their own," Bradford told Fred Hager, who ran the label. "I reminded him not to expect any fast sales up here in the North, but the Southern whites will buy them like nobody's business. They understand blues and jazz songs, for they've heard blind-men on street-corners in the South playing guitars and singing 'em for nickels and dimes ever since their childhood days."[42]

Bradford argued that both blacks and whites would buy the same records, displaying a race-blind attitude toward marketing that would be considered radical were it introduced today, much less in the 1920s. Music made by blacks did find a white audience and continues to do so, but only because whites sought and continue to seek it out. While Jim Crow was killed in the 1950s and 1960s in the American South, it survives in the music industry of the twenty-first century. Beginning in 1935, when "Your Hit Parade" first started tracking record sales, the recording industry relegated music made by African-Americans to the "race record" category, a term that lasted until 1949. At that point, with the U.S. military officially desegregated and African-Americans increasingly confident in asserting their civil rights, "race records" started sounding awkward. One former Billboard employee frankly admitted the problem: "Maybe 'race' was too close to 'racist.'" Industry executives managed to hit upon another, equally unhelpful name for the category, "rhythm and blues," a term used to describe almost all forms of music made by black people, though eventually an emphasis on blues-based dance music evolved, and genres such as gospel and jazz were granted their own charts.[43]

Back in the late teens, Perry Bradford claimed that the major labels were constantly being threatened by white Southerners intent on keeping blacks out of the recording industry. If not, "Okeh Products— phonograph machines and records—would be boycotted." Despite this pressure, Hager agreed to give a black artist, Mamie Smith, a shot— but, unsurprisingly, only after his first choice, Sophie Tucker, had declined the opportunity to record the songs herself. "That Thing Called Love" and "You Can't Keep a Good Man Down" were vaude-villesque pop songs, and they sold well—in the South, as Bradford had predicted, but also in Philadelphia, Chicago, and other Northern cities. Hager was pleased, and he agreed to record Mamie Smith again. It was this, Bradford and Smith's third collaboration, on August 10, 1920, that ignited a phenomenon. "Crazy Blues" was something new: the first-ever black blues record. It sold 75,000 copies in its first month alone. It was the first but not the last time a single woman singer would secure the financial stability of a recording company.[44]

The 1920s

> I learned the blues off of records. My mother used to buy Mamie Smith, Bessie Smith, Ma Rainey; all these songs she likes to sing, and I would sing along with her. We had one of these old Grafonola that you wind up. So if we was cleaning house—if we were in the bedroom, it was on the stairs. If we were outside washing clothes we'd bring it there, see? So I heard these records and I'd sing along with Mama—so that's how I learned to sing the blues.
>
> —Blue Lu Burke, blues singer[45]

Blues records traveled. While Burke's mother's example prepared her for the life of a cleaning woman, the records showed her another, inspiring and instructing Burke in her drive to become a singer. Before Mamie Smith's "Crazy Blues," singers such as Ma Rainey relied upon personally witnessing others' performances for their chance to add new sounds and songs to their repertoire. Without the chance meeting of that nameless young girl in Missouri in 1902, for example, who could say when she would have next heard the blues? And the foremost interpreter of the blues, Bessie Smith, had herself learned the blues in person from Rainey.

Records courted an audience that live performances couldn't reach: the extremely rural, the extremely poor, and those barred from live performances because they had the wrong color skin. Young white men such as John Hammond, one of the most influential record industry personages of the twentieth century, as a teenager in the 1920s realized "[T]he best stores sold Victor, just as the best people bought them, but I discovered my favorite music on other records. In the rear of the house the servants had a Columbia Grafonola, a wonderful phonograph."[46]

Hammond developed his musical taste through these records and went on to become an important early champion of jazz and blues as well as a public figure in the fight for black civil rights. He played key roles in the careers of many of America's finest recording artists in the twentieth century, from Bessie Smith and Count Basie to Billie Holiday and Fletcher Henderson, to Aretha Franklin, Bob Dylan, and Bruce Springsteen. In 1920, when Perry Bradford was told that "Victor just couldn't afford to lower their prestige" by recording a black woman singer, John Hammond—Park Avenue resident and an heir to the Vanderbilt fortune—was turning to smaller labels such as Okeh to hear the same music that Blue Lu Burke and her mother were enjoying as they cleaned houses. Records allowed Hammond access to the black music scene he so admired, bringing the music, if not the black servants, from "the rear of the house" to the front parlor.[47]

The servants in John Hammond's household may well have been recent arrivals to New York. During the period from 1910 to 1940, it is estimated that nearly two million blacks moved from the Southern states to the North, going there to find jobs initially created by World War I and later staying on to work in the industrial centers eager for labor in the wake of restrictions on European immigration imposed in the 1920s and 1930s. Many hoped that the journey northward would bring an end to the discrimination they faced in the South, but as Hammond's comments reveal, the long shadow of the South and Jim Crow often followed the migrants wherever they moved.

Finding themselves in the new world of the postwar North, black musicians realized that work in fledgling industries such as music recording unfortunately offered no relief from the racism and oppression they had left behind. Describing the New York jazz and blues scene of the 1920s and 1930s, Hammond recalled that while "[t]here was no white pianist to compare with Fats Waller, no white band as good as Fletcher Henderson's, no blues singer like Bessie Smith, white or black . . . the best jazz players barely made a living [and] were barred from all well-paying jobs in radio and in night clubs." Bessie Smith's "Florida Bound Blues" expressed a feeling shared by many who had moved north in the hope of a better life: they wanted to go back. "It's so cold up here that the words freeze in your mouth."[48]

Royalties were another area in which black performers were disappointed and often defrauded. "I didn't even know what he meant when he said royalties," piano player Memphis Slim admitted in an interview intended for broadcast, remembering his recording sessions in Chicago in the 1930s. "You know, the kind of deal I got I would not want to say over the radio." Depressingly, the long history of the record industry's exploitation of black performers begins with the very first black stars. Historian William Barlow estimates that the nearly $20,000 Perry Bradford earned in royalty fees for "Crazy Blues" was less than half the amount he should have received, given Okeh Records' own sales figures, which counted one million copies of the record sold in the first year of its release alone. As for Mamie Smith, the singer herself received no royalties at all, apart from $1,000 as a "gift" from Bradford and a token recording fee (probably $50 or less).[49]

In general, black performers in the early years of recording were totally ignorant of the arcane and ever-evolving copyright laws concerning recordings, and both black and white company executives took advantage of this fact. For many artists who had gone north to Chicago and New York, leaving the plantations and farms of the South to make a career in music, the inequities of this new world were depressingly familiar. "You wasn't gonna get no royalties anyway," Memphis Slim explained. "It was like a sharecropper, you always almost got out of the hole, but not quite."[50]

1920–1939
The Doll-Baby Woman Is a
Thing of the Past

Black women experienced their own special set of challenges. Facing potential prejudice on many fronts—by virtue of their sex, their class, and their skin color—black women in the post–World War I period strove to create a stronger vision of black womanhood in this new era. "The doll-baby woman is a thing of the past," Amy-Jacques Garvey, the wife of black nationalist leader Marcus Garvey, wrote in 1925, "and the wide-awake woman is forging ahead prepared for all emergencies, and ready to answer any call, even if it be to face the cannons on the battlefield." According to one report, in 1922 two million black women were working in three general areas: domestic service, agriculture, and the manufacturing industries. Black women were by no means "doll-babies"; they were compelled to work in occupations that required great stamina, and they were often the main breadwinners for their families, having access to many jobs in white households from which black men were excluded.[51]

Their strength as laborers, however, did not earn them the respect of white society. Although the status of white women was changing during this period, with women winning the vote in 1920 and experimenting with new, freer expressions of sexuality in the celebrated figures of the flapper and the vamp, the definition of womanhood was to a large extent still defined by Victorian standards: the true lady did not work at all. She was a creature of leisure, by and large confined to the domestic sphere and entrusted with the moral uplift of society by virtue of her isolation from the evils of the outside world. Very few black women could afford this lifestyle, and accordingly they were shut out of this ladylike world. Bessie Smith's "Washwoman's Blues" testified to the drudgery of the job: "Oh, the washwoman's life, it ain't a bit of good."[52]

Relegated to the toughest, least "feminine" occupations, and branded as sexually depraved by a Southern white regime that regarded the rape of black women as a conceptual impossibility, black women struggled to assert their civil rights through establishing their respectability according to mainstream white terms. The National Association of Colored Women (NACW) founded in 1896, was led by Mary Church Terrell and formed part of a broad church-based movement in the black community to elevate the status of black women according to the tenets of Christianity. Its motto, "Lifting As We Climb," expressed the NACW's ambition to include the largest group of black women, the working-class "washwomen" of Bessie Smith's song, in its mission. In addition to the common laborers, the churchwomen also hoped to help "the lowly, the illiterate, and even the vicious to whom we are bound by the ties of race and sex, and put forth every possible effort to uplift and reclaim them." If Terrell's attitude toward the less fortunate members of her sex appears harsh, it may be put in perspective when compared with the following comment, published in a white-owned newspaper in 1904: "Negro women evidence more nearly the popular idea of total depravity than the men do. . . . I cannot imagine such a creation as a virtuous black woman."[53]

The efforts of the church-based women's movement were helpful to black women to a degree, in that they established a visible image of black female morality that could be appreciated by mainstream white culture. Yet that image could also be stifling, restricting the expression of a more potent sexuality and a desire for a less proscribed way of life in general. It was against this kind of historical backdrop that the early blueswomen performed for their black and white audiences. As women seeking both respect and commercial popularity, they charted a sometimes-treacherous course through the prevailing stereotypes of their day—celebrated by their audiences for their brash statements of who and what they wanted and chastised by the churchwomen and others for their willful embodiment of the wild and sensual aspects of black culture that seemed to encourage white criticism of the black community as a whole.

For many decades to come, black singers were to be confronted with a choice: achieving the approval of the churchgoing community through singing religious music, or facing criticism and even social exile through the performance of secular music, whether blues, jazz, or rhythm and blues. Of course, not everyone in the black community adhered to these categories of approval—many fans and performers appreciated both types of music and indulged in them with equal enthusiasm. The 1920s blues singer and pianist Ida Goodson was among them:

> I can be playing the blues, and I can feel something going all over and the next thing I know, I'm feeling good—that's the devil in me then! Then I play a church song, and . . . that Christian feeling coming back on you. And so that's just the way it is: the devil's got his work, and God's got his work.[54]

Others took a harsher view. Dave Peyton, of the widely circulated black newspaper the *Chicago Defender*, was an important black music critic in the early days of recording. Peyton led the campaign against jazz and blues music, which, he argued, "appealed only to the lower classes of Race folk." In his opinion, this music was "crude, barbaric, vulgar, and suggestive . . . appealing only to the animal emotions." Proper music, in his opinion, was that of the European classical composers, and the occasional stately spiritual hymn. Not all critics shared his opinion, however. The writer Langston Hughes was one of the most prominent black critics to praise blues and jazz, and he celebrated its working-class creators as well: "the low-down folks, the so-called common element . . . the common people [who] will give to the world its truly great Negro artists, the one who is not afraid to be himself."[55]

Or herself. As the twenties progressed and the blueswoman Bessie Smith began to emerge as one of the first great black artists of the twentieth century, Hughes would continue to defend her against the Dave Peytons of the world. "Let the blare of Negro jazz bands and the bellowing voice of Bessie Smith singing the Blues penetrate the closed ears of the colored near-intellectuals," he wrote, "until they listen and perhaps understand." What Hughes loved about Bessie Smith was the very thing she had learned from Ma Rainey: her self-acceptance as a strong, black woman. Racial pride, the foundation of the twentieth century's civil rights movement, was embodied in Ma Rainey—from the way she looked to the way she sang to the things she sang about. Rainey—and Smith after her—insisted on being, simply, herself. "If white people are pleased, we are glad," Hughes wrote. "If they are not, it doesn't matter. We know we are beautiful. And ugly too. . . . If colored people are pleased, we are glad. If they are not, their displeasure doesn't matter either. We build our temples for tomorrow, strong as we know how, and we stand on top of the mountain, free within ourselves."[56]

Ma Rainey stood on top of that mountain for most of the 1920s; though her protégée Bessie Smith achieved a wider following, Rainey's fans did not desert her. Rainey was a living link to the Southern lives they had left behind but had not forgotten. Her gruff, earthy voice was full of the weather, the food, the feelings of the South they once knew. Rainey made her last recording—her ninety-second!—for Paramount in 1928. With the crash of 1929 and the ensuing Great Depression, Rainey and the other stars of the Classic Blues era struggled to maintain their careers. The T.O.B.A. circuit closed shop in 1930, and Rainey toured for a while in the old tent shows and even in carnivals. No longer the "Paramount Wildcat," Rainey by the mid-1930s was billed as "the Black Nightingale." Her tour bus was gone; in its place was a one-woman trailer with flimsy wooden walls and a canvas roof. She stopped touring in 1935, bought two theaters in Rome, Georgia, and ran them successfully for several years, though she never again performed—perhaps because she embraced religion and joined the Baptist Church. Whatever her reasons, by the time of her death in 1939, her achievements in music were simply seen as part of her wild past, footnotes to musical history drowned out by the new sounds of jazz. Despite a brief revival of interest in the blues in the 1940s, it was not until the 1960s that Rainey's Paramount recordings were reissued in their entirety. Gertrude "Ma" Rainey's death certificate listed her occupation as "housekeeping."[57]

Yet her fans did not forget. They treasured her records and continued to enjoy them, through the Depression and through World War II, until the grooves wore through the shellac. They shared their memories of her performances, and they told stories of her wild life and the way she made them feel. Ma Rainey was not a housekeeper. She was the Assassinator, the Godmother, the Wildcat, the Mother of the Blues.

Chapter Two

THE AIR AND HOW TO FILL IT: BESSIE SMITH, BLUES SINGER

1912

Moan them blues, holler them blues,
let me convert your soul.
—Bessie Smith, "Preachin' the Blues" (1927)[1]

The South

In the beginning, there was attitude. In the years just after Emancipation, when the old folks were still hopeful and the young ones still innocent of the past, a girl with a will and The Voice started life full of high spirits, hard work, and the assumption that her feelings not only were just as important as those of anyone else, but also that they could be shared and, through sharing, understood by the whole world. The girl grew and so did the world around her, and soon neither was as innocent as before, but she held on to the feelings, the will, and, of course, The Voice. And though the world was bigger than she'd ever dreamed it could be, so was her success at sharing herself with it. Bessie Smith created a life that no one could have imagined for her, using the only tools she had: her will, The Voice, and her songs.

The Voice of Bessie Smith was recorded for posterity, but the facts of her early life as a girl in Chattanooga, Tennessee, slipped away, as they often do when a family is more concerned with subsistence than self-celebration. Few documents of the Smith family have survived the passage of time, but the memories of old friends offer clues to the childhood of the future "Empress of the Blues." Born in a "ramshackle cabin" in Chattanooga and orphaned by the age of nine, Bessie Smith (1894–1937) displayed a sense of self-confidence that defied her circumstances and her apparently grim prospects for the future. Bessie and her six older siblings began working as children, keeping the family together by pooling their earnings. Just one generation out of slavery, African-Americans made up half of Chattanooga's thirty thousand residents. They had come to the busy little city from plantations, looking for better lives. What they found was disappointing: crowded conditions in the black ghettos, virtually no social mobility, and more hard work. Chattanooga was a growing city in the so-called New South, a South that hoped to work its way out of the industrial shadow of the North.[2]

So Bessie and her brother Andrew took to the streets—he on guitar, she singing, dancing, and cracking jokes for coins from passersby. Some of the locals remember those sidewalk performances around 1904 and recall a girl whose strong personality was evident even then. As one passerby threw money in appreciation of the young Smith children, ten-year-old Bessie was heard to respond, "That's right, Charlie, give it to the church."[3]

Impious, perhaps, but not necessarily inaccurate. Even at the age of ten, Bessie Smith felt a bond with the local black preachers. Whether

The irrepressible Bessie Smith (1894–1937), in a publicity shot from the 1920s.

through sermon or secular song, they both transported their audiences from the everyday into a different dimension—one of pure, unmediated feeling. Church was an important place for black Southerners at the turn of the twentieth century, being one of the only places they could congregate without attracting police attention. Church was a haven from the constant surveillance of whites, and it was in church that blacks could vent their pent-up emotions and were indeed exhorted to do so by their ministers, the best of whom transported their congregations to emotional heights unreachable in the buttoned-down daily lives of a race under siege.

"The South had fabulous preachers and evangelists," remembered one Bessie Smith fan. "Some would stand on corners and move the crowds from there. . . . If you had any church background, like people who came from the South as I did, you would recognize a similarity between what she was doing and what those preachers and evangelists from there did, and how they moved people."[4]

The power to "move people," to help them express their inner emotions, was a rare and valuable gift. Although the Civil War had brought freedom from slavery, nothing had changed the rule of white supremacy. It wasn't that they were unwanted in the South, exactly; blacks had an important role to play. The purpose of their existence was to work for white people. "What good does it do to teach a negro Shakespeare, Latin, or Greek when all that he will ever be is a day laborer and a field hand?" one white Southerner asked around the turn of the twentieth century, expressing a typical attitude. "A negro can succeed in the South if he is content to be a negro and remain in a negro's place." That place was at the bottom of Southern society, and any upward aspirations were quickly and aggressively confronted and stifled. One professor at Southwestern Presbyterian College in Memphis, Tennessee—just upriver from Chattanooga—argued that blacks needed to be restrained if America were to progress as a nation: "The black man is to be restrained, hampered, brow-beaten, discouraged within the next quarter of a century as never before in all the bitter years of his existence on this continent." White Southerners knew that only constant vigilance, repression, and terror could keep blacks from claiming what was rightfully theirs.[5]

This was the South of Bessie Smith's youth, and like many black Southerners, she looked for a way out. On the crowded streets of Chattanooga's black neighborhoods, she began to sing her way toward a different life. Although blacks generally were forced to remain quiet, apart from the occasional "yes, sir" or "no, ma'am," while in the presence of whites, exceptions were made for singing—on the public sidewalk (though not in all-white neighborhoods) and in the church. Bessie Smith never had much interest in the religious message the black preachers delivered, but she loved the emotion they expressed and brought out in their flocks.

The preachers may have had a more direct line to God, but no one had a greater access to the inner emotional landscape than Bessie Smith, with a voice that was not merely heard but felt. "She was a natural singer," say those who heard her in the early days. "She was just a teenager, and she obviously didn't know the artist she was. She didn't know how to dress—she just sang in her street clothes—but she was such a natural that she could wreck anybody's show." That was the point, after all: "wrecking" the show meant breaking through the veneer of composure, coaxing—demanding—a response that was visceral, that meant something. For the preacher: speaking in tongues, women fainting, sometimes even the men fainting. For Bessie Smith: people rising up from the seats, shaking their heads, shouting back at her—"Say it, sister!"—the old call-and-response. What they "wrecked" was the fragile web of public behavior, exposing the naked emotional life that pulsed below it all the time. She would continue to respond to the church in her career, courting scandal in songs such as "Preachin' the Blues," which spoke to both religious and sexual fervor in the same breath.[6]

She had natural talent, but she also had the will to transcend her background. Where she got the idea—and the courage—to aspire to a life beyond manual labor will never be known. But she spent her youth working on her act with Andrew and making enough money to contribute to the household. But by 1912, at the age of eighteen, she was ready to get out from under her family obligations. She convinced her oldest brother, Clarence, to get her an audition with the Moses Stokes Company, a traveling vaudeville and minstrel show in which Clarence worked as emcee. She was hired on the spot—albeit as a tap dancer, not a singer—and she took off for a life on the road. Dancing, singing, it didn't matter; she was finally getting out of Chattanooga. Though it was just the first of many touring shows in which Smith worked, it forged a link in the tradition of great blueswomen, for the star of the Moses Stokes Company was, of course, the great Ma Rainey. At this point, Rainey was just on the cusp of her greatest success, and she no doubt set a striking example of the potential for a career in show business.

Touring with Ma Rainey exposed a whole new world to Smith. She reveled in the freedom of travel, a luxury that few black women were able to enjoy. The pragmatist in her was thrilled, too, as the touring revealed town after town filled with folks eager to pay for entertainment. For Smith, this was the equivalent of running away to join the circus. Life was faster and looser, and the rules were different on the road. Ma Rainey and Bessie Smith cemented a relationship—possibly romantic, but certainly warm—that lasted throughout Smith's career. Maud Smith, the wife of Bessie's brother Clarence, told stories of going with Bessie to visit Ma Rainey in her retirement. According to Maud, Rainey was "like a mother" to Bessie. As already noted, there was always speculation as to the true nature of their relationship, and they may have been both friends and lovers.[7]

After touring with Rainey for a few months, Smith left the company for unknown reasons. She never returned to the sidewalks of Chattanooga, though, and instead was able to get work in the T.O.B.A. circuit of black theaters, traveling throughout the South, where she perfected her routine for the next seven years. Through

Rainey, Smith had learned a vaudevillian repertoire of song, dance, and comedy. Smith adopted Rainey's bawdy, good-times style and made it a part of her singing, something Janis Joplin would later pick up on. The earthy, nurturing-yet-saucy mother figure of Joplin's "Tell Mama" (1970) channeled this legacy directly.

Ma Rainey's playful, bickering "Ma-and-Pa" routines were the cornerstone of her success, and Smith recognized their appeal. Like Rainey, Smith's great theme was the man–woman relationship. Each song was another opportunity to reexamine love in all its glorious and devastating forms. This approach would become the central theme of American popular music in the decades to come, for female and male singers alike. As the twentieth-century love song fluctuated between dark and light, Smith explored both sides and so, in turn, did her successors: Billie Holiday pierced the heart's deepest chambers with songs like "The Man I Love" (1940), while Etta James laughed and challenged her lover in "Roll with Me, Henry" (1955).

In 1920, however, Smith was alone among singers, having cultivated her own personal style, omitting most of Rainey's minstrel-stage gags and focusing on her voice and the elements of pure singing: vocal power, range, phrasing, and tone. Smith made these changes and then left the South for good. Her move to the North was a signal event in the development of the blues, for Smith aimed to take the sound of the South with her on a journey far from tent shows and all-black theaters and to bring it to a wider audience. All art hopes to speak of universal human truths, but this can be achieved only by giving voice to the particular. Bessie Smith's voice was rich with Southern history, weathered by the Southern air; it was rough with emotion, wise with sorrow and a childhood of hard work. Bessie's voice was hers alone.

Around 1920, at the age of twenty-six, Smith moved to Philadelphia and began performing along the eastern seaboard. The Jazz Age was dawning and Prohibition had just begun. The twentieth century's first bloom of "youth culture" was in ascendance, and though Bessie

Smith was edging her way past "young," she embraced its spirit of hedonism, began to fudge her age, and went looking for fame and good times. Her early tours with Ma Rainey were no doubt instructive in living what might now be called the "rock star" life. Always up for a good time, Smith was headed to Harlem, home to the liveliest nightlife in the country.

When Prohibition went into effect in January 1920, its direct consequence was to make Harlem's after-hours clubs even hotter, as they attracted more and more rebellious blacks and whites to their now-underground revels. Many Southern-born blacks, like Bessie Smith, were less affected by the ban than whites, having had more experience with homemade alcohol as a matter of economic necessity. Smith claimed that "anything sealed" (i.e., factory-made) made her sick, and she was known to carry a flask of moonshine in her purse. As with most Americans in the 1920s, Prohibition did not stop Bessie Smith from drinking—it merely channeled her budget for alcohol into the black market.[8]

Post–World War I Harlem was home to much more than speakeasies, however. It was quickly becoming the capital of Black America. When black veterans returning from Europe faced unexpected racism from their fellow Americans, the cultural elite of Harlem responded. Black cultural leaders such as scholar W. E. B. Du Bois, the writer Alain Locke, and others promoted the concept of "The New Negro," highlighting the sensitive, compassionate, and intellectual qualities of African-Americans that were often obscured by the clichés of minstrelsy: the childlike, simple-minded Sambo; the "coon" figure of the lazy slave; and Mammy, the icon of benign, uncomplaining maternal servitude. Du Bois, Locke, and other members of the Harlem Renaissance devoted themselves to rehumanizing African-Americans.

Harlem was also home to Marcus Garvey's Back-to-Africa movement, which encouraged black pride in the face of mounting disillusionment due to unmet, post-slavery aspirations. From 1917 on, race riots had become a staple of the national political scene, with newly arrived Southern blacks scapegoated for all that was wrong with the nation's economy.

Harlem was an oasis for African-Americans, a place where they, as the majority race, could feel secure expressing themselves politically and artistically. When Harlem's white counterparts downtown in Greenwich Village discovered this cultural flowering, Harlem became a magnet for the white avant-garde, as well. Harlem gained a reputation as a place where both blacks and whites could lose their inhibitions. It was the perfect setting for Bessie Smith and her songs of emotional emancipation. Decades later, as women flocked to the concerts of Aretha Franklin and Janis Joplin—"lookin' for liberation," as Joplin put it—they would participate in a ritual that began at the feet of Bessie Smith. Her booming voice; wide, swiveling hips; and wicked laughter gave the modern American woman a whole new way to feel free.[9]

1922

> Miss Smith is known from the Atlantic to the Pacific and from the Gulf of Mexico to the Hudson Bay as one who really sings the "blues" as they should be sung. She is the girl who put the blue in "blues."
>
> *Pittsburgh Courier,* 1924[10]

The North

Zutty Singleton, the great early jazz drummer, played with Bessie Smith ("Miss Bessie," he called her—"I could never get up enough nerve to call her just 'Bessie'") in New Orleans in 1922, a year before her first released record. She was touring, as usual, and had drawn a sold-out crowd, as was also normal for Smith by this time. Years of working the theater circuit throughout the South, and occasionally in the North, had earned her an audience that was more urban and possibly larger than that of her mentor, Ma Rainey. Though they had a lot in common—a deep, soulful voice; an earthy sense of humor; an ample silhouette; and a taste for the wild side of life—Smith and Rainey were growing apart, stylistically. Rainey never gave up her down-home, country blues style, with its rural subject matter and minstrel-show influences. Smith crafted a stage presence and singing style that was a bit more refined. She wore opulent, draped gowns, and while they often were gaudy, they could not rival Ma Rainey's chaotic, gypsylike assemblages of silk and velvet, long ropes of (faux) pearls, and all that gold: gold necklaces, gold earrings and gold teeth. Compared to Ma Rainey, Bessie Smith, in her ostrich-plumed headdress and fringed shawl, looked demure.

Smith was edging away from Rainey's influence in other ways, too. Zutty Singleton's memory of her 1922 New Orleans performances offers some clues as to why she moved north, away from the South of her formative years and its secure audience base. "At that time her stage set-up was like the old-time recording studios," he recalled, "with the old-fashioned horn. And she would explain to the audience how she made records, and sing the tunes she had recorded, like 'Gulf Coast Blues,' 'Aggravatin' Papa,' 'Baby Won't You Please Come Home,' and a whole gang of blues."[11]

The image is striking, reminiscent of Ma Rainey's "Phantom" performance, stepping out of a giant Victrola and onto the live stage. For here was Bessie Smith, with no records to her name, preparing the audience to hear her in a new medium, allowing them a glimpse not only of her private life offstage (recording songs by day), but also into the private world of her own ambitions—she was going to be on records, she was going to be a star. For an audience of Southern blacks accustomed to hiding their own aspirations in the public sphere, this would have been exhilarating, and it must have been for Smith, too.

In this world, only "uppity" blacks shared their aspirations publicly—ambition itself was a white prerogative. Those who did succeed were careful not to flaunt it, for fear of white retribution. "The more a Negro owned," recalled the educator and black leader Benjamin Mays, who was born the same year as Bessie Smith, "the more humble he had to act in order to keep in the good graces of white people." Failure to do so could be deadly; fifty-one blacks were lynched in 1922, the year of Bessie Smith's New Orleans performance. Lynchings were public reminders of the consequences of black aspiration; they usually were held in public with the support of the local law enforcement and an audience of men, women, and children. Between 1882 and 1946, at least 4,715 blacks were lynched in the United States.[12]

The spectacle of a black woman onstage bragging about her accomplishments was an act of real courage. Bessie Smith had dreamed of getting out of Chattanooga and having a career, and there she was on the stage, telling other black folks about how she had done it and how far she was going to go, instead of keeping quiet and trying to get ahead while no one was looking. This was perhaps her greatest gift, something beyond vocal power. It was her ability to share herself with her audience, the way she allowed them to commune with her emotional reality for the duration of a song and the conviction it took to deliver it. Bessie Smith, in other words, had soul.

The metaphysics of American popular music begins and ends with the question of soul. This is the otherworldly aspect of music, the part of a song that is separate from the mechanical issues of melody, tempo, time signature, and timbre. Soul is what is felt, not merely heard. A perfect song can be soulful, but to have soul, it must be performed by a special singer. Soul is a quality in a singer that is both innate and acquired; the deep understanding of life implied in her song speaks to both a personal sensitivity to the world and often a personal history marked by lessons in pain. A performer either has soul or she doesn't, but it can't be bought or even convincingly learned, though sometimes it is found, later, after the performer has had a moving experience and suddenly feels it deep down inside. In Bessie Smith's case, it was there from the beginning. It made up the largest part of Smith's presence, for even those who never heard her sing live could testify to the corporality of her recordings, the very insistence of The Voice filling a room. Her voice was a medium, delivering soul. It never evoked just one feeling, but a multitude, rich with ambiguities, personal testimonies to the way life really was. And although she was not a political person as such (nor did she call herself a feminist), Bessie Smith nevertheless lived politics in the way few people do: by acting according to her principles. It has become commonplace to assert that the personal is the political, but it's not quite that simple. Only the personal—made public—becomes the political, and that's just what Smith spent her life doing. She put it all out there in public: her mind, heart, and soul.

One of the curious aspects of Smith's faux–recording-studio set on that 1922 New Orleans stage was the fact that the earliest known recordings of Bessie Smith were not made until 1923. (There have been rumors of earlier ones: the Chicago Defender reported in 1921 that Smith had been recording with the Emerson Records company, and an advertisement in the Defender a few months later promoting Smith's appearance onstage in Philadelphia contains a reference to Columbia Records, but no recordings have ever been found.) Smith may very well have concocted the set as a personal vision of what was to come; self-esteem would never be a problem for Bessie Smith.[13]

The Defender may have been confused by talk of Smith's early and unsuccessful auditions for record companies. In 1921, for example, Smith is known to have auditioned for Black Swan Records, but had not been offered a recording contract. Black Swan was the first black-owned record company, a fact that was deployed as a marketing strategy in advertisements reading, "The Only Genuine Colored Record. Others Are Only Passing for Colored." Set among the numerous advertisements for hair-straightening tonics and skin-bleaching solutions in this 1922 black newspaper, Black Swan's reversal of the "passing" phenomenon (in which light-skinned blacks "passed" as whites) is striking. Despite its posturing, Black Swan decided that Smith's earthy sound was too rough for its taste.[14]

Black Swan's decision not to sign Bessie Smith was both an artistic and a commercial mistake, for within a few years her voice became emblematic of the African-American experience. In the 1920s and 1930s, the voice of Bessie Smith and the trumpet of Louis Armstrong came to represent Black America—or at least how it sounded. Two years after that audition, Smith finally got her opportunity to record, and in New York City in February 1923, Bessie Smith began her life-long relationship with Columbia Records.

Competing stories exist, each telling how Bessie Smith came to Columbia's attention. Frank Walker, the executive at Columbia in charge of black artists, claimed that he was the one who brought her north for her first recording. Clarence Williams, a music-industry player who attached himself to Bessie Smith in much the same way as Perry Bradford had to Clara Smith, the first black recording star, recalled that it was his initiative that brought Bessie Smith to Columbia Records. Whatever the case, they both eventually profited from her success, with Williams receiving an especially large share as the self-credited "author" of many of Smith's songs, a designation that remains unclear to this day.[15]

In early 1923, however, Smith's priority was securing a recording contract. By this time, she had moved to South Philadelphia and was living with Jack Gee, another name that would mysteriously appear from time to time in the composer credits for her songs. John "Jack" Gee and Bessie Smith met in 1922, when he had gotten the courage to ask her out after going to see her sing several times. After he chased a robber and was subsequently shot on their first date, Smith spent weeks at his hospital bedside. He was a tall, handsome man with an open face and a big, dimpled smile. By the time he was released, their relationship was solid. They shared a few things in common: Jack Gee had grown up in the South (Virginia) but had moved to Philadelphia in search of better opportunities. They also shared a propensity for high drama, drinking, luxury items, and spousal violence. All these became fixtures of their marriage.[16]

Gee was working as a night watchman (though he preferred to let people believe he was a Philadelphia police officer) and hocked his uniform and a pocketwatch in order to buy Smith a fancy dress for her audition with Columbia. (It was his last such act: when it became clear that Smith was a success, he quit his job and began buying himself expensive clothes.) In preparation for the audition, Smith and Gee traveled to Harlem and stayed with Gee's family. It was Bessie Smith's first time in New York.

In 1923, the offices and studios of Columbia Records were in Columbus Circle on West 59th Street—across the city and far downtown from the Gee home in East Harlem and a world away from the tent shows and sidewalks of Smith's Chattanooga beginnings. Columbia was the big time, a leading company in its field. Yet its recording practices were still relatively primitive, awaiting the introduction of electrical recording tools that would arrive two years later. In the meantime, Bessie Smith arrived at the studio to find a huge horn— much like a giant version of that on an old Victrola—protruding from a curtain, behind which sat the recording engineer. The recording was purely acoustic, the volume of each performance dependent upon the strength of the singer's voice, with attention paid to balancing it against the instrumental accompaniment, so that both could be heard. Singing into the new recording equipment was unnerving for many vocalists, and probably for Smith, too; she tried eleven times to make a good recording but finally gave up and returned the next day.

On her third try on the second day, Bessie Smith successfully recorded her first "side" (each successfully recorded song was called a "side," as each of the 78 rpm records had only one song on each side). The song was "Downhearted Blues." The song is slow, with an easy, rolling beat, much of its rhythm coming not from Williams's piano playing, which is rather stiff, but instead from Smith's assured timing, the way she begins to sing just before the beat in some cases, leaning back behind it in others.[17]

"People, it's hard to love someone when that someone don't love you." With this line, Smith began her recording career. It was an auspicious start. Her voice was pure authority, nothing in it betraying more than a day's worth of failed takes, nothing to suggest that this was anything but the first time she had sung it, or that she may have been making it up as she went along. The first emphasis in this line was on the word *love*. She stretched it out, emphasizing it, then in the very next word, took it further, with the *someone* reaching an even higher range before dropping back into the last half of the line. It was an idiosyncratic reading that immediately grabbed the attention of the listener. The next three lines were interesting, too, but the song didn't really start to swing until the second stanza, when it changed into a standard blues verse format with two repeated first verses followed by the response of the third:

> *Trouble, trouble, I've had it all my days (2x)*
> *It seems like trouble's going to follow me to my grave*
>
> *I ain't never loved but three men in my life (2x)*
> *My father, my brother, the man that wrecked my life*
>
> *It may be a week, it may be a month or two (2x)*
> *But the day you quit me, honey, it's coming home to you*
>
> *I got the world in a jug, the stopper's in my hand (2x)*
> *I'm gonna hold it until you men come under my command*[18]

It is here, at "Trouble, trouble," when the power of Smith's voice came to the fore. Jumping in on the phrase just before the measure began, she invested the word with real meaning: *trouble*—chaotic, jarring, her voice an arc from one word to the next, and the listener believed that this woman knew what she was talking about. In each subsequent verse, the pattern was the same, with the first reading of the line heavy and dark, its repetition a fainter echo but impregnated with the portent of the first, the repetition of the words allowing the listener the opportunity to reflect upon their meaning.

The lyrics described an emotional journey from being "downhearted," and "heartbroken" to the final two stanzas, when Smith seemed to take charge of the situation, threatening her lover: "The day you quit me, honey, it's coming home to you," and that final, enigmatic verse. "I got the world in a jug," she sang, creating an image of a woman literally holding the world and all its problems and contingencies. Only she could cork it, with "the stopper" in her hand, thus controlling the very pulse of life and refusing to do so until "you men come under my command." This is a song about control, the control that Bessie Smith meant to exert over the men in her world.

What was so powerful about the verse is not only the vivid imagery but the way she delivered it: her singing conveyed power, yes, but it was a complex sound, one full of ambiguity, not merely anger or determination ("I'm gonna hold it . . .")—but also sadness at having been put in this position ("I ain't never loved but three men in my life . . .")—and a little bit of fear, as if this is all a bluff, hoping she wouldn't be called on it. The depth of feeling never sounded like merely one thing: just anger; just fear. It was all of those things at the same time. Her voice flows—a rich, thick sound with its own momentum, ribboning out through the speakers like heavy cream. She sang it slowly, each line almost at a spoken pace, allowing the listener to feel the impact of the words in real time: sad, determined, strong. Eighty years later, lasered onto a CD, the voice of Bessie Smith still rings with authority.

The song's narrative in fact foreshadowed the next fourteen years of her short life: the problems with men ("the man that wrecked my life"), her growing power as an artist ("It may be a week, it may be a month or two"), and her conquest of the recording industry ("I got the world in a jug"). From this perspective, she did succeed. By the end of 1923, "Downhearted Blues" had sold three-quarters of a million copies—more than Ma Rainey or any other blues artist had dreamed of, and Smith would dominate the blues and jazz scene for the rest of the decade.[19]

Bessie Smith's recordings quickly became an important part of black American life. By the mid-1920s, the cost of a record player had dropped below $10, a price that was within reach of many black Americans if they used the installment plan. Phonographs became a standard feature in the homes of middle-class black families, and Bessie Smith 78s were the main thing they played. Smith's voice was a part of the fabric of everyday black life in the 1920s, entertaining and inspiring her audience in the parlor, in the barrooms, and onstage. In 1924, the *Chicago Defender* promoted her live performances, writing that "Bessie is making thousands of friends on her present tour," and indeed that was exactly how many blacks perceived her—as one of their own. "Of course," another *Defender* journalist wrote, "her recording has made her prestige rise higher, but glad to say she is the same Bessie, wearing the same size shoes."[20]

Smith's fans, both black and white, appreciated her lack of affectation and felt that the public image of Bessie Smith was essentially the same as the offstage one: "A kind of roughish sort of woman," as her clarinetist, Buster Bailey, described her. "She was good-hearted, and big-hearted, and she liked to juice. . . . For Bessie, singing was just a living. She didn't consider it anything special." Her rough style was a big part of her appeal. Smith helped to establish the precedent of the singer-as-glamorous-rebel that so many popular music stars—from Billie Holiday to Elvis Presley to Madonna—went on to replicate. Smith's endless touring schedule afforded her many opportunities to interact with her fans—for better or for worse. Ruby Walker recalled an incident in Baltimore in 1923 when Smith and her chorus girls stopped by a nightclub after performing their own show. Though she had recorded only a few songs at this point, Smith was immediately recognized by the crowd, and they clamored for her to get onstage. Amidst all the commotion, they were confronted by a few drunken revelers, angry that their seats had been given to Smith and her entourage. When the leader pulled a switchblade on Walker, Smith jumped up, grabbed the knife, and starting punching. "When it comes to fighting," Walker said, "she is the best." The drunks were led out by security, the crowd cheered, and Smith placated them with a chorus of W. C. Handy's "St. Louis Blues." It was stories like this one that burnished Smith's reputation as a wild woman, and they were passed along the grapevine from Baltimore to Harlem to Chicago and beyond.[21]

Though excluded from the inside gossip of the black community, Smith's white fans nevertheless picked up on her earthy personality—oftentimes the lyrics to her songs were the tip-off—and were drawn to it, too. The 1920s culture maven Carl Van Vechten, one of Smith's most vocal white fans, concurred: "This was no actress; no imitator of a woman's woes; there was no pretence." Van Vechten made an effort to see Smith wherever she performed, even though many of those shows were intended for black audiences only. Harlem's after-hours nightclubs were among the few that welcomed integrated audiences, though not all Harlem nightclubs were so open (most served either blacks or whites exclusively). For her part, Smith made no great effort to appeal to whites, even once they started buying her records and going to her shows. If they happened to like her, fine. If not, that was okay, too. It was this lack of "pretence," as Van Vechten put it, that appealed to whites in the first place.[22]

Some of Smith's songs articulated experiences that were applicable exclusively to the lives of black Americans, such as "Bo-Weevil Blues" (1924), whose pestilential subject was common to black folk songs dating back to slavery times, and "Backwater Blues" (1927), which described the effects of a flood and quickly became associated with the tragic 1927 Mississippi Valley Flood, in which more than 300,000 blacks lost their homes. "Washwoman's Blues" (1928) was one of the few recorded Bessie Smith songs to mention white people specifically, referring to working as a cook in "some white folks' yard." The reference here is deliberate yet relatively neutral—in this case, working for a white person as a cook is depicted as preferable to washing their clothes. "Bo-Weevil Blues" and "Washwoman's Blues" spoke to the lives and work of many black Southerners, but the majority of Smith's songs pertained to the new reality for African-Americans in the 1920s: life in the urban North.[23]

Whether in search of work or simply as an escape from the terrors of southern Jim Crow, millions of African-Americans began moving north around the beginning of World War I and continued to do so for decades, in a domestic diaspora that came to be known simply as the "Great Migration." Cities such as Chicago and Detroit, and New York City's Harlem neighborhood, quickly became centers for the new black culture, and Bessie Smith found enthusiastic audiences in all of them.

As more blacks left their rural lives behind, blues songs increasingly depicted life in the North and the new pressures there. Blues singers wrote fewer songs about farm work and more about the worries of finding new jobs and the loneliness of their new lives in the big cities. Smith captured the sentiment in her "One and Two Blues" (1926), singing about a love that "starts way down home below the Dixon line." Like most of her songs, this one is humorous and yet speaks to a deeper truth, describing the challenges in adapting to the industrial North, with its "eight-hour days" and hard-cash economy (even the title phrase, "One and Two," is a euphemism for money).[24]

All the inevitable challenges of life in the big city—the fast pace, the constant interaction with strangers, the intimacy of living in close quarters with so many others, the difficulty of finding a loving mate—found their expression in Bessie Smith's music. In "Keeps On A-Rainin' (Papa, He Can't Make No Time)" (1923), she even gave voice to the Southerners' reaction to one of the biggest differences between the North and the South: the weather. "In the wintertime when it's ice and snow, you know your pretty mama's got to have some dough."[25]

Apart from the climate, there was one other aspect of the South that persisted in the songs of newly Northern blacks, and that was the sense of home that the South continued to represent. Bessie Smith's "Louisiana Low Down Blues" (1924) typified this feeling. "My home ain't up North," she sang, "it's further down the road." Life in the North was often much more difficult than Southern blacks had expected. Racism extended north of the Mason-Dixon Line; it was just more subtly expressed. Disappointment with their new lives in the North fueled idealized dreams of the South. Mostly, these displaced people yearned for a sense of familiarity, what Smith called the "solid ground" of the Southern communities they had left behind.[26]

Bessie Smith's blues drew upon traditional melodies, chords, and lyrics—those that had previously been used in songs about the experience of slavery, and later the disappointments of post-Emancipation life—and adapted them to the new African-American experience of life in the Northern cities. Her music had a profound influence on the writer Langston Hughes, one of the central figures of the Harlem Renaissance. Hughes considered her a serious artist well before most of his contemporaries did, probably because of his respect for traditional African-American cultural forms, such as jazz and blues. (Most leaders of the Harlem Renaissance preferred European musical styles.) Like Langston Hughes, Bessie Smith was interested in the real lives of African-Americans, and both artists gave voice to their disappointments and dreams. Though the Harlem Renaissance was largely an elite literary phenomenon, the music created by Bessie Smith was the soundtrack playing along in the background of working-class Harlemites' everyday lives.

While many of her songs were based on the experience of African-Americans, the emotional content of the music was accessible and appealing to listeners of any race. For Bessie Smith's white fans, the fact of racial segregation posed a greater problem than her lyrics. Smith toured the South and Northeast constantly throughout her career, returning to New York intermittently to record and perform there, and to Philadelphia to relax at home with her family. Whites generally were admitted to predominantly black theaters in the North, though their attendance never matched that of Smith's black fans. In the South, however, she performed to strictly segregated audiences, usually all-black, with the occasional "whites-only" shows later in the evening if the demand was high enough. "On Saturday night she played a special show for white only [sic]," wrote one reviewer in Nashville in 1923, "and knocked all the tin off the roof of the theater. Trouble was had in getting the people to leave the theater as they cried for more."[27]

Smith's popularity with Southern white audiences kept growing. Apart from Northern enclaves like Harlem and Chicago's South Side, the South contained most of Smith's white fans, because it was Southern whites who were most familiar with black culture, from the days of slavery on. Nowhere did white and black people live closer together than in the South, and this was the irony of post-Reconstruction segregation—it developed because of this closeness, not despite it. Southern whites had heard the blues since childhood—from their washwomen, cooks, nannies, and gardeners. A fondness for black music was nothing to be ashamed of in the Jim Crow South; the musical talent of blacks was acknowledged even in slavery times, and it continued into the twentieth century. In 1924, Bessie Smith performed for an all-white audience in Atlanta, where one of the prominent white music dealers reported that her records "actually outsell everything else in the catalog." Like many other black artists, Bessie Smith was celebrated as an entertainer in the South, but the fruits of her success were limited: her records may have occupied a prime spot in the drawing rooms of white Southerners, but Smith herself could never be invited in.[28]

While the color line was more obvious in the South, New York had its own version of Jim Crow, a subtler set of expectations for the behavior of each race that was enforced through the urban geography of neighborhood segregation as well as psychological and social pressure. This was the young John Hammond's New York. His mother, Emily Vanderbilt Sloane Hammond, was the great-granddaughter of Cornelius Vanderbilt, the original railroad tycoon. She was a progressive reformer in the classic sense: "The social order she found was the one she accepted. Racial minorities were beyond her reach. Blacks were porters and laundresses. The poor existed and were to be helped," wrote John Hammond of his mother's well-meaning but often condescending views, which were typical of the upper classes in the Progressive Era.[29]

As Hammond's interest in black music grew, his unquestioning acceptance of his mother's racial attitudes faltered. "My record collection demonstrated the unique talents of Negro artists," he wrote, "while what I saw and heard about Negroes denied my growing respect for them." He finally confronted his mother with the contradiction. "John, you're old enough to know the facts of life," she told him. "I realize that you're fascinated by colored people, and I want you to know that everybody is alike. But with Negroes . . . their skulls harden when they are twelve. There *is* a difference." Hammond meditated on this, but after listening to his favorite jazz records, he came to a different conclusion. "I wanted to believe her," he admitted, "but I simply could not."[30]

Bessie Smith was instrumental in changing the racial outlook of this young Vanderbilt. As a seventeen-year-old boarding student at Connecticut's Hotchkiss School, Hammond was permitted to travel to New York City once a week to take violin lessons in Morningside Heights, the West Side neighborhood just south of Harlem. One Friday, Hammond noticed Bessie Smith's name on a theater marquee in the neighborhood. After his lesson, he raced across town to his family home on the Upper East Side, told them he was going out to play in a string quartet, then "hurried uptown to hear Bessie. I had her records then, and I considered her the greatest blues singer I had ever heard." This became Hammond's regular pattern—pretending to be a student of classical European music while secretly indulging his passion for Harlem's blues and jazz. "I went to every theater and club in Harlem and was usually the only white person there."[31]

Or was he? By the late 1920s, when Hammond became a regular at Harlem's nightclubs, the uptown neighborhood had already become a destination for white New Yorkers seeking an exotic thrill or even a glimpse of the real lives of African-Americans. But many of the clubs Hammond frequented, such as Small's Paradise, Connie's Inn, and the Cotton Club (named for its Southern plantation interior design motif), were known for their overwhelmingly white audiences, and blacks were welcomed only as performers or as waiters. There was much more to African-American life than singing, dancing, and serving, but the grimmer realities of daytime life in Harlem were literally invisible to whites who made the evening trips uptown.

Bessie Smith, with her dark skin and down-home voice, was an exception to the type of female performer who usually was seen onstage in these clubs. Much more desirable to management were the fair-skinned, straight-haired chorus girls who were also popular in the musical theater of the time—Josephine Baker was the aesthetic ideal—but Smith's talent and recording successes earned her a spot on the cabaret stage. Northern whites may have seen a limited view of black life there, but it was more than they had seen before, and it was a first step toward the integrated audiences that would later applaud Billie Holiday at Café Society and Aretha Franklin at the Fillmore West.[32]

In the 1920s, Harlem's nightspots were an important venue for interaction between blacks and whites. The growth of the recording industry in that decade brought black artists into the homes of many whites who later sought out their live performances, and the cycle profitably reversed itself, as well. The most famous of these white enthusiasts was Carl Van Vechten—New York Times music and dance critic, essayist, and longtime fan of Bessie Smith. His patronage of Harlem and its artists embodied the contradictions and controversies inherent in this uptown/downtown cultural exchange. Van Vechten was a sincere supporter of African-American artists. He bought their artwork, attended their performances, and introduced them to wealthy white patrons at his famous cocktail parties. He also presumed to speak for them, as in his 1926 novel, Nigger Heaven, which, despite its now-shocking title, was an attempt to illustrate the more genteel side of Harlem. (The novel was criticized by blacks but quite popular with whites.) Van Vechten always seemed a bit self-congratulatory, but he was well-meaning despite his often-patronizing tone.

"It would seem incredible to me that anybody with any feeling—

musical or otherwise—could listen to Bessie Smith's recording of 'The Weeping Willow Blues' . . . without becoming a convert," wrote Van Vechten in a typically glowing passage. Along with his friend Langston Hughes, Van Vechten felt that the best of black artistry could be found in its folk culture: spirituals, jazz, and the blues. Like much of his work, Van Vechten's writing on Bessie Smith shows its age—rapturous praise for "this elemental conjure woman," and her "rough Ethiopian voice" resonate with condescension to the contemporary ear. But in 1926, the year those words were written, mainstream appreciation for black blues singers in the white or black press was a rarity, and Van Vechten's numerous pieces on the blues for *Vanity Fair* were respectful, admiring, and serious critical works.[33] Van Vechten was a true fan and a relentless socialite. He succeeded in insinuating himself into Smith's personal circle a few times, and his recollections of these experiences, along with his photographic portraits of the singer, have become his most enduring contribution to Smith's legacy.

He first saw Smith perform live at the Orpheum Theatre in Newark, New Jersey, in 1925. According to his own account, when he announced his destination to the white driver of the cab, the man replied, "Going to hear Bessie Smith? . . . No good trying. You can't get in. They've been hanging on the chandeliers all week"—which, if true, gives some indication as to the popularity of Smith among whites of all strata of society, from cab drivers to Park Avenue cultural critics. (Van Vechten, the consummate insider, somehow found his way to a box seat.) Her white audience may have been substantial, but at this show in Newark the crowd was almost all black, apart from Van Vechten and his entourage—"a vast sea of happy black faces," he wrote, "[n]ever before had I seen such an audience save at a typical Negro camp meeting in the South."

Bessie Smith finally took the stage, following a comedy act. "A great brown woman emerged . . . very large, and she wore a crimson satin robe, sweeping up from her trim ankles, and embroidered in multicolored sequins in designs. Her face was beautiful with the rich ripe beauty of southern darkness, a deep bronze-brown, matching the bronze of her bare arms." Van Vechten's description seems to emphasize the darkness of Smith's skin tone, which may have made her, in his eyes, an even more "authentic" black artist; he turns to African motifs several times, as well, to describe her power.

He also paid attention to the reaction of the crowd, providing an unusual perspective on the dynamics of Smith's performance:

> And now, inspired partly by the lines, partly by the stumbling strain of the accompaniment, partly by the power and magnetic personality of this elemental conjure woman and her plangent African voice, quivering with pain and passion . . . the crowd burst into hysterical shrieks of sorrow and lamentation. "Amens" rent the air. Little nervous giggles, like the shivering of Venetian glass, shocked the nerves.

Smith was in complete control of her audience, drawing out the emotional impact of every line. "It's true I loves yo', but I won't take mistreatments any mo'." "Dat's right," a girl cried from the audience. Smith's effect on her female fans was explosive and emotional. When Smith sang the next line: " 'O, Lawdy, Lawdy!' the girl beneath us shook with convulsive sobbing," wrote Van Vechten, who was as moved by the crowd's reaction as he was by Smith's singing. On meeting her backstage for the first time, he wrote, "This proved to be exactly the same experience that meeting any great interpreter is likely to be; we paid homages humbly and she accepted them with just the right amount of deference. I believe I kissed her hand. I hope I did."[34]

The coolness of Smith's interaction with Van Vechten was typical of her reaction to anyone who made a fuss over her: she accepted it as her due and then got on with her business. The class, race, or status of the admirer made no difference to her. "She would tell anybody to kiss her ass," said her niece, Ruby Walker. "Nobody messed with Bessie, black or white, it didn't make no difference." Another interaction between

Smith and Van Vechten proved Walker's point, and in the process became an essential element of Bessie Smith's larger-than-life legend.[35]

It was 1928 and by now Bessie Smith was one of the most famous black people (and one of the richest black performers) in America. Her appearance at one of Van Vechten's parties was undoubtedly a social coup for Carl and his wife, the former Russian ballerina Fania Marinoff, for Smith was known for mingling almost solely within the black community. Van Vechten, on the other hand, was famous for his salons, parties stocked with the cream of New York's artistic elite, from Broadway to Harlem—the twentieth century's first wave of Radical Chic. Among the guests that night were the composer George Gershwin, opera singer Marguerite d'Alvarez, and Adele Astaire, the popular Broadway dancer (and sister of Fred).

Bessie arrived sober but seemingly annoyed by her surroundings; her niece said that she had always disliked "dicty" people, those who tried to act superior to others. She hated snobs. She may have been paid by Van Vechten to perform at the party, or she may have gone as a personal favor to Porter Grainger, her pianist, who had an interest in gaining the kind of social acceptance that his attendance at a Van Vechten salon would bring. In any case, she was in no mood for small talk.

"How about a lovely, lovely dry martini?" asked Van Vechten with a smile.

"Whaaat—a dry martini?" she replied, "Ain't you got some whiskey, man? That'll be the only way I'll touch it. I don't know about no dry martinis, nor wet ones, either." Upon receiving her drink, Smith marched to the piano with Grainger and prepared to sing. When asked what songs she intended to perform, she replied, "Don't you worry about it. My piano player knows." Van Vechten may have provided the setting and the liquid fuel, but Smith dictated the terms.[36]

She began with "Work House Blues," a song whose lyrics about hard work, plowing, and cooking couldn't have been farther from her uptown surroundings. "She got down to the blues," Van Vechten wrote later, "really down to 'em. . . . It was the real thing: a woman cutting her heart open with a knife until it was exposed for us all to see, so that we suffered as she suffered." No doubt the suffering she inflicted on her audience was intentional: Smith was clearly uncomfortable at Van Vechten's soirée. She performed six or seven more songs with a drink break between each one. By the time the performance ended, she was totally inebriated. Her friends attempted to get her out of the party as quickly as possible, fearing the outrageous behavior they had seen so many times before. "Let's get her out of here quick," one said, "before she shows her ass."[37]

The two had escorted Smith through the party and almost to the door when Fania Marinoff stopped them. "Miss Smith," she exclaimed in her brightest show-business style, "you're *not* leaving without kissing me goodbye." Marinoff draped her thin arms around Smith's neck and pulled her close.

Smith screamed, "Get the fuck away from me, I ain't never heard such shit!" and pushed her hostess off, throwing her to the floor. Horrified, Smith's friends dragged her out to the hallway and toward the elevator. As they struggled in the hall, Carl Van Vechten rushed out of his apartment and came toward them. "It's alright, Miss Smith," he said quietly. "You were magnificent tonight."

Van Vechten may have fawned over Smith that night, but in later years he declined to circulate the story in its entirety, perhaps embarrassed by its retelling in the black community. Smith herself was known to repeat it, mimicking Van Vechten's offer of a "lovely, lovely dry martini," and telling her listeners, "Shiiit, you should have seen them ofays looking at me like I was some kind of singin' monkey!" This comment revealed Smith's general impression of the white community's newfound interest in black artists. She was wary of their attention and refused to go out of her way to please them. If she was concerned about being accepted, it was only the acceptance of the black community. As Ruby Walker understood it, "She pretended she didn't care about how people felt about her, but she really felt left out sometimes—not by white people; she *really* didn't care how they felt—

she just loved her own people, and she hated to see them trying to act so dicty and white." This quality in Bessie Smith—her down-to-earth attitude and sense of self-worth—endeared her to her black fans, who admired her strength, and it earned the respect of whites such as Van Vechten, who could not buy her friendship.[38]

The story of the night at the Van Vechtens' soon became a legend in Harlem, and Smith became its heroine. Her response to Marinoff ("I ain't never heard such shit!") helped transform Smith's own name into a new euphemism, as in, "I ain't never heard such Bessie Smith," and "*some* Bessie Smith"—all of which only served to enhance her reputation as a tough woman. Like the black folk hero Stagger Lee, Bessie Smith's name was acquiring the glamour associated with challenging the status quo. And, like Stagger Lee, Bessie Smith was becoming well known for her willingness to use violence—even against whites—if it was required to maintain her own sense of personal integrity. This was power.[39]

Bessie Smith had become a new kind of heroine. She was a beloved scoundrel, wicked and wise. She had come to represent an African-American alternative to those twin female rebels of mainstream white culture, the flapper and the vamp, whose devil-may-care pursuit of pleasure and career was a slap in the face of middle-class morality. Unlike white women, black women had never been confined to the home; they couldn't afford to stay there, anyway. Black women had been out in the world, working, before and after Emancipation. They were the breadwinners, church organizers, and community leaders, and with Bessie Smith, they began to contemplate the possibility of commanding attention as outspoken rebels, too.

Smith's reputation as a wild, often violent woman spread with her fame as a singer. There was the story of how she ran off the Ku Klux Klan at a tent show in North Carolina ("What the fuck you think you're doin'?" she was reported to have asked them. The question was rhetorical; the hooded Klansmen fled.) At a party in her hometown of Chattanooga that same year, Smith was stabbed by a man she had cussed out earlier in the night after he harassed her chorus girls. The local papers reported that Smith chased him for three blocks with the knife still lodged in her side before turning to one of the young women and saying, "Baby, take this thing out of me." Public reaction was swift and fierce. According to Ruby Walker, the attacker was beaten to death by Smith's fans upon his release from jail. "This was Bessie's hometown," Walker explained. "They loved her there." Bessie's fans were intense.[40]

She was well loved—by everyone, it seemed, but her husband, Jack Gee. Having married Gee just a few months after signing her first contract with Columbia in 1923, their marriage was always complicated by her career: the constant traveling, the long periods apart, the astonishing success that changed their financial status overnight. The marriage seemed to bring her happiness for a couple of years, after which the relationship became a series of arguments, jealous quarrels, and physical confrontations. Smith was tempted by partying, drinking, and younger men, and she shared her husband's weakness for other women. "She was a strong woman with a beautiful strong constitution," Ruby Walker said of her aunt, "and she loved a good time . . . but Jack couldn't see it that way, that's why every time you looked he was knocking her down."[41]

The domestic violence that Smith suffered at the hands of her husband was well known to her immediate circle of friends and family, but it seemed to be the one aspect of her life that was not shared with her audience. In a well-publicized life of sex, drugs, and other indiscretions, Smith's own abuse at the hands of her husband was the only taboo subject. In retrospect, the contrast between Bessie Smith's public image as a strong, proud, self-possessed woman and the violent reality of her marriage is striking. Unlike Billie Holiday, whose violent private life clearly informed her wounded, fragile public image, Smith consistently projected the persona of an invincible woman.

Smith was indeed strong; while she feared her husband's outbursts, she was not immobilized by that fear. Smith took steps to distance herself from her husband by touring without him, and she continued to make arrangements in her personal and professional life that preserved her independence. She was good at keeping her husband at a distance when the situation demanded it.

Bessie Smith's lesbian relationships were a case in point. These liaisons were well known to her inner circle as well as to virtually anyone who followed her career closely, but she always had these affairs while on tour, when her husband couldn't interfere. One such romance attracted the attention of a columnist for the *Interstate Tattler*, a black gossip rag published in Harlem that collected tips from all over the country. Signed "I. Telonyou," the "Town Tattle" column of February 27, 1925, read: "Gladys, if you don't keep away from B., G. is going to do a little convincing that he is her husband. Aren't you capable of finding some unexplored land 'all alone.' " While he must have heard the rumors, it is not known whether Jack Gee ever learned of his wife's relationship with Gladys Ferguson, a male impersonator— or of her liaisons with other women, such as the chorus girls in her show with whom Smith was known to fool around.[42]

While Ma Rainey sang openly of lesbianism in her "Prove It on Me Blues" (1928), Smith did not, although several of her songs, including "Soft Pedal Blues" (1925) celebrated the "buffet flat," a private club (often run by a woman) located in a private home or rooming house in which alcohol, gambling, sex shows, and prostitutes were made available to a select clientele. As Ruby Walker described it, "It was nothing but faggots and bulldykers, a real open house . . . [and] Bessie was well known." Smith was a regular customer of these establishments, and her lyrics illustrate her enthusiasm: "I'm drunk and full of fun— Yahoo!" Clearly, the only thing giving Smith the blues here is the need to "soft pedal" the entertainment—to keep down the noise.[43]

A hallmark of Bessie Smith's style was her determination to do exactly as she pleased. Even in the my-man-done-me-wrong songs so typical of the women's blues genre, Smith usually gets her way in the end. While the authorship of Smith's songs is not always clear (it seems almost certain, for instance, that Smith was not credited with many of her own compositions), it is notable that so many of her songs feature this theme of eventual triumph, suggesting that those who wrote songs for her did so with this concept in mind.[44] And because of Bessie Smith's success with this theme, it became a template for other women singers, as in Tina Turner's "You Should'a Treated Me Right" (1962) and, of course, Aretha Franklin's anthemic "Respect" (1967).

Many of Smith's songs describe the pain a woman feels when disappointed by a lover, but the image she projected was never merely that of a victim. A strong theme of justice runs through her work, as in her 1928 song, "Put It Right Here (Or Keep It Out There)," in which she tells her man that he'll "have to find another place for to park his old hips." This was justice explained in layman's terms.[45]

Smith's righteous indignation, the emotion that fueled so much of her best work, usually was inspired by her demand for equity in a relationship. While she often expressed it humorously, it was nevertheless the foundation of her performance style, and an important part of her public persona. The songs that describe a lover's rejection are almost always resolved with Smith's affirmation of her own self-worth. In "I Used to Be Your Sweet Mama" (1928), Smith completes the title phrase with: "But now I'm just as sour as can be." She does the same in "I Ain't Goin' to Play No Second Fiddle" (1925)—"'cause I'm used to playin' lead."[46]

Smith's insistence on fair play was significant not only as it related to equality in male–female relationships, but also in the broader scope of black–white relations. Just as African-American slaves' songs masked their objections to servitude beneath a veil of acceptable biblical references (the story of Moses leading the Israelites out of Egypt being a popular cover story for their own desire to escape slavery), Bessie Smith's songs could also be interpreted as the demands of black citizens for their share of the American Dream. Her songs' themes— refusal to accept mistreatment from men, sharp comebacks to put-downs and the like—could also vent feelings that her audience had about mistreatment from white employers and the white mainstream society in general. Although direct confrontation was still too dangerous (a more militant form of black musical expression was still forty years away), Smith's songs were important early sounds in the twentieth-century struggle for black civil rights.[47]

～

By 1929, Bessie Smith was a legend in her own time: a best-selling recording artist with more than 130 recordings to her credit; one of the most popular stage performers on the T.O.B.A. circuit; a celebrated public figure well loved for her rowdy, down-to-earth personality; and one of the highest-paid black entertainers in the country due to her high recording and performance fees (and despite the fact that she never received a cent in royalty fees for her songs). She stood out even among the great black stars of her day: trumpeter Louis Armstrong, dancer Bill "Bojangles" Robinson, and fellow blueswomen Ethel Waters, Ida Cox, Alberta Hunter, and Victoria Spivey. But she was more than merely famous, she was a living symbol of personal freedom: she did what she liked; she spoke her mind, no matter how outrageous her opinion; she flouted bourgeois norms and indulged in alcohol, drugs, and recreational sex.

She had set a precedent, establishing the protocol for future musical artists in her fusion of personal style and professional demeanor. Her career marked the beginning of a new aesthetic premise in American music: the singer *was* the song. When Bessie Smith sang, "Come on and rock me with a steady roll," this was no coy burlesque show, but a strong woman with a big appetite whose audience knew she was serious.[48] It was a persona that worked for Smith but would wreak havoc on the lives of many performers who followed—singers such as Etta James and Janis Joplin, who found themselves bound to wild onstage images that sapped their private emotional lives.

Smith's erasure of the boundary between the personality of the artist and the delivery of the song constitutes one of the most significant

contributions of African-American music style to mainstream American popular music. Suddenly, popular music was personal. It cut deeper
than the Tin Pan Alley moon-spoon-June lyric, and it spoke to real
pain and real desire. There would be plenty of silly pop tunes in the
decades to come, but when the charts became too unbearably light,
someone like Aretha Franklin would come along, working within the
Bessie Smith tradition, and deliver, "I Never Loved a Man (The Way
That I Love You)" (1967), guiding her audience back to a more intimate place, and, like Smith, leading them there with her voice.

1929

Now comes the big hush. Just the piano goin'. It's the blues.
Somethin' tightens up in me. Man, what will she look like? I
ain't never seen her before.

Then I hear her voice and, gosh, I know this is it . . . my
lucky day. I'm hearing the best and I'm seeing her, too . . . a
great big woman and she completely dominates the stage and
the whole house when she sings the "Yellow Dog Blues." Ah!
I don't know, she just reaches out and grabs and holds me.
There's no explainin' her singing, her voice. She don't need a
mike; she don't use one. . . . Everybody can hear her. This gal
sings from the heart. She never lets me get away from her
once. As she sings she walks slowly around the stage. Her
head, sort of bowed. From where I'm sittin' I'm not sure
whether she even has her eyes open. On and on, number after
number, the same hush, the great performance, the deafening
applause. We won't let her stop. What a woman. . . .

Outside it's still cold. I don't know when I get up to go
and I'm sure I'm not sure where I'm goin'; just walkin'. But
there's a record playin' back somethin' that was recorded;
recorded in my head. There's that one woman's voice, "Oh,

you easy rider, why don't you hurry back home. . . ." So help
me, I still hear it.

—Art Hodes, jazz pianist and historian[49]

The Death of the Blues

It was a cold night in Chicago, and Art Hodes—a young, white jazz
pianist—was alone on the South Side, looking for a warm place to go
inside and hear some "colored music." He came upon a theater adver-
tising a few different forms of entertainment that night: a long-
forgotten movie, followed by a live performance by the black
Hollywood star Stepin Fetchit, and ending with a performance by
Bessie Smith. It was a microcosm of American entertainment in the
late 1920s, encompassing the past, present, and future paths that culture would travel. Movies were in their infancy, still sharing the stage
with live performance, but racial stereotypes had already insinuated
themselves in cinema as early as D. W. Griffith's *Birth of a Nation*
(1915), and the great success of Stepin Fetchit's (aka Lincoln Theodore
Monroe Perry) recurring role as a lazy, dimwitted fool testified to that
fact. Smith's singing performance that night was a holdover from the
pre-movie era, and although some had predicted "the death of the
blues" as early as 1925, Smith retained a loyal following. Radio exposure and massive record sales had boosted her career and ensured that
her legacy would survive.

Though her records were powerful on their own, her fans loved to
see her perform. For Art Hodes, seeing Bessie Smith for the first time
was a big event. Upon finally seeing her, he said, "[R]esplendent is the
word, the only one that can describe her. Of course, she ain't beautiful,
although she is to me." Hodes's qualified praise was significant. His
feeling that he had a special appreciation of her beauty was a common
one among Bessie Smith fans, who recognized that her physical attrib-
utes clashed with the prevailing standards of beauty for the era yet

loved her all the more for it. This special understanding between fan
and star would recur in the 1960s, when Janis Joplin became the first
unruly, frizzy-haired, braless woman superstar, each fan believing s/he
was the only one to know her full worth. Like Smith, Joplin defied
contemporary boundaries for female attractiveness and in the process
revealed a whole spectrum of society ready to adore women on their
own terms.[50]

Among the anorectic flappers and slinky vamps of the age, Smith's
ebony skin and generous size set her apart, proudly. As she put it, "I'm
as good as any woman in your town/I ain't no high yellow, I'm a deep
killer brown." The self-satisfaction that Smith exuded was a huge part
of her appeal to her listeners, male and female.[51]

Smith was fortunate to have such a devoted following for her live
performances, because in November 1931, Columbia declined to sign
her again due to a downturn in the blues market. It was the first time
in nine years that Smith was without a recording contract. It was bad
news, but it didn't mean the end of her career. Bessie Smith was a real-
ist. She had helped create the blues as a popular genre, but she was
willing to experiment with more popular music if the times demanded
it, and they did. All blues artists were hurting, and record companies
usually found it easier simply to hire new artists than to develop new
styles in the performers who were already known as blues singers.
Bessie Smith tried to adapt, however, and by 1933 she had incorporated new songs into her repertoire, including two songs taken from
hit Broadway musicals: "Smoke Gets in Your Eyes" and "Tea for Two."
The image of the "Empress of the Blues" performing squeaky-clean
songs was a stretch, but Smith did it for the obvious reason: she needed
the money. Although she had earned hundreds of thousands of dollars
in the 1920s, the combination of her lavish spending habits, expensive
touring show, and Jack Gee's financial mismanagement had left her
with little in the bank. And with the onset of the Depression, many
record companies not only were ditching their old artists—they were
going out of business entirely.

So Bessie Smith continued to tour, changing her style to suit the times, and she remained popular. Her original fans never forgot her, either. Two years after splitting from Columbia, Smith was asked to record there again. A fan since childhood, John Hammond in 1933 finally saw a chance to work with his idol. The young jazz fan had turned his back on the Social Register in order to become a record producer at Columbia Records, and he eagerly paid Smith and her backing musicians out of his own pocket when the label grew nervous about its investment. This kind of dedication led to one of the music industry's most phenomenal careers; Hammond went on to discover and record many of Smith's successors, including Billie Holiday, Aretha Franklin, and Janis Joplin, among other music legends. From the 1930s to the 1970s, John Hammond was instrumental in bringing the century's most talented women singers to public attention and preserving their legacy through recordings.

For this session, Hammond handpicked his musicians: trombonist Jack Teagarden, saxophonist Leon "Chu" Berry, bassist Billy Taylor, and clarinetist Benny Goodman were among the stellar lineup. None had ever worked with Smith before, and they were excited about working with her. "Jack Teagarden was flying," Hammond recalled. "He had dreamed of recording with her and thought he never would."[52] Four songs were recorded that day, the best of which was "Gimme a Pigfoot," a classic Bessie Smith tune in its celebration of good times and in her lusty delivery.

The song begins with a condemnation of the Cotton Club scene and its pretensions, describing the pretentious "highbrows" there and her refusal to enter such a place. The scene shifts to "Hannah Brown's" party, which sounds like a typical buffet flat. As she sings about Hannah Brown's, her voice loosens into its beautiful, powerful roar, and the song really starts to swing. Her trademark phrasing is in full effect, slowing down on some words and then piling them on top of one another to add depth and variety to the performance. In a line describing a piano player, she sings, "He's got rhythm, *yeah*, when he stomps his feet," emphasizing the "yeah" with such unreserved enthusiasm that the song as a whole is propelled forward, pushing through the amplifiers and grabbing the listener by the ear. Improvising on the last chorus, Smith is singing full bore, still totally at ease, not straining, her voice an almost solid object. Although no one knew it at the time, the spectacular "Gimme a Pigfoot" was her last recording. Unabashed, forceful, and full of life, it was a fitting finale to her recording career.[53]

~

Though the songs from the Hammond sessions were not big sellers when first released, Smith continued to perform live and draw an audience. With Hammond's help, she began performing at several downtown clubs—notably, Connie's Inn, where a white audience heard her new songs. Even in the subdued 1930s, Bessie Smith found an audience. The times had changed but Bessie hadn't; the same sass that she had flaunted in the 1920s was now interpreted as sheer defiance, and she projected an image of strength in the face of adversity. Popular culture in the 1930s was, in fact, full of such women, from Smith to the smart-aleck heroines of Hollywood films such as Tallulah Bankhead and Myrna Loy. Bessie Smith's tough persona turned out to be much more resilient than that of the 1920s ingenue.

Despite the decline in the popularity of the blues, Bessie Smith was in ascendance, having found a new sound and an expanded audience for her still-powerful singing. At forty-two, her years of experience had only increased her stylistic range, and she was by now a legendary figure in the music world, even among the new generation of jazz players. "I introduced her to the members of the band," recalled Lionel Hampton of a visit she and his uncle Richard Morgan (her companion, post–Jack Gee) paid to him while he was touring with Benny Goodman, whose band was then the biggest draw in the country. "[S]he really didn't need an introduction—*she* was the star. I'm convinced that if she had lived, she would have been right up there with the rest of us in the swing music." *If she had lived.*[54]

1937

You ever hear what happened to that fine, full-of-life female woman? You know how she died? . . . They brought her to the hospital but it seemed like there wasn't any room for her just then—the people around there didn't care for the color of her skin. . . . *See that lonesome road, Lawd, it got to end,* she used to sing. That was how the lonesome road ended up for the greatest folk singer this country ever heard—with Jim Crow directing the traffic.

—Mezz Mezzrow, jazz clarinetist[55]

The Death of Bessie Smith

Music always comes from somewhere. People live, love, work, and die in particular coordinates of space and time. A map can be drawn of every life, indicating where on earth all the events of that life took place. Because music is a product of human life, it too has a geography, and in the geography of American music there is arguably no more central an axis than the straight line drawn through Mississippi, north to south. It is called Highway 61. Stretching from just below Memphis, Tennessee, and right through Mississippi down to the Louisiana border, the straight, flat road follows the path of the Mississippi River. The land through which it passes remains a living palimpsest of the history of black America, having served as the physical site for so many important achievements and disappointments of African-American culture. It was on cotton plantations along Highway 61 that slaves became freedmen, then became sharecroppers. It was along this road that the first blues songs were born, created by those same farmers. It was up this road that some of those blues-playing laborers traveled, taking their music north with them. And it was on this road,

Highway 61, driving south from Memphis toward Clarksdale, home of the Delta Blues, that Bessie Smith died. In the map of her life, Bessie Smith had completed the circle.

> JACK: **This woman is badly hurt. . . .**
> 2ND NURSE: **You cool your heels.**
> JACK: **Ma'am—I got Bessie Smith out in that car there. . . .**
> 2ND NURSE: **I don't care who you got out there, nigger. *You cool your heels!***
> —Edward Albee, *The Death of Bessie Smith*[56]

The death of Bessie Smith in many respects became nearly as important, in terms of her legend, as her life. Through the rituals of mourning, mythmaking, and eulogy, Bessie Smith came to symbolize more than just the triumph of one woman's artistry. She became an important symbolic figure for the aspirations and disappointments of blacks, and of women, and she seemed also to stand for the best and the worst that America could ever be. The significance of Smith's life, work, and death was well understood by Ralph Ellison, who wrote:

> There are levels of time and function here, and the blues which might be used in one place as entertainment . . . might be put to a ritual use in another. Bessie Smith might have been a "blues queen" to the society at large, but within the tighter Negro community where the blues were part of a total way of life, and a major expression of an attitude toward life, she was a priestess, a celebrant who affirmed the values of the group and man's ability to deal with chaos.

For this "priestess," it was not only her music that was put to ritual use but also the narratives of her death. The disputed circumstances of Bessie Smith's demise cast her life in a new light and forever affected the way she was remembered by future generations.[57]

The facts—or at least the best approximation of them—were these: At around 1 A.M. on September 26, 1937, Bessie Smith and Richard Morgan left Memphis and began driving to Clarksdale, Mississippi, along Highway 61. They had gone about seventy-five miles when Morgan, who was driving, saw a pair of taillights ahead, tried to brake, and lost control of the car, which smashed into the rear of a parked delivery truck and flipped over, coming to rest on the passenger side, where Smith was sitting. The injuries were severe. The truck and its driver, who has never been identified, left the scene.

Almost immediately, Morgan and Smith were joined by two white men, Hugh Smith and Henry Broughton, who had been driving to a favorite fishing hole three hours south of their hometown of Memphis. Smith was a doctor, and he quickly assessed Bessie Smith's injuries: her right arm was almost completely severed at the elbow; her entire right side had been crushed; and she was no doubt bleeding internally. Not quite unconscious, she moaned and gasped for breath, and then went into shock. Dr. Smith and Broughton moved her to the side of the road and then went to a nearby house to call an ambulance.

The delay in the arrival of the ambulance prompted the men to move Smith into their own car and drive her to the hospital themselves. Incredibly, just as they were about to move her, yet another car arrived on the scene, speeding down the highway, and promptly crashed into Dr. Smith's car. The white couple in this fourth vehicle was injured but not seriously, and at that moment an ambulance, a sheriff, and two policemen arrived. A second ambulance pulled up, apparently summoned separately by the driver of the now-vanished truck. Bessie Smith and Richard Morgan left for Clarksdale in one ambulance, the young white couple in another.

It is at this point that the mythologizing begins: was Bessie Smith taken to a white hospital, only to be refused service and thus killed by Jim Crow? Dr. Smith insisted that this was not true. "The Bessie Smith ambulance would *not* have gone to a white hospital," he said. "You can forget that. Down in the Deep South cotton country, no colored ambulance driver, or white driver, would even have thought of putting a col-ored person off in a hospital for white folks." Dr. Smith recalled that the separate hospitals for "colored" and white were about a half-mile apart, an insignificant distance when one considers the severity of her injuries. The black ambulance driver, Willie George Miller, claimed to have driven Bessie Smith directly to the black hospital, and he said that, in his memory, she was dead on arrival. According to hospital records, however, Bessie Smith died at 11:30 A.M. of internal injuries.[58]

Bessie Smith's son, Jack Gee, Jr., gave an interview to the *Baltimore Afro-American*, which he claimed to be based "in part" on Richard Morgan's own account. Morgan himself was never interviewed. Gee's version conflicts with those of Dr. Smith and Willie Miller. According to Gee, Dr. Smith refused to put Bessie Smith in his car because it "would get too bloody." He also claimed that when the ambulance arrived, the white woman hurt in the second accident was treated first. Finally, he said that Smith was taken to a white hospital, refused serv-ice, and then transferred to an ill-equipped black hospital, where doc-tors "had to run all over the town to get the proper equipment."[59] John Hammond spoke with a black musician who had been traveling with jazz bandleader Chick Webb in the South at the time of Smith's death. A few weeks later, Hammond published his own account in *Down Beat* magazine, entitled, "Did Bessie Smith Bleed to Death While Waiting for Medical Aid?" Needless to say, it mirrored the version that Smith's son had told. Hammond did request more information from his read-ers, "realizing that such tales can be greatly magnified in the telling." Apparently no one contacted him, although Hammond later admitted that he regretted his rush to print, and he wished he had taken more care with his sources at the time of writing.[60]

Both Dr. Smith's and Gee's versions are plausible. The reality of Jim Crow actually adds credibility to each story in a different way. Racial segregation was so deeply ingrained and so strictly enforced in Missis-sippi in 1937 that it seems unlikely that anyone, black or white, would attempt to force a white hospital to treat a black patient, no matter how severe the injuries. From this perspective, Dr. Smith's version seems sound. On the other hand, it also seems plausible that someone at the scene of the accident may have insisted, as Gee claims, that the white woman be treated first, thus exacerbating Bessie Smith's condition. It is also probable that the black hospital was poorly equipped, at least by comparison to the white hospital. "Separate but equal"—the legal standard that had sustained the Jim Crow system since 1896— virtually guaranteed lower-quality facilities for blacks, whether in schools, train stations, or medical facilities. From this perspective, then, Gee's story is both compelling and logical. Except for the issue of which hospital she was delivered to, Dr. Smith's and Gee's stories are not necessarily contradictory . . . and the shadow of Jim Crow remains.

Stories of her death, and the role of racism in it, began to circulate almost immediately thereafter. Even with the accounts of Dr. Smith, Willie Miller, and the hospital staff, the failure on the part of the original truck driver and Dr. Smith himself to transport Bessie Smith immediately to the hospital remains suspect, if not inexcusable. Thus, perhaps even among the well informed, these lingering details have contributed to the suspicion surrounding her demise. The *Baltimore Afro-American*, a prominent black newspaper at the time, in December 1937 published a feature story entitled, "Entertainers Find Perils Along the Road," which described not only Bessie Smith's death but also the racism and violence experienced by other traveling performers, such as Billie Holiday, Lionel Hampton, and Blanche Calloway (the jazz singer and bandleader and sister of Cab). When Calloway tried to use the restroom at a filling station in Yazoo, Mississippi, her husband was pistol-whipped by policemen and the couple was sent to jail and subsequently fined for "disorderly conduct." All African-Americans had either heard or personally experienced such stories—this was the context in which Bessie Smith's death was understood. As John Hammond told the *Baltimore Afro-American*, "Although the story might not be true, there is the possibility that it could have happened."[61]

Subsequent accounts of Smith's death were eventually published, but they made no impression. Dr. Smith made a statement to the *Afro-American* a few weeks after the "Perils Along the Road" story, but it was buried on page five and attracted little notice. They lacked the impact of the original story—"Bessie Smith Killed by Jim Crow"—with its sad, dark logic. It made sense to most people, in an awful way, and it had become a parable for the black experience in America.[62]

In 1963, LeRoi Jones wrote: "Bessie Smith was not an American, though the experience she relates could hardly have existed outside America; she was a Negro." Clearly, no eyewitness interview could seriously alter this view of Bessie Smith: an exile in her own country, murdered by racism. It was a view shared by many blacks and whites in the years following her death. Edward Albee's play, *The Death of Bessie Smith* (1959), literally dramatized the story for audiences worldwide, and subsequent magazine articles repeated the Gee version. Smith became a martyr, a secular saint among American artists—her life a beacon for singers inspired by her work, her death a warning about the limits of fame and talent in a flawed world.[63]

Like all martyrs, Bessie Smith continued to live even after death. Thousands attended her funeral, and the event was covered in all the major black newspapers. In 1938, Columbia Records, capitalizing on the publicity, reissued many of her recordings, something they subsequently repeated nearly every decade as the company changed hands from Columbia to CBS to Sony. The reissues were a gift to the public in that they kept her music available for successive generations of fans, and they were of course a windfall for Columbia, which became the sole proprietor and beneficiary of her recordings after her demise.[64]

The disembodied voice of Bessie Smith took on a new life through these records. Some were collected in archives by jazz aficionados such as Carl Van Vechten; others were passed down within families. Still others ended up in places such as the St. Vincent de Paul charity shop in Philadelphia in the mid-1960s, where the biracial playwright August Wilson first discovered a record devoid of context, with merely a faded yellow label reading, "Bessie Smith: 'Nobody in Town Can Bake a Sweet Jelly Roll Like Mine.'" When Wilson put the record on a turntable, "the universe stuttered and everything fell to a new place." Wilson kept playing it, over and over, twenty–two times in a row. It was a pivotal moment: "A birth, a baptism, and a redemption all rolled up into one. . . . It made me look at the world differently. It gave the people in the rooming house where I lived, and also my mother, a history I didn't know they had. It was the beginning of my consciousness that I was the carrier of some very valuable antecedents."[65]

Smith's ability to communicate this sense of timeless connectedness, what Wilson calls "the conduit of ancestors," was noted by others who heard her after her death. Ralph Ellison wrote of listening to an upstairs neighbor who was a professionally trained opera singer. "If she polished a spiritual to a meaningless artifice," he wrote, "I'd play Bessie Smith to remind her of the earth out of which we all came." The reminder was always potent, though its meaning was not always easy to accept.[66]

James Baldwin perceived Smith in a similar way, effectively using her music and her biography as a tool for deeper self-understanding. When Baldwin went to Europe in the 1950s, he had never listened to Bessie Smith. Yet he took with him two of her records as a kind of experiment, "to try to re-create the life I had first known as a child and from which I had spent so many years in flight."

> I had never listened to Bessie Smith in America (in the same way that, for years, I never touched watermelon), but in Europe she helped me to reconcile myself to being a "nigger". . . . I realized that I had acquired so many affectations, had told myself so many lies, that I really had buried myself beneath a whole fantastic image of myself which wasn't mine, but white people's image of me.

For Baldwin, it all came down to the beat. "It was a cadence; it was not a question of dropping s's or n's or g's, but a question of the *beat*. Bessie had the beat." Listening to Bessie Smith—forcing himself to listen to her—was a rite of passage for Baldwin. In Ralph Ellison's phrase, it was a "ritual" that facilitated his own self-understanding.[67]

For Baldwin, as with many others, the suspicion surrounding Smith's death was an important part of her influence. "[L]ife is very difficult, very difficult for anybody, anybody born," he said:

> [P]eople cannot be free until they recognize this. Bessie Smith was much freer—onerous and terrible as this may sound—much freer than the people who murdered her or let her die. . . . That's what the Blues and Spirituals are all about. It is the ability to look on things as they are and survive your losses, or even not survive them—to know that your losses are coming.

From Baldwin's perspective, Bessie Smith's death, in an "onerous and terrible" way, somehow justified her life, and her art. As the preeminent blues interpreter, she had communicated a certain vision of life—a grim one, but also a courageous, realistic one. The fact (as he understood it) of her murder simply added to the power of her vision and the impact of her art.[68]

~

Despite her spiritual legacy, Bessie Smith's grave in Mount Lawn Cemetery outside Philadelphia remained unmarked for thirty-three years. In 1970, Barbara Muldow, a black Philadelphia native, brought the situation to the attention of the *Philadelphia Inquirer*, whose staff solved the problem by making two phone calls: one to Juanita Green, the owner of two nursing homes who had once worked for Bessie Smith as a maid, and the other to Janis Joplin, the nation's reigning queen of rock 'n' roll.

Just as many black artists had found in Bessie Smith a touchstone for their own identity, so too did many women, regardless of race, who saw her as an icon of courage and aspired to her fierce attitude toward life. Janis Joplin idolized Bessie Smith, and as an aspiring singer, she told friends that "she felt she was Bessie Smith reincarnated," which no doubt revealed more about her artistic ambitions than about her spiritual beliefs. Joplin learned to sing by listening to Bessie Smith's records, and later covered Smith's songs in the studio and in concert. Smith's "Black Mountain Blues" was one of the first songs Joplin ever performed live. Its lyrics expressed some of the essential Smith qualities that Joplin, in her own words, "copped": the urge to rebel, to drink too hard, and to feel too deeply. Thirty years after her death, Smith remained the preeminent icon of female bravado.[69]

Like James Baldwin, Joplin also found meaning in Smith's death, and she identified with the difficulties experienced by Smith throughout the cycle of her life. Joplin seemed to see in Smith's death the same nobility that Baldwin did: a resolute acceptance of life's disappointments. Joplin copped that, too. "I ain't got no choice but to take it like I see it," she said. "Let it happen, man!" Joplin recognized the "romantic mystique" of Smith's death but nevertheless subscribed to its seduction herself. "People, whether they know it or not, like their blues singers miserable," she said. "They like their blues singers to die afterwards."[70]

~

There is no denying the power of Bessie Smith, but it has always been a challenge to see beyond that power. The strength of her voice and her personal charisma remain so seductive that it's tempting to forget just how extraordinary she was in her own time. All her recordings are still in print; listening today, we hear the voice of the Jazz Age—a deep, brassy sound communicating all the creativity and excitement of a culture pushing itself to the edge. But not every woman in the 1920s and 1930s sounded like that, and certainly not most African-Americans. This was a time when women—white women—were still getting used to the idea of voting. When birth control was illegal and even discussing it was dangerous. When the concept of a college education for women was considered radical. When forty thousand unmasked Ku Klux Klansmen marched on Washington, DC, in support of white supremacy. This was Bessie Smith's reality, a world in which, to most of the population, the idea of a woman taking the stage to air her feelings was considered brazen and impolite. The idea that a black woman would have the audacity to do such a thing was beyond the comprehension of many. But the great artists always make it look easy. On CD today, Smith sounds invincible. It's why they loved her then, and still do now.

Bessie Smith had always had a talent for understanding the needs of her audience. She simply assumed they felt the same thing she did, and she put that into song with a voice as authoritative as a thunderclap, announcing to the world that these thoughts and feelings were worth listening to. This combination of emotional depth and performative power produced soul. In this sense, then, Bessie Smith was the first recorded soul singer, the first to communicate the universal feelings of pain, joy, fear, and despair into art that flowed out of the phonograph, through the living room, down the alley, into the dance hall, through the car radio, and eventually into the headphones of her most recent listeners. As one of her early fans recalled, "[S]he just upset you." Her death was just one more blow. For the singers who followed, she was the great influence, a never-ending fountainhead of inspiration, and her singing became the standard by which they would judge themselves. This is what Janis Joplin meant when she said of Bessie Smith, "She showed me the air and how to fill it."[71]

The cemetery headstone made possible by Joplin and other Smith devotees reads:

> THE GREATEST BLUES SINGER
> IN THE WORLD WILL NEVER
> STOP SINGING
> BESSIE SMITH
> 1895–1937

Chapter Three

JAZZ NOIR:
BILLIE HOLIDAY

On Friday, November 24, 1933, Bessie Smith took
the subway downtown to the Columbia Records
studios at 55 Fifth Avenue in New York City. It was
to be her last recording session. The following
Monday, a young singer made the same trip down
from Harlem, found her way to the same studio and
the same microphone, and made her very first
recording. That young singer was Billie Holiday.
Historical hindsight makes the question inevitable:
was this the day the torch was passed? Four years
later, Bessie Smith was dead; four years later, Billie
Holiday was the new dark star of jazz singing.

Those four days in November 1933 were the closest the two ever came to sharing a room, a microphone, or a conversation. Yet they shared a great deal
else. Holiday's emotional power—understated but
lethal—was a recalibration of Smith's unchecked passion. The expressive trumpet sound of Louis Armstrong

was also a big influence. "I liked the feeling that Louis got and I wanted the big volume that Bessie Smith got," Holiday famously said. "But I found that it didn't work with me, because I didn't have a big voice. So anyway between the two of them I sorta got Billie Holiday." Bessie Smith had given voice to African-Americans in the second and third decades of the twentieth century, as they moved from the South and into new lives in the great Northern cities. Billie Holiday, who was born in the North, sang to an even broader audience of black and white women and men, elucidating the sorrows and joys—though mostly sorrows—of Americans as they lived through depression, war, and all the changes of the modern world.[1]

~

Bessie Smith and Billie Holiday shared something else, too: the enthusiastic support of record producer John Hammond. It was Hammond who arranged both recording sessions in November 1933.

A mere twenty-two years old, John Hammond was just beginning to develop his career, one that was unique in its combination of music producing, writing, marketing, and social activism. His passion for jazz and blues was increasingly linked to his desire to combat racism. The Depression was now underway. The few paying gigs in the music industry were taken by whites, and blacks faced "insurmountable odds . . . against achieving any sort of recognition without help." Hammond saw his opportunity. "I was an entrepreneur at heart. . . . I wanted to bring my discoveries to the world." Hammond used his growing power in the industry to showcase black artists. "The music and the radical press gave me a platform for constructive criticism," he wrote. Young, energetic, and unencumbered by financial constraints, Hammond found a moral justification for his obsessive fandom. He was one of the first to establish a link between jazz and blues and civil rights, an idea that rippled across American culture throughout the rest of the century.[2]

While Hammond "thought nothing of traveling hundreds of miles

Billie Holiday (1915–1959) where she was happiest, singing with a band—shown here performing in England in 1954.

to visit a jazz club or a theater where rumor or a friend had told me I would find someone worth hearing," he also made frequent visits to Harlem's speakeasies, where budding jazz artists played every night. "Most of the time I was disappointed, but now and then it all became worthwhile," he recalled. Hoping to hear blues singer Monette Moore one night early in 1933, Hammond dropped in at her eponymous club on 133rd Street. But Moore was somewhere else that night, and Billie Holiday, a virtually unknown seventeen-year-old, sang in her place. Hammond had expected a blues singer to fill in for Moore, but he quickly realized that, although she was not really a blues singer, she sang from a blues point of view—not merely voicing the lyrics but endowing them with the emotional timbre of her own experience. She sang jazz with a blues intention, and Hammond was thrilled: "I decided that night that she was the best jazz singer I had ever heard."[3]

Hammond was eager to be the first to record Holiday, but it took a few months of negotiating with his contacts at Columbia Records— and the success of another of his recent "discoveries," clarinetist and bandleader Benny Goodman—before he could convince them to take a chance on the untested young singer. Through Hammond's introduction, Goodman himself was soon a fan of Billie Holiday, and he agreed to record with her on her first few records. In fact, the first release, "Your Mother's Son-in-Law," was issued under Goodman's name. An indefatigable musical matchmaker (he used the term *jazz catalyst*), Hammond managed to get Goodman to play on Bessie Smith's final recordings in those historic four days as well—the jazz world's version of a harmonic convergence. Smith and Holiday apparently never crossed paths, though; as Hammond no doubt realized, the once-celebrated, now-struggling Empress of the Blues would not have enjoyed meeting Hammond's Next Big Thing. Whether Smith heard Holiday's singing in the four years of her life after those recordings is not known.[4]

Billie Holiday was the future, with a sound especially suited to the uncertain era of widespread poverty, social unrest, and world war ahead. Hers was the voice from the edge. "Billie's appeal to theatrical people, the gay crowd, and others outside the social norm was tremendous," Hammond noted. Holiday, both during her life and after, became an icon in these worlds, a beacon to those who felt left out of the American mainstream. Holiday sang from a place of pain—the pain of the outsider—and this was evident to her listeners. Whereas Bessie Smith projected a fun-loving, extroverted enthusiasm, Billie Holiday's onstage personality was far more reserved, almost detached. Yet they did have something in common, both broadcasting an unusual strength of spirit and a hard-won emotional wisdom, singing with seemingly so much at stake that audiences couldn't help but draw closer and share the experience. It was this quality that earned Holiday the title of "blues singer," though she almost never sang traditional blues.

Not long after her first recording session, the word about this unusual young singer began to spread. "You never heard singing so slow, so lazy, with such a drawl," Ralph Cooper, the emcee at Harlem's Apollo Theater told his boss, "—it ain't the blues—I don't know what it is, but you got to hear her!" Holiday's career was underway.[5]

1915–1948

> You know the kind of people that say, "I'm gonna get cussed
> out anyways, so what's the difference? What the hell?" Well,
> Eleanora just went out and done what she felt like doing
> 'cause she was just don't care-ish.
>
> —Mary "Pony" Kane[6]

Not Too Young and Not Too Nice

Just don't care-ish. There may be no better definition of "cool" than Pony Kane's homemade phrase. Kane was a close childhood friend of Eleanora Fagan, a girl who embodied all that was cool long before she changed her name to Billie Holiday. Born in Philadelphia in 1915, about twenty years after Bessie Smith, she was the illegitimate child of two teenagers: Sadie Fagan, a housemaid, and Clarence Holiday, a musician. Her father was an inconsistent presence in her life and certainly never spent any time encouraging his daughter to follow his artistic path, though if musical talent is inherited, she must have gotten it from him. The exact details of her childhood are disputed; Holiday contradicted herself many times in interviews and conversations over the years. Her autobiography, *Lady Sings the Blues* (1956), co-written with journalist William Dufty, is a less-than-perfect factual record of her life, but as a window onto Holiday's self-image, it is quite revealing. She felt no compunction about portraying herself as a wild young girl—"a real hip kitty," as she put it. She was pretty, too. Holiday was tall and shapely, with high cheekbones and distinctive, almond-shaped eyes. Her skin was light brown—her maternal grandfather was biracial—and her hair was thick, black, and wavy. Holiday "didn't straighten [her hair]," Pony Kane recalled, "didn't have to." Holiday's beauty got her attention from an early age. "[A]ll the women was jealous of her. Used to beat her up sometimes." Violent behavior—by men and women—was a fact of life from Holiday's earliest days.[7]

Holiday described a childhood spent shoplifting, ditching school, fistfighting, and hanging around whorehouses, "the only joints fancy enough to have a victrola and for real enough to pick up on the best records." By "the best records," she meant those of Louis Armstrong and Bessie Smith. She also recounted being raped at age ten by a neighbor, and again at age twelve by a musician. She was working as a prostitute by her early teens. "They slap her around a lot, her men did," recalled Kane. "I seen her come back to Durham Street looking like she be put through the mill. Her eyes was made up so you won't notice too much." Seeking work, Sadie Fagan had left her daughter in Baltimore with relatives, but eventually she was forced to bring her up to New York, where she was working as a domestic, in order to remove her daughter from an increasingly dark life in Baltimore. The plan failed, for Holiday was working as a prostitute in Harlem within a few months.[8]

~

Not much had changed in the three decades since Bessie Smith's childhood in turn-of-the-century Tennessee: African-Americans were still struggling to forge meaningful lives at the lowest levels of American society. They continued to face a fearsome lack of employment opportunities and were still expected to fill the most menial jobs. For the young Billie Holiday, future career options were essentially the same as they had been for Bessie Smith: washwoman, cook, or prostitute . . . and perhaps entertainer, if she were bold enough to consider it. She had already tried and quit all three professions by the time she began working for tips as a singer in Harlem in the late 1920s.

The problems faced by blacks in the post–World War I period were easier to tolerate in Harlem, the capital of African-America, where black people were in the majority and owned the businesses and the real estate; black people were everywhere. It was easy to find the music scene, too. Legendary composer, bandleader, and pianist Duke Ellington remembered Harlem in the Depression: "There wasn't nearly enough work for everybody that could blow horns, and what musicians didn't have steady jobs would spend their days standing out on the street gabbing, always arguing about the respective merits of everybody else." Jazz pianist and Baltimore native Joe Turner recalled that upon arrival he found his way to Harlem by "ask[ing] the first person I met where I could find the colored people in town." Advised to take the train to 130th Street, he started looking for musicians. For many, Harlem was a nonstop party: no curfews, no rules, and plenty of great musicians: trumpeter Louis Armstrong, pianists Mary Lou Williams and James P. Johnson, singer Ella Fitzgerald, and innumerable other legendary jazz men and women were gigging in Harlem in the 1920s and 1930s. Harlem was famous, and it attracted both blacks and whites.[9]

Even the thirteen-year-old Eleanora Fagan had heard about the scene. Taking the train from Baltimore alone, she was supposed to meet her mother in New Jersey, but instead she took it upon herself to go to Harlem: "Nobody was going to stop me from getting to Harlem." Reunited with her mother after getting picked up by a social worker, Eleanora moved to Harlem with her mother and loved her new home. "Every night the limousines would wheel uptown," she recalled, characteristically attuned to both the trappings of the wealthy and the contrast between the lives of blacks and whites. "The minks and ermines would climb over one another to be the first one through the coalbins or over the garbage pails into the newest spot that was 'the place.'"[10]

Despite her initial experience in the Harlem brothel, the move from Baltimore to New York was the beginning of a new life for Holiday, one she worked toward relentlessly from the moment she arrived. Eleanora Fagan was a striking young woman, but as she became Billie Holiday, she aspired to adult glamour. She achieved a specific kind of nightlife elegance with her marcelled hair, powdered face, highly arched and penciled eyebrows, carefully lacquered and outlined lips, pearl necklaces, hoop earrings and long gowns made of clinging fabrics whose drapes and folds pooled around her feet. Since the days of Mamie Desdoumes in Storyville, female blues and jazz singers had played up their sex appeal, but Holiday's look was relatively restrained. She worked on projecting an image of carefully groomed sophistication rather than the blatant sexuality of some of the "exotic" entertainers at nightspots such as the Cotton Club, where stereotypes of a savage Africa were an excuse for daringly revealing costumes.

Like Bessie Smith, Holiday appreciated fine clothes and jewelry. She devoted entire interviews to describing her wardrobe, onstage and off. "I always do my own hair. . . . I do my own nails, too," she told the *Baltimore Afro-American* in an article entitled, "What Does Billie Holiday Wear?" in 1937. The story was filled with lavish descriptions of Holiday's "peach colored dressing gown, trimmed in turquoise blue, with satin turquoise mules"; a "soft fleece sport coat in a dark gray with a blue fox collar"; a stage costume of "black chiffon fitted evening gown, with a black satin underslip trimmed with rhinestones"; Max Factor makeup and Emeraude and Evening in Paris perfumes. No aesthetic detail went unnoticed—from the "tearose"-colored satin underwear she favored to her penchant for white furniture. She even tried to paint her black telephone white, which destroyed the phone. Those around her in later years claimed that even when Holiday was broke, she still managed to show up in a fur coat. Fashion was a kind of protective armor for her.[11]

Renaming herself was another essential step in Holiday's transformation. She claimed to have taken the name "Billie" from the popular silent film star, Billie Dove. Dove was a blonde, glamorous, successful white actress who was called "The American Beauty" after appearing in a 1927 film of the same name. By reclaiming "Holiday," her father's name, Fagan legitimized herself both as a daughter and as a musician. As a name, "Billie Holiday" evoked many things: a masculine toughness, sex appeal, glamour, and the promise of escape.

The Depression was well underway and Americans were just beginning to suspect that it might go on for a long, long time. It was an inauspicious time to start a career in entertainment. The depressed economy was forcing the closing of many small nightclubs and cabarets and the demise of independent record labels. Columbia Records producer John Hammond was able to continue recording his jazz favorites only by bankrolling the sessions himself. Fewer records didn't spell the end of radio, however; live broadcasts of ballroom concerts by the new swing bandleaders such as Benny Goodman and Artie Shaw were a cheap solution to radio programming, and they proved enormously popular. The economy may have been depressed, but talented individuals like Billie Holiday were determined to pursue their ambitions. For a girl from the Baltimore ghetto, the Depression wasn't a big change: money was still scarce, living was still hard, and luck was what one counted on.

The Depression notwithstanding, the interwar period was a time of raised expectations for American women—expectations that rarely were met. Women had successfully fought for the vote in 1920 (though the franchise remained off-limits to almost all Southern black women until the passage of the federal Voting Rights Act in 1965), and the twentieth century stretched out before them, full of promise and raised expectations even for black women, who had the most ground to gain. While many of the most notable changes affected white women—better-paying work in the new pink-collar jobs of modern bureaucratic business as typists and telephone operators, new contraceptive choices popularized during the Great War, and more opportunities to go to college than previously—the specter of so many women staking a claim in the spheres of business, professions, and the world of art was exciting to young women like Eleanora Fagan, who saw the blonde Billie Dove as a role model. The title of one of Dove's most popular films, *Sensation Seekers* (1927), captured the spirit of interwar women perfectly.[12]

During the Victorian era, women had often been labeled "hysterical" for their inability to cope with the restrictions placed upon the sensitive sex. With the turn of the twentieth century, this began to change. These highly intelligent, ambitious women were now regarded as a new model of modern woman: complicated, mysterious, and interesting. Women such as writer Zelda Fitzgerald, English shipping heiress and art patron Nancy Cunard, and the African-American writer Zora Neale Hurston were seen as romantic figures. Doomed or not, there was room for them in a world that had been turned upside down by global war and its attending social upheaval. Things were different now, or at least they looked as though they might be.

Billie Holiday wanted to be one of those new, modern women. Bessie Smith—who had successfully claimed all the perks allotted to the new, twentieth-century woman—died too soon to be a hands-on mentor to Holiday (not that Smith would ever have considered it, given her aloofness toward other singers). Though inspired by Smith and Louis Armstrong, Holiday's personal style was something new in popular music. She embodied a coolness that was new to the medium.

Hollywood played a large part in shaping Holiday's public persona. As her interest in Billie Dove made clear, Hollywood was always a touchstone for Holiday. She was an avid fan of its films, its stars, and its scandal magazines, which were the only form of literature she was ever known to read (apart from comic books). Billie Holiday took her musical lessons from the jazz greats but adopted the rest of her style from the same place every other American was going in the late 1920s and 1930s: the movie theater.

~

The years during which Eleanora Fagan was reinventing herself coincided with a golden era of women in American film, known as the "pre-Code" era, a brief interlude between the advent of "talkies" and the 1934 introduction of the puritanical Film Production Code Administration, also known as the Hays Code, which censored American filmmaking. Between 1929 and 1934, Hollywood actresses challenged older notions of how women should behave, talk, and appear. Norma Shearer, Jean Harlow, and Greta Garbo literally embodied— onscreen, larger than life—the new freedoms of the post-Victorian age, reveling in every new opportunity for excess. The titles say it all: *A Woman of Affairs* (1929); *The Divorcee* (1930); *Laughing Sinners* (1931); *This Modern Age* (1931); *A Free Soul* (1931); *Faithless* (1932); *Love Is a Racket* (1932).

As a talented and beautiful young woman, Holiday was attracted to all the pleasures of "this modern age," whether depicted on film or through the racy hits of the 1920s women blues singers. "We have tremendous vitality of body and complete emancipation of mind," proclaimed actress Dorothy Mackaill in *Safe in Hell* (1931). "None of the old taboos . . . mean a damn to us. We *don't care*."[13] Mackaill's pronouncement held true for Holiday and so many other "just-don't-care-ish" young women of the era. The wide-eyed John Hammond, for example, was surprised by the young Billie Holiday's tough personality: "I discovered that her beauty surpassed her disposition, which could be remarkably moody." Holiday's adult identity was more or less fully formed by the mid-1930s, when the Film Production Code Administration, the Depression, and rumors of war began to tame the wildness of the women in American popular culture, in Hollywood and the music world alike.[14]

But the Production Code didn't apply to the music industry, and Billie Holiday couldn't and wouldn't have changed her style anyway. Tough yet vulnerable, sexy and sinful, Holiday kept on being herself, honing her craft as a strange, laid-back singer and drifting farther and farther from the increasingly pious image of womanhood that the mainstream culture—and certainly the popular music culture—was eager to promote. (Even in the strong images of women during the 1940s, such as Rosie the Riveter, the emphasis was on women's selfless contributions to the war effort and their resolve to stay true to their country and overseas husbands—no "laughing sinners" here.) And in any case, the reality of her life as a singer struggling to succeed in the nightclubs of Harlem was wilder than any Hollywood film. Though Holiday had chosen Billie Dove as her namesake, it was another pre-Code star who seemed to embody Holiday's world-weary aspect and languorous self-destruction. Greta Garbo, "a woman whose capacity for love and sacrifice made every other human emotion or endeavor seem small," was a better fit.[15]

Like Garbo, Billie Holiday projected through her performances a vision of womanhood that was utterly modern in its emotional freedom and absolutely doomed in its consequences. The tension between the two would fuel the art of both singer and actress throughout their careers. "It might sound sadistic, the idea of an audience's lapping up stories of women surrendering to some punishing fate," wrote one of Garbo's critics, in an analysis that applies equally well to the experience of listening to Billie Holiday. "It seems that way only until you watch the films [or hear the songs]. To see the films is to know something stronger and deeper was going on . . . the redemptive power of love, to be sure. But what was being redeemed in these films wasn't just a soul from sin. It was sex from judgment." Holiday was no ingenue. Like Garbo, she was a mature woman with all the complexity that implied. Love and sex were complicated, too; neither Garbo nor Holiday was capable of reducing them to mere boy-meets-girl routines.[16]

Holiday struggled with the judgment of others all her life, yet she continued to express herself in a raw, nakedly honest way that exposed her deepest parts to an often-unfriendly world. Her fans loved her for it. As the decades wore on, both Garbo and Holiday found themselves ever more alone with their expressions of serious, deep emotions in a world of increasingly bubbly, ever-agreeable actresses and singers. They weren't necessarily evil women, Holiday and Garbo, just a little outside the comfortable box of female sweetness and cheer. Garbo put it best in her 1931 film, *Inspiration:* "I'm just a nice young woman. Not too young and not too nice—I hope."[17]

～

In 1933, Holiday was just getting started, "trying to kick and scratch out a living in Harlem," when John Hammond first heard her sing. "My discovery of Billie Holiday was the kind of accident I dreamed of," he later said, "the sort of reward I received now and then by traveling to every place where anyone performed." Though Holiday was an unknown in the record industry, many others had heard her before Hammond's "discovery." By 1933, Holiday's unique drawl of a voice was well known to most of the important jazz musicians working in New York.[18]

From the beginning, Holiday enjoyed a status among her instrumentalist peers that was unusual for a female vocalist. In an era when the music magazine *Down Beat* ran stories with headlines such as "The Gal Yippers Have No Place in Our Jazz Bands," she was accepted as a fellow musician by the men with whom she performed. "You know, with most singers you have to guide 'em and carry 'em along—they're either layin' back or else runnin' away from you," pianist Bobby Tucker recalled. "But not Billie Holiday. Man, it was a thrill to play for her. She had the greatest conception of a beat I ever heard. . . . With Lady you could relax while you were playin' for her. You could damn near forget the tune." Holiday's innate, swinging sense of time was one of her greatest musical gifts, giving her the ability to transform an already-popular song into something brand new.[19]

And how to describe her voice? "[M]agnificent . . . a searching, sobbing, exciting voice that whispered along the heart strings when she sang," wrote one critic. Emotions were always brought up in descriptions of her singing, since so many of them seemed to be wrung out of each slow phrase. Her range was not vast, especially when compared to some of her virtuosic peers such as Sarah Vaughan, but hers was an intimate style that made great use of the microphone and recorded well. Innovations in electric microphones changed the terms of singing; no longer was it necessary to belt a song for it to record well, as Bessie Smith had done. Billie Holiday was naturally suited to the newer, more sensitive microphones of the 1930s, which picked up every whisper and sigh.[20]

The power of her voice came not only from its sound but also from its unadulterated intention. "She was open," said soul singer Jill Scott, "completely willing to be human in front of a microphone." This was the blues coming through, for the raw sound of emotion splintering a real human voice has always been central to the blues aesthetic. Holiday's voice exerted a great influence on future generations of singers, showing them a way to reinvent music as a quieter, subtler experience that had more to do with the privacy of a small, smoke-filled room than with the big stages of vaudeville and Broadway. Her sound was nontraditional in its softness and its feathery tone, and she paved the way for future jazz, rhythm and blues, rock, and soul singers who made the most of their unusual soft or raw voices in their own genres.[21]

Slightly rough (and increasingly so toward the end of her life), Holiday's voice was subtle and sounded like none of the more conventional, clearer-toned singers of the day. *Time* magazine described her, with evident bemusement, as a "young woman with a hump in her voice," but the jazz press recognized her gifts right away, and she drew ever larger crowds in Harlem's nightclubs once her recording career began.[22]

According to jazz critic George Frazier, Billie Holiday was "not one of those specious performers who catch on like a forest fire, she is instead, a profound artist whose talents are too subtle for immediate consumption by the mob." Holiday's offbeat aesthetic particularly appealed to the jazz cognoscenti, who by the late 1920s were already beginning to establish themselves and the genre itself as existing apart from and slightly above the American cultural mainstream. For many white jazz musicians and critics, jazz music was a language understood by the hip, rebellious few. Those in the know heard the blues in her voice and approved, understanding that blues and jazz were part of the same tradition (and only recently starting to be divided as separate musical genres). The fact that not everyone appreciated Holiday's singing made her even more attractive to the critics, who encouraged jazz musicians to see themselves as true artists beholden only to their own standards.[23]

Just as John Hammond had found in Bessie Smith a passport to a wholly new way of experiencing the world, many of his white contemporaries romanticized jazz not only as beautiful music but also as a link to a superior, somehow more authentic way of life—the life of black Americans. "I wonder why white musicians are so corny?" Bix Beiderbecke, the legendary 1920s (white) jazz cornetist, asked a friend. "[I]n a colored café. . . . The band always has something that keeps your ear cocked all the time. . . . Goddamn, those people know how to live." These white jazz fans admired black people for their music, and for their courage in the face of racial prejudice. To them, black musicians were heroic; the passion in their music was fueled by pain that could be pointed to and named.[24]

Milton "Mezz" Mezzrow, a white clarinet player who performed with Beiderbecke, described his embrace of black jazz as a "nose-thumbing at all pillars of all communities, one big syncopated Bronx cheer for the righteous squares everywhere." Mezzrow, Beiderbecke, and other white musicians were sincere in their appreciation of black culture and devout in their worship of great black artists, but they also gained something by aligning themselves with the art form: hipster credibility. The birth of Beat culture in the 1950s and its taste for Bebop would constitute a second flowering of this cultural exchange. But between the eras of Louis Armstrong and John Coltrane, the talents of Billie Holiday were uniquely suited to the tastes of jazz hipsters; she was a young, beautiful black woman from the Baltimore ghetto with a voice as contradictorily tough and sweet as her personality, a singer who thought like a horn. She embodied all their values and expressed all the pain. Mezz Mezzrow tried to explain the peculiarities of jazz musicians, and in doing so shed light on Holiday and her appeal. "[J]azz musicians have an off-center perspective on the world," he explained. "You can't blame them for walking around with a superior air, partly because they're plain lonely and partly because they know they've got hold of something good, a straight slant on things, and yet nobody understands it." Billie Holiday would never achieve the widespread acclaim and acceptance she desired—at least not in her lifetime—but the cognoscenti picked up on her talents right away. "I grant that certain icky souls haven't found Holiday to their taste," *Down Beat*'s George Frazier wrote in 1938, as Holiday's reputation among her peers was in ascendance, "but I feel reasonably certain that she appeals to the people who count." He was right. Holiday was a critical favorite long before she found a mainstream audience.[25]

As John Hammond had recognized early on, Holiday was also a hero to those "outside the social norm," including lesbians and gay men. Like Ma Rainey and Bessie Smith, Holiday was known to have sexual relationships with women, and this was surely responsible for some of her appeal to the lesbian crowd. Her affair with actress Tallulah Bankhead was no secret to those who saw them together in the nightclubs in the late 1940s, and she was involved with other women as well. Count Basie's nickname for her was "William," a name she herself often used when interested in other women. "She ha[d] this reputation for being a fabulous les," said her friend and accompanist Carl Drinkard. He remembered the many women who showed up at Holiday's shows and spent "a baby fortune" on drinks in the hope of securing an introduction from the maître d'. Holiday responded to this not-so-subtle form of procurement in her typically jaded way, telling Drinkard: "These people expect me to take these broads out of here, and I'm not going to disappoint them" (though she did not always end up in bed with them—sometimes she pawned them off on her male accompanist). Holiday didn't enjoy being told what to do, or with whom to sleep. "Sure, I've been to bed with women," she told Drinkard, "but I was always *the man*."[26]

As Rainey and Smith's experience demonstrated, the world of show business—particularly the African-American music scenes on the road and in the nightclubs of Harlem—was a place where sexuality was openly expressed and experimentation was the only norm. Bisexuality was merely one aspect of the erotic tableau. This tolerance of homosexuality was in fact much more common in American culture in general in the years before World War II than it was immediately afterward. This is not to say that lesbians and gays were not persecuted (police raids on gay and lesbian bars were common in large U.S. cities, and health officials warned against the dangers of same-sex relationships), but the inevitability of, at the very least, homosexual experimentation was tacitly accepted by many Americans. The lesbian and gay civil rights movement that started with the Stonewall riots of 1969 tends to confuse the narrative of American homosexuality. The common yet often false presumption that American history is one of relentless progress leads many to the conclusion that homosexuals must enjoy greater liberty in the twenty-first century than they did in the previous one, but the story is not as simple as that. As the romantic lives of Ma Rainey, Bessie Smith, and Billie Holiday suggested, many women and men in the early twentieth century were inclined to view human sexuality as a broad spectrum, rather than as an either/or option. They allowed themselves to express their desires at various points along the range of sexual possibilities without the need to categorize their identities as either "straight" or "gay," as is so often the case today. Of course, certain circles—such as the nighttime world of jazz clubs and theater—were more welcoming to sexually adventurous lifestyles than others, and, generally speaking, an openly homosexual man or woman in the 1930s was still marked as an outsider. Yet the fact that the excruciatingly prim John Hammond would make a point of Holiday's appeal to "the gay crowd" proves that, if nothing else, a "gay crowd" existed and was acknowledged even by those who found it distasteful. Years after her death, Billie Holiday would come to be celebrated as a gay icon, but in her own era she was seen simply as a woman with broad tastes, no different from many other men and women in her milieu.[27]

Like Rainey and Smith, Holiday pursued men as well as women, and she was married twice. Just like Smith, Holiday's choice of husbands dismayed her friends, as she repeatedly linked herself with men more interested in her money than her love. Holiday married her first husband, Jimmy Monroe, in 1941. Monroe was a playboy with no discernible career or talent apart from his ability to attach himself to successful women. Many of Holiday's friends believed Monroe was the first to introduce her to opium, yet for all his problems, Monroe was a better husband to Holiday in their brief time together (their actual relationship lasted less than one year, though fifteen years passed before a legal divorce) than most of the other men she chose. A long list of relationships with musicians, hangers-on, and managers followed, including one with an exceptionally violent man named John H. Levy, her manager in the late 1940s and early 1950s. This was followed by her second marriage to the equally abusive Louis McKay, who made Jimmy Monroe seem angelic by comparison. Memry Midgett, who played piano for Holiday, described McKay as "one of the most ruthless men I have ever met; he exploited her completely."[28]

This description fits most of the men with whom Holiday was involved—the various managers and handlers who tried to control her life and, most important, her earnings. Midgett remembered Holiday talking about "nice guys who would have been kind, protective, providing, and she said herself she didn't know why she didn't like those kind of men, but she didn't." All who knew Holiday acknowledged her attraction to mean, violent men. To chronicle all of her relationships—brief and long term—is to retell the same sad story of the lure of the moth to the flame.[29]

Bassist John Levy (not to be confused with Holiday's abusive boyfriend/manager during the same period) worked with her in the late 1940s and considered her a friend, and he was baffled by the pattern he saw. "Why would you punish yourself, put yourself in that position?" he wondered. He speculated that Holiday equated physical violence with masculinity and was attracted to that—or at least felt that she deserved it. Considering the facts that her father was absent from her childhood and that the majority of her experiences with men, from the age of ten onward, were abusive, Holiday probably did not know what a healthy relationship felt like, much less how to create one or seek one out. Those who admire Holiday's artistry have warily approached the problem of her toxic romantic history: To what extent was Holiday a victim? To what extent was she responsible for her own physical and emotional security? There are valid arguments for both perspectives. Her friends urged her to avoid violent men, and she had innumerable opportunities to choose a partner who would have treated her with love and respect, but some inner emptiness drove her toward catastrophe nearly every time. She was human, after all, and rational explanations have no bearing on the human heart and soul.[30]

This didn't stop people from looking for reasons behind human tragedies—nor should it. As it happened, Levy (the bassist) later went on to work with Ike and Tina Turner, whose relationship paralleled many of Holiday's. "Without [Tina], [Ike] was just another guitar player—she was the act—but that same kind of male dominance existed that doesn't allow her to express herself except in what he allows her to say—she's completely dominated." Was the abuse a form of self-punishment, a way of proving one's inner suspicion of worthlessness? Or was it a way of allowing one's partner to feel powerful even as he was left out of the limelight of stardom? Or perhaps Billie Holiday and Tina Turner simply saw abuse as a form of paying their dues; after all, many other women singers had the same experience, among them Ella Fitzgerald and Sarah Vaughan. These were dues that men rarely had to pay.[31]

While her relationships with women seem to have been less destructive, they did not appear to be significantly more nurturing or supportive—and in any case, none of them lasted as long as those with men. Her persona, onstage and off, evolved into an uncanny combination of vulnerability and cynicism, as she infused sad and tender love songs with the knowledge of her own painful affairs. Her appeal to gay men became more pronounced in the late 1940s and 1950s as her problems with drugs, alcohol, and abusive relationships increased. Her hardened attitude toward life's disappointments was familiar to gay men who, like Holiday, were increasingly forced to recalibrate their own aspirations and desires in the face of society's restrictions on sexuality and emotional expression—restrictions that became ever more harsh as the conservative 1950s wore on. Holiday's glamorous pose—carefully curled and oiled hair, perfect makeup, glittering gown, and pristine gardenia tucked behind her ear—embodied the attempt to stave off the world's ugliness through the mindful construction of a personal aesthetic. In the gay subculture, this would come to be known as "camp," and certain women entertainers became icons to American gay men—Holiday, Judy Garland, Bette Davis, and Mae West, to name a few. These women challenged social norms by caricaturing women's roles, sometimes enacting almost grotesque versions of the idea of femaleness, just as some gay men cultivated an extravagant image of effeminacy. Billie Holiday exemplified the "survivalist spirit" that gave camp its resonance, while at the same time earning the affection of homosexual men and women through her other obvious features: talent, charisma, and beauty. To both heterosexual and homosexual audiences, Holiday exemplified outsider chic.[32]

~

New York in the 1930s was a city of contrasts. Many of the city's landmark buildings—the Chrysler Building (completed in 1930), the Empire State Building (1931), and Rockefeller Center (1939)—were erected even as the newly homeless pitched their tented Hoovervilles in the middle of Central Park. New Yorkers were not immune to the Great Depression, but they managed to devise an array of brilliant distractions to keep the country entertained. From Harlem's Savoy Ballroom to Times Square's Paramount Theatre, New York exulted in an unparalleled nightlife. Billie Holiday had found herself in the right place at the right time, and soon she was a staple of the city's nightclubs, ballrooms, and radio broadcasts.

Like most musicians of the postwar era, Billie Holiday's recording sessions were valuable to her mostly as a way of publicizing her live performances (singers and musicians usually received a flat fee for the recording and no further royalties). Her first recordings with John Hammond, therefore, were helpful to her career in allowing other musicians to hear her and consider hiring her to sing with their bands.

From the late 1920s, jazz bands had been getting larger, with entire sections devoted to different types of instruments like a small orchestra. The Big Bands were popular draws in large ballrooms and college halls around the country, where they would play their new jazz music at dances. These dance concerts quickly became a staple of radio broadcasts, as well, thus popularizing the Big Band sound even more. And then there were the canaries.

Described as "a singing cheerleader for the team behind her in uniform," the generally underrated female singer who accompanied a Big Band was known as a canary: a decorative songbird who sat still and only occasionally provided a vocal accompaniment. The aesthetic advantage of having a young woman on the bandstand was often the primary incentive for hiring a "girl singer." Her job was to sing in between the "real" music—the instrumental arrangements and various solos performed by the male musicians. Most of these women singers were much more talented than the term *canary* implied; they were serious vocalists, but they quickly learned that a pretty face, a frilly gown, and a willingness to perch decoratively on the edge of the stage while the men played were the rules of the game. Peggy Lee, Ella Fitzgerald, Carmen McRae, and Lee Wiley were just a few of the talented canaries who escaped their cages and went on to bigger careers in jazz and pop music.[33]

Though beautiful, charismatic, and happy to wear an expensive dress, Holiday was miscast in the canary role. The ever-present John Hammond had been the agent of Holiday's move into touring with the Big Bands. It was he who had brought Count Basie's Kansas City–based band to the attention of New York aficionados, and it was he who suggested that Basie hire Billie Holiday—the band's first female singer—to polish the act. Basie's New York debut had not been a great success; part of the reason may have been the poor condition of the instruments themselves, many of which were said to have been held together with rubber bands. This might have been a clue to Holiday that life on the road with the Basie Band was not going to be luxurious. She learned that for herself soon enough.[34]

"I joined Count Basie's band to make a little money and see the world," said Billie Holiday. "I didn't see anything but the inside of a Blue Goose bus and I never got to send home a quarter." Holiday's stark description of life on the road was no exaggeration. The constant traveling was exhausting enough, but checking into a second-class hotel reserved for blacks was even more demoralizing. In her autobiography, Holiday described her time with the Basie Band (1937–38) with a mixture of pride and bitterness. The music was wonderful; the touring was hell.[35]

Count Basie's band was stocked with future jazz legends, from Basie

himself to drummer Jo Jones, bassist Walter Page, and tenor saxophonist Lester Young, among others. Young was especially important to
Holiday. They had met in 1934 and immediately recognized each
other as soulmates, maintaining a platonic, loving, and deep relationship that was unique for both of them, one that lasted until they died
within four months of each other in 1959. She called him "Prez," short
for "President," acknowledging him as the greatest of the jazz saxo-
phonists. She was his First Lady, "Lady" for short. Holiday, with her
penchant for reinvention, immediately adopted the new name, adapting it to "Lady Day." For once, the names and the relationship lasted.

Holiday's stint with Count Basie became one of those jazz legends.
Those who saw her performances recall a band that swung like no
other, and a singer perfectly suited to her band. No recordings were
made to document the groundbreaking combination, however,
because Holiday and the Basie Band were signed to competing music
labels and were unable to come to an agreement. A few radio
airchecks survive, however, and they substantiate the power of the
Holiday–Basie union. Holiday first sang publicly with Count Basie
only a week after joining the band. They performed at the Apollo
Theater, and Holiday was a smash: "She just couldn't get off the stage,"
Basie remembered.[36]

The musical rewards were great, but the financial and emotional
ones were meager, and Holiday left the band in 1938, just shy of one
year into the tour. She was immediately recruited by Artie Shaw to
sing with his Big Band, another arrangement resulting in wonderful
(again, mostly unrecorded) music and trying personal experiences for
both Holiday and Shaw. As the first black singer hired by an all-white
(and, of course, all-male) band, Holiday was immediately faced with
racism in a more pronounced form. When touring with Basie, the
entire band was black; they all stayed in the same hotels and ate at the
same restaurants. When Shaw's band toured the South, Holiday was
often forced to leave the bandstand after singing her part. "They didn't
care if she sang," remembered saxophonist Les Robinson, "as long as

after she finished she returned to her place, as they would say. She just sort of took it in her stride. The South didn't bother her; it was the North where she flipped. . . . the guys [band members] stood behind her. Artie did too."[37]

As Robinson makes clear, Holiday's expectations regarding Southern hospitality toward blacks were already low, and she expected the racism she encountered there—which is not to say that she endured it silently. In one incident in Kentucky, someone in the audience shouted, "Let the nigger wench sing again!" Holiday called him a "motherfucker," and a near-riot ensued. Like Bessie Smith dressing down the Ku Klux Klan, Holiday knew just how dangerous it was to curse a white man in the South, especially when standing onstage as the only black in sight. The band defended her, though, and they all survived the incident.

The treatment Holiday received in the North, however, was a shock to her and the entire band, and she patently refused to stand for it. Shaw's band had released its soon-to-be-classic "Begin the Beguine," and its success was making the band more and more visible. In October 1938, *Billboard* raved about her performances with Shaw: "The ebony-colored Billie Holiday . . . is of that phenomenal species of singer who has no true singing voice yet can sell a song with a lot of passion and restrained emoting. In her field she is probably tops." *Billboard*'s blessing didn't mean much outside the music world, however. When the band returned to New York that same month to play at the Lincoln Hotel in the center of Manhattan's Theater District, the hotel manager insisted she use the freight elevator so the white guests would not think she was staying in the hotel. Holiday was incensed, and so was Shaw, but apparently she went along with it that night. When their performances at the Lincoln were broadcast over the radio, however, the show's sponsor, Old Gold cigarettes, refused to air a black singer, and the show aired without her. Holiday quit the band. It was a loss for Shaw, for her audience, and for jazz in general: Holiday never returned to the Big Band format.[38]

In truth, Holiday had never exactly fit in with the Swing Era's notion of what a girl singer should be. "You were supposed to do eight popular songs," Artie Shaw explained later, "and we did a half-hour of the blues. . . . Maybe a third of it would be Billie extemporizing, making up her own blues lyrics. And we would start slow, build it up, change tempos, do all kinds of things. . . . Something happened, some kind of chemistry happened up on that stand." Shaw and Holiday shared a mutual respect for each other's musicianship. Shaw recalled his attitude toward the audience during the time Holiday was working with him; it described her own style, too. "The audience was totally irrelevant," Shaw explained. "You do what you do for the love of what you're doing. And if it works, fine." Shaw stressed that Holiday and, later, the talented Helen Forrest, who took Holiday's place, "were the only singers I could relate to musically."[39]

The attitude Shaw described was the classic Holiday "just-don't-care-ish" cool, and it informed all aspects of her life. It was during her trying experience with Shaw's band that Holiday began to acquire her status as an icon of black pride—among both blacks and whites. Holiday often rode to gigs with Shaw's bass player, Sid Weiss, and his wife, Mae. "She was living 'black is beautiful' before it was fashionable," Mae Weiss recalled. "Her whole stature and the way she carried herself is what you see today, the pride in being black. She did it before she even knew what it was; that's the way she lived."[40]

Holiday's stint with Artie Shaw was her last attempt to become a mainstream singer, and it failed. Not because she wasn't talented enough, but because she couldn't and wouldn't conform to the mainstream's increasingly narrow definition of female musician. She was too black for Old Gold but too white for black audiences in Detroit, where she was asked to "black up" her light complexion. She could sing pop songs, but they never sounded the way their songwriters had written them, and there was tremendous pressure on the Big Bands to play the songs chosen by the industry as "hits." Holiday wasn't alone in her distaste for the iron grip of the industry's promoters: Artie Shaw abandoned his own band—now a phenomenal success—shortly after Holiday did, and although he made several successful comebacks, he stopped playing for good in 1954. Holiday never stopped. Singing was it for Holiday—she just needed to find the right venue. Her best work lay ahead.

1938—1948

> Her whole life had taken place in the dark. The spotlight shone down on the black, hushed circle in a café; the moon slowly slid through the clouds. Night—working, smiling, in makeup, in long, silky dresses, singing over and over, again and again.
>
> —Elizabeth Hardwick[41]

The Miracle of Pure Style

Leaving the Big Bands proved to be a greater artistic loss for the bands than for Billie Holiday. She returned to New York City, her spiritual hometown, with its hundreds of nightclubs, after-hours bars, and jam sessions; thousands of aspiring jazz musicians; and thousands more aficionados who were longing to hear and see her again after her years on the road. The tours with Count Basie and Artie Shaw had been exhausting, but Holiday had continued making records between gigs. By 1938, she had established herself as one of the most important voices in jazz, at least among those who heard the records. She wasn't being played much on the radio, but she had developed the beginnings of an adamant cult following.

Holiday's voice was striking in its sense of restraint. Like her idol, Bessie Smith, Holiday experimented with phrasing, timing, and dynamics (changes in the speed and volume of her singing) in order to

personalize her interpretation of each song. Like Smith, she emphasized unexpected words and dramatized the lyrics by waiting until the
last possible rhythmic moment to sing. But whereas Smith's dominant
vocal style was the sheer power of her hearty voice, Holiday took the
opposite approach, singing delicately, with precision. Her tendency to
hold back when other singers would let it rip gave her singing a
tremendous emotional tension, and she accentuated this quality as her
career progressed. She had begun recording with Teddy Wilson's
orchestra in 1935, and the nearly one hundred sides they produced
broke new ground in the world of jazz vocals. Songs such as "Long
Gone Blues" (1939), one of Holiday's own compositions, set the pattern for her cool style.

"Talk to me, baby, tell me what's the matter now," Holiday begins in
the breathiest possible whisper, sliding into the phrase and sliding back
out again as she repeats the words in the classic blues format. "Are you
trying to quit me, baby, but you don't know how?" This line is delivered
with an audible pout, but the volume of her voice is still soft, framed by
the steady, muffled chugging of the rhythm section behind her. Were a
typical blues singer to attempt "Long Gone Blues," it might come off
like a typical rant against a mistreating man—"I've been your slave
ever since I was your babe/But before I'll be your dog, I'll see you in your
grave"—one can easily imagine Bessie Smith belting out these lines.
But in Holiday's interpretation of these standard blues, the statements
fall from her lips gently, her intimate, sad phrasing of the words *slave*
and *grave* sounding as though she has a little too much familiarity with
both. Holiday's style is hesitant and questioning rather than threatening. By the last stanza, Holiday's lyrics and voice conspire in a prophecy
of things to come: "I'm a good gal, but my love is all wrong."[42]

This was a voice rich with the emotional history of the blues, but
not a blues voice per se. By the time Bessie Smith died, Holiday had
already taken her place, creating blues music for the newer, darker era
of the late 1930s and 1940s. Holiday had achieved many of the bench-
marks of Bessie Smith's career: she was a successful singer, leading the

tough but glamorous life of a jazz musician, and while the mainstream went on ignoring her, it also ignored her transgressions, allowing her a degree of personal freedom unavailable to the average American woman at the time. She had consciously modeled her life on that of the glamorous and wild blueswomen before her, but she was trying to live Bessie Smith's life without Smith's self-esteem, and it didn't quite work. Observed longtime *New Yorker* film critic Pauline Kael, "There was one thing her voice could never do: heal, the way a rich, full voice can—as Bessie Smith or Aretha Franklin can . . . she meant to wound, not to heal." In fact, Holiday often seemed wounded herself. In her earliest recordings her thin, high voice sounded almost jaunty, but by the late 1930s, she had modified her sound, elongating the beats in her always unexpected phrasing and evoking a deeper, more melancholy quality. As longtime fan and rock star Bryan Ferry later put it, "Even when she sings of hope, her message is despair."[43]

Returning to the nightclubs of Manhattan she seemed to find her true environment in the textures of life lived after dark. This Billie Holiday is the one whose image lasted long after death—a talented, tormented, seductive performer with a sinister aura. Fittingly, for a woman enthralled by Hollywood, the qualities of that era's newest movie genre captured her style the best: film noir. Every archetype of the form was contained within her, her setting and her songs—the femme fatale, the smoke-filled rooms, the stories of love and corruption. Noir defined 1940s American popular culture and Holiday, too, with its vision of an aesthetically striking world without pity. Holiday's elegant appearance and chilled delivery gave voice to a kind of jazz noir—"music for lovers and thieves," to paraphrase the great sax player (and occasional, abusive lover of Holiday's) Ben Webster. This was the new, noir Billie Holiday, a singer who had come fully into her power and was capable of transforming almost any song into a searing lament, her way.[44]

Overt political commentary was never part of film noir, nor was it, for the most part, an element of Billie Holiday's repertoire. She made one exception, though, starting in 1939, when she began performing at a new club far downtown in Greenwich Village: Café Society. With its multiracial audiences and Left-leaning atmosphere, Café Society was a long way from the Cotton Club and its segregated white audiences. Café Society was meant to be more than a nightclub. It was a venue for expressing the Left-leaning ideals of its owner, Barney Josephson, and his clientele. Café Society prided itself on its progressive policies, giving the best seats in the house to its black patrons and employing veterans of the Abraham Lincoln Brigade as its bartenders. It was the perfect setting for Billie Holiday to sing a song about lynching written by a Jewish schoolteacher in the Bronx named Abel Meeropol (pen name Lewis Allan).[45]

Meeropol taught high school English to pay the bills but devoted his creative energies to politics and art. He was known in New York's leftist artistic circles as a writer of poetry and songs reflecting his passion for social justice. He and his wife, Anne, were Communist Party members who later adopted the children of Ethel and Julius Rosenberg after their 1953 execution for espionage. In 1936, however, the problem of lynching—in which blacks were murdered and often hung from a tree for public viewing—was foremost in Meeropol's consciousness, due to the attention paid by the liberal press as well as the NAACP's campaign to pass an anti-lynching bill in Congress (it never passed). Originally written as a poem and published in a teachers' union newspaper, "Strange Fruit" was set to music by Meeropol and began to be performed by various progressive singers around New York without attracting much notice—until it caught the attention of Barney Josephson, who had recently hired Holiday to sing at his club. It is hard to know how Holiday initially reacted to the song, since everyone involved told a different story about the fateful event. According to Meeropol, she seemed indifferent and unmoved. Josephson reported that after hearing it, she asked him, "What do you want me to do with that?" For whatever reason, Josephson took this to mean that Holiday "didn't know what the hell the song meant," which hardly seems possible. For her part, Holiday claimed that it was she who had encouraged

Meeropol to set the poem to music in the first place ("I dug it right off," she claimed), and that she had even helped to arrange the music. In any case, it soon became Holiday's "personal protest" song.[46]

"Strange Fruit" was unlike anything else Holiday ever performed. It was politically topical and musically strange: slow, even by Holiday's languid standards, and it did anything but swing. The song was a description of lynching whose central image depicted its victims as grotesque yet commonplace aspects of the lush Southern environment: magnolias, poplars, and "black bodies swinging in the Southern breeze." Even the left-wingers at Café Society were surprised by the grotesque imagery and the obvious rage fueling the lyrics. Until this point, the entertainment featured at nightclubs—even the politically minded Café Society— tended to be much more escapist love songs. Protest songs were performed at union rallies and political marches, not in nightclubs.[47]

The song was given special status from the beginning and performed only at the very end of Holiday's set. Barney Josephson carefully directed the song's staging, insisting that all bar service stop, all lights go dark, and all noisy patrons leave the place before a single spotlight shone down on Holiday as she began to sing. She sang it slowly, almost gently, giving life to the lyrics' gruesome details. It was not only the lyrics and the singing but also the sight of this beautiful black woman onstage so intimately engaged with such a revolting topic that gave the Café Society patrons a jolt.

The effect was total: an emotional shock and then release that left the audience (often literally) crying for more, but more never came. Josephson and Holiday insisted that there be no encore after "Strange Fruit," no matter how loud the audience cheered. The song left Holiday emotionally and physically spent. "I finished a set with 'Strange Fruit' and headed, as usual, for the bathroom. I always do," Holiday said. "When I sing it, it affects me so much I get sick. It takes all the strength out of me." "Strange Fruit" is perhaps the clearest example of Holiday's power to channel emotions through her songs. "Holiday was putting into words what so many people had seen and lived through," said Lena Horne. "She seemed to be performing in melody and words the same thing I was feeling in my heart." Hearing the song was a kind of catharsis for her audience.[48]

The NAACP was quick to capitalize on the song and its message, and Walter White, the organization's leader, wrote a personal letter to Holiday expressing his congratulations on "one of the most stirring and grim songs I have ever listened to." The NAACP issued a press release a few days later. *Time* magazine featured a small piece on Holiday and the song, which they dubbed a "prime piece of musical propaganda" for the NAACP. "Strange Fruit" was neither written nor performed for the purposes of propaganda, but the sensational content of the song, as well as the press attention, convinced Holiday to record it.[49]

Afraid of controversy, her own label, Columbia, refused to record the song, but they allowed her to do so with Commodore Records, a small label operating out of a record shop on East 42nd Street. Columbia made a mistake: the record was a hit, due to the popularity of the less-controversial Billie Holiday composition, "Fine and Mellow," which was pressed on the record's flip side. While "Fine and Mellow" was popular, it was "Strange Fruit" that became Holiday's signature piece. No one could have predicted it; despite her self-proclaimed status as a "race woman," Holiday was never political in the standard sense. She did not follow the news, nor did she seek out other songs with political content. But her own experience on the road with Artie Shaw, and performing for mixed audiences, had made her the target of overt racism many times. She dealt with it the way she dealt with every other depressing aspect of her life: with grim humor. Pianist Joe Springer recalled walking with her once as someone called out, "How are you doing, Lady Day?" Holiday responded: "Well, you know, I'm still a nigger." Billie Holiday was always aware of racial injustice. And as for lynchings, all African-Americans were aware of them. The NAACP published its annual reports on lynching statistics through the 1960s; there were three reported in 1939, the year "Strange Fruit" was recorded, and more than 100 lynchings over the course of the decade.[50]

"Strange Fruit" is significant as an aesthetic achievement but also for its status as one of the first protest songs in the popular music genre. The only earlier popular song to openly address racism was 1929's "Black and Blue," performed by Holiday's idol, Louis Armstrong. The blues queens of the 1920s had addressed injustice obliquely, as in Bessie Smith's "Poor Man's Blues" (1928), yet these songs didn't approach the intensity of "Strange Fruit," a song about a topic that was rarely discussed in polite company, described in imagery that left its listeners sickened and moved. "It was really the first time that anyone had so explicitly and poetically transmitted the message of black people," producer Ahmet Ertegun believed. "It was always guarded in the blues: hidden language. But this was quite open."[51]

Of course, "Strange Fruit" was written not by a black blues artist but by a white Jewish man. Given the dismal state of black civil rights in the late 1930s, however, only a white artist could expect to write a song like "Strange Fruit" without suffering serious consequences. Even though Holiday was black, the fact that a white person was responsible for the song's composition made her performance easier to swallow for whites and certainly safer for Holiday, since the performance was an alliance between blacks and whites, rather than simply an anti-white tirade. It was not until the civil rights movement of the 1960s that black composers such as Nina Simone, with her searing "Mississippi Goddam" (1963), dared to unveil a song as overtly challenging to the racist status quo as "Strange Fruit." Surprisingly, Meeropol's radical politics got little attention from the mainstream press. *Time's* article on the song mentioned only that it had been written by "a libertarian New York public school teacher named Lewis Allan."[52]

Holiday's recording proved to be just as affecting as her live version. Journalist Samuel Grafton wrote about it in the *New York Post* several months after its release:

This is about a phonograph record which has obsessed me for two days. It is called "Strange Fruit" and it will, even after the tenth hearing, make you blink and hold onto your chair. Even now, as I think of it, the short hair on the back of my neck tightens and I want to hit somebody. And I think I know who.[53]

The emotional resonance of Holiday's performance transformed lynching into a pain that could be experienced by anyone who heard the song, and few who heard it were left unmoved. As one of the first mainstream protest songs, it set a standard by which its followers would be judged.

~

The flip side of "Strange Fruit" contained another gem, "Fine and Mellow," a Holiday composition that went on to become one of her biggest hits. The irony of sandwiching the two songs on opposite sides of the same record didn't seem to bother anyone at the time: "Strange Fruit" is a dirge-like protest against injustice, while "Fine and Mellow" is at first glance another bad-man-but-I-love-him lament in the established women's blues tradition. Surely a woman strong enough to sing out against lynching would be strong enough to stand up to a man who mistreated her? Holiday's history of abusive relationships with men never ceased to confound her fans, friends, and family, but her role as romance's victim became a large part of her persona. "Murderous dissipation went with the music," writer Elizabeth Hardwick, an acquaintance and fan of Holiday's, wrote, "inseparable skin and bone. And always her luminous self-destruction." By the early 1940s, Holiday had already acquired an aura of nihilistic glamour that at once protected her from the vicissitudes of fame and sealed her destiny as a doomed antiheroine of the American musical scene.[54]

"My man don't love me/Treats me awful mean." The first lines of "Fine and Mellow" contain the standard contradiction: why is he still "her man" if he mistreats her? But Holiday's phrasing complicates the lyrics, her soft voice swings with blues sass and lilts in a teasing way, as if she knows that she is mouthing another of life's funny contradictions and doesn't take it too seriously herself. "Love will make you drink and gamble/Stay out all night long," she sings. "Love will make you do things/That you know is wrong." These lines get to the heart of the song; drinking and gambling are the least of it, she implies, but love will make you do other, more serious things—like staying with a dangerous man, for instance—even though you know that's wrong. It is in this line, "you know is wrong," that her emotion seeps out, as if she is pressing this wisdom on her listener.

Yet the last stanzas take a subtle turn, making a thematic shift away from the seemingly masochistic lyrics of other Holiday songs such as "My Man" (in which she sings, "I know I'll come back on my knees someday"). In "Fine and Mellow," which was written by Holiday herself, the end of the song suggests a stance taken against her no-good partner. She threatens him, and finishes with a sexy and humorous metaphor that continues the threat. "Love is like a faucet," she sings. "It turns off and on/Sometimes when you think it's on, baby/It has turned off and gone." She won't tolerate mistreatment forever. With this resolution in mind, "Fine and Mellow" makes a suitable pairing with "Strange Fruit."[55]

When Holiday performed "Fine and Mellow" at Carnegie Hall in 1946 with her old friend Lester Young on sax, her rendition of the song brought down the house. The bluesy swing of the song got the crowd roaring, and the song's final line was delivered with an almost gleeful snap that recalls Betty Boop in its playful sexiness. The audience went wild. Unlike Bessie Smith, Holiday withheld her emotions, using restraint as her key dramatic element, so when she let go of that restraint, even for a moment, the effect was electric. No matter when she performed it, "Fine and Mellow" always delivered that charge.

~

Billie Holiday's emotional style was one of her defining features. Her tendency to underplay the emotional aspects of the love songs and laments she performed was unique, and her fans saw an authenticity in her delivery that was absent in other singers, who strove to enact the emotions of the lyrics in a musical-theater mode. Holiday's understated affect simultaneously influenced and reflected the emerging emotional style of American culture in the late 1930s and 1940s, a period when women and men alike adopted an emotional coolness that continued through the rest of the century. Early blueswomen such as Ma Rainey and Bessie Smith performed in an emotionally unrestrained manner that provided a vicarious thrill for their audiences, but Billie Holiday did the opposite, showing how alluring emotional detachment could be.

This emotional coolness was characteristic of 1930s popular culture. *The Fountain* (1932), a novel by Charles Morgan, was one of the decade's most popular books, particularly among women, and it reflected a similarly cool ideal. The novel's heroine strove for an internal stillness that was invulnerable to outside forces, a form of subtle psychological strength. Women readers yearned for the same self-control. "Stilling the soul . . . this is what I want," Anne Morrow Lindbergh wrote in her diary after reading the novel. Modern women had shaken off Victorian charges of sentimentality and hysteria in order to take on more responsibility within the public sphere. Keeping one's emotional composure was the price she paid for that new role (a price that men paid, as well, though to a lesser degree). As one woman wrote after reading *The Fountain*, "The desire to be invulnerable is flawless." Billie Holiday's unflappable demeanor—her rigid, unmoving stance onstage, head slightly cocked, one hand gently snapping in time to the beat, soft voice rising ever so slightly and then returning to equilibrium—embodied the new appeal of invulnerability. "Never was any woman less . . . attached," Elizabeth Hardwick wrote. But she held that frosty pose at the edge of an emotional precipice, and she always seemed on the verge of slipping over it. This was the force behind her magnetism. Like the femmes fatales of film noir, Billie Holiday's allure was purely modern, and like the rest of the modern world in late 1939, she was headed toward a dark, uncertain future.[56]

~

Billie Holiday's life had changed since those early days in Harlem. She was, by 1940, well known and greatly admired by those in her circle—mostly other jazz musicians, critics, and fans. It wasn't enough. Holiday was frustrated with her status as merely a cult favorite. Other jazz vocalists such as Ella Fitzgerald had started their careers around the same time but were now gaining mainstream acclaim and much higher record sales than Holiday. In August 1939, she quit her high-profile standing gig at Café Society, hoping to revive her career with new recordings. Some, like producer John Hammond, claimed that she left Café Society because she was too unreliable: drugs were getting in the way, and she either failed to appear at scheduled performances or showed up intoxicated. Barney Josephson asserted that Holiday got around Café Society's "iron law" against marijuana by smoking it in cabs between shows, driving through Central Park in the middle of the night, alone.[57]

Drugs accessorized, fueled, and influenced the jazz scene. They were as ubiquitous as late hours and constant practice. Bessie Smith smoked "reefers" throughout her career, as did many others in the music industry. Marijuana helped to define a new subculture of "hipsters" (also called "hepsters" or "hep cats") in the 1920s: African-Americans who scorned the Puritan work ethic, preferring to indulge their pleasures and live for the moment rather than work toward some American Dream that had never included them anyway. The romance of the (apparently) carefree life of the black hipster had attracted the young, white, Jewish Mezz Mezzrow, who speculated on the reason whites had oppressed blacks for so long: "Were they [white Southerners] afraid that if the Negro was really set free he would make us all look sick with his genius for relaxed, high-spirited, unburdened living?" This view of blacks was in fact a stereotype promoted by whites since the days of slavery, and one that persisted in the caricatures of minstrelsy and in depictions of happy Sambos in the popular culture through the 1950s.

But Mezzrow saw something admirable even here. He was sincere in his admiration for blacks and in his respect for their ability to create meaningful, rich lives outside the white mainstream. Mezzrow yearned to be part of that life, and he succeeded—partly through his clarinet playing but primarily as a reliable drug connection; by the mid-1930s, "mezz" was slang for high-quality marijuana.[58]

There were two sides to drugs: using them for the first time was a sociable activity, an entrée into a well-populated underground world, but self-exile often was the end result. With milder drugs, such as marijuana, the illegal status (effectively criminalized in the federal Marihuana Tax Act of 1937) was the cause of the alienation; with harder ones, such as heroin, the addiction itself further isolated the user from all other desires and relationships. Billie Holiday's drug use probably started with marijuana—even her idol, Louis Armstrong, was a lifelong smoker. Among her friends, Holiday's stage fright and general insecurity were well known. Using drugs and alcohol before a gig was a common way to overcome that fear. "We used to smoke pot a lot together," one friend recalled of their time together in the mid-1930s. "She was kind of a shy girl, until she got loaded." Another friend from that era remembered Holiday as "a little shaky in what she had to offer [as a singer] . . . a sort of a shy approach to audiences, that hesitation, like 'Who wants to hear me?' . . . this may be one reason—aside from associations—that got her on drugs, to give her that false courage." Holiday needed drugs to share herself with people, but once she became a regular heroin user, she had a greater need to get away from people, in order to use the drug.[59]

Holiday's "associations" were often blamed for her drug use: the boyfriends, husbands, managers, and hangers-on who introduced her to, or supplied her with, drugs. But Holiday would have been surrounded by drugs even without these pushers; drugs were an inescapable feature of the jazz world. Not everyone used them, but many did, and their use did not always lead to ruin. In Holiday's case, drugs seem to have merely sealed her fate, not written it. "This woman was only feelings," one of Holiday's friends, Marie Bryant, explained. "Billie was only quivering nerves, quivering emotions. That's why she couldn't make it in this world, she could never make it. She was just too gentle, too honest, too emotional." Like the heroine of *The Fountain*, Holiday sought to rid herself of the intensity of her emotions, using drugs as a tool for becoming "invulnerable." Bryant compared Holiday to other sensitive and thereby doomed artists, among them Marilyn Monroe. "All they wanted to do was their thing, and God had given them this pure way of expressing themselves, but . . . they did everything they could to get out of the crassness. Today they'd be gone even faster."[60]

1940–1959
The Grand Destruction

By the time Billie Holiday left Café Society in late 1939, she had established herself as an artist and as a personality in the jazz world. She had paid her dues, earning the respect of her fellow musicians through her unerring sense of swing. She had also begun to develop a reputation as a wild woman who could hang with the bad boys of jazz. By the mid-1930s, even before marijuana was criminalized, Holiday's name had become a kind of password among marijuana smokers who had formed an ad hoc network of users across the country. "[W]henever you went to different cities," Marie Bryant remembered, "soon enough a guy would knock on your hotel door with a phonograph and Louis's [Armstrong] and Billie's records . . . and a little thing of pot. . . . And this happened all over the country, a society of people who just loved Billie." Holiday had been an icon for outsiders from the beginning; when her drug of choice became illegal, she became an icon for outlaws, too.[61]

Moving from marijuana to heroin was a big step. Heroin was a drug associated with whites, and also with a type of addict whose life was clearly out of control. The 1940s saw the first wave of heroin wash over the jazz world, greatly inspired by the artistry and addiction of the brilliant saxophonist Charlie Parker (1920–1955). Descriptions of Parker's musical style are strikingly similar to those of Holiday's: "He could do anything he liked with time," wrote critic Whitney Balliett, "and in his ballads he would lag behind the beat, float easily along on it, or leap ahead of it." Holiday possessed this quality, too. "The blues lived in every room of his style," Balliett explained, echoing similar observations of Holiday's blues influence. Charlie Parker and Billie Holiday had similar, exquisite musical instincts (Holiday's close friend Lester Young was Parker's boyhood idol), and they shared a desire to evade the world and its pressures, both turning to heroin as an escape hatch.[62]

By the early 1940s, her friends began to notice a change in Holiday's behavior. At first, heroin seemed to help her in all the ways she hoped it would: it calmed her nerves before performances, and allowed her an emotional distance that afforded some relief from the chaos of her insecure financial situation, odd hours, and abusive relationships. It was at this time that her characteristic, near-frozen stage attitude was fully realized.

Her performance began even before she sang the first note. After injecting herself with heroin in her dressing room, then making sure every detail of her appearance was correct—from the gown to the gardenia in her hair—she would slowly walk through the nightclub, talking to members of the audience seated at their tables, sometimes allowing them to buy her a drink. By the time she arrived onstage, she was primed and ready to perform. The single spotlight first used during her performance of "Strange Fruit" became a permanent part of her onstage aesthetic, isolating her from the band and preventing her from seeing the faces of the audience as she sang. "Going off[stage]—she'd nod just to the side to the right, just a nod and a pretty smile—" recalled comedian Harold Cromer, one of her fans. "She walked off regal—Rosalind Russell stole Lady Day's walk—that tall royal sweep thing. Oh, she didn't do it fast, because she'd be in tempo with the music, always."[63]

Billie Holiday couldn't fully control her career—no performing artist ever could—too much of her fate lay in the hands of the general public, the critics, and the recording industry, with all their whims and favorites. In fact, Holiday had never known stability; she had never felt secure. A childhood of abandonment, sexual assault, prostitution, and poverty prepared her only to expect more of the same. The security she craved was temporarily restored by drug use; while she was high, she could imagine that none of that mattered, that everything was going to be just fine. The schism between these realities contributed to an emotional and performative style that grew increasingly baroque.

Each aspect of her self-presentation began to acquire iconic dimensions. "I had the white gowns and the white shoes," wrote Holiday in her memoir. "And every night they'd bring me the white gardenias and the white junk." Like Marlene Dietrich's androgynous suits, and Joan Crawford's shoulder pads, Holiday's pencil-thin eyebrows, defined, glossy lips, sparkling gowns, and, of course, the gardenia tucked behind her left ear, soon became trademarks. Holiday's style was evolving into a perfect representation of the cool, emotionally unassailable woman she perhaps dreamed of being—it was probably more achievable than a dream of calm domesticity as a wife and mother. She needed props to make the vision real, though; the flowers, the makeup, and the dresses were a part of it, as were the dogs.[64]

Beginning in the 1940s, Holiday was often photographed with her pet dogs, upon which she lavished attention. They accessorized her dramatic appearance and also served various practical purposes. "Her animals were really her only trusted friends," recalled the younger singer Lena Horne. Well, they were everything her men were not: faithful, obedient, and nonjudgmental. Holiday was known to hide her drug stash in her dog's collar, and have the dog deliver it to her at the club. Gladys Palmer, who played piano for Holiday in Chicago in

1938, recalled an evening when the singer asked her to watch her dog, a Chihuahua. The dog wore a collar with little jingle bells attached. When Palmer's bracelets hit the jingle bells by accident, the bells split open and four caps of heroin spilled out. "All my friends are sitting there thinking I'm on this junk. . . . I didn't know the stuff was in there," she protested. "So in order to prove to them that I wasn't on the stuff, I had to take them back to the hotel and give Billie her dog, her stuff. . . . I don't need this!" cried Palmer. Holiday was upset, but she kept the dog and lost the piano player.[65]

The dogs remained an important part of her persona. In an April 1953 article in the magazine *Tan*, entitled, "Can a Dope Addict Come Back?" a photograph of Holiday holding the Chihuahua covers the left side of the page, while an illustration of a giant hypodermic needle and three huge pills floats in the air beside the pair. "Holding her pet Chihuahua, Chiquita, whose painted toenails match her fingernails, Billie Holiday leans reflectively on her piano," read the caption. The dogs, the drugs, and even Holiday's "reflective" mood combined to perfect the image of the strange, glamorous, dangerous singer.[66]

Holiday was playing nightclubs in the early 1940s, traveling from New York City to Chicago, Los Angeles, and even Europe, where she was treated like a bona fide star. In 1944, Holiday finally won the *Esquire* magazine jazz poll for best vocalist: the poll had been voted by critics rather than by *Esquire* readers. In 1945, Holiday was released from her longstanding contract with Columbia and began recording with Commodore. The recordings were among her very best: "I Cover the Waterfront," "He's Funny That Way," and a remake of her own "Billie's Blues" all became Holiday classics. She soon moved to Decca, where she recorded "Lover Man," which became a hit. Her career was stronger than ever—stronger, in fact, than it would ever be again.

~

By 1945, Billie Holiday had become a target for the narcotics squad of the New York City Police Department. They hired a black officer to trail her, go to her performances, watch who came and went from her apartment. She was well aware of the surveillance and seemed to take it in stride. She invited friends to her house, knowing they would have to pass the phalanx of police standing by the stoop. None of it made her quit using drugs. It merely forced her to become ever more creative in hiding her activities. She had stashes all over town: bouncers in the nightclubs, elevator operators in her hotels, fawning fans—all these functioned as "holders" of her stash at one time or another. And she was still drinking. "She was never at any hour of the day or night free of these consumptions," remembered Elizabeth Hardwick, "never except when she was asleep. And there did not seem to be any pleading need to quit, to modify." Holiday's accompanist, Carl Drinkard, concurred: "Lady could not kick any habit. Lady did not *want* to kick any habit. . . . Lady was a very simple person to understand; all she wanted was to wake up in the morning feeling beautiful, and to feel beautiful to Lady meant waking up knowing that she had enough drugs to feel beautiful." Feeling beautiful was costing her up to $1,000 a week—perhaps more.[67]

Kicking the habit was finally forced upon her. Busted by federal narcotics agents in Philadelphia in May 1947, Holiday pleaded guilty, was convicted of possession, and was sentenced to a year and a day in a West Virginia women's prison. The trial was well publicized, and during her incarceration Billie Holiday achieved a new kind of celebrity—one based as much on her scandalous life as on her artistic achievements. Though she kicked heroin while imprisoned, by the time she returned to New York from West Virginia, she was using again.

The scandal of her imprisonment, combined with the sympathy of her original fans, created a huge demand for Holiday upon her return to New York. Due to a local law, convicted felons could be denied cabaret cards—licenses to perform in establishments serving liquor—which meant Holiday could no longer sing in nightclubs. She worked around it, scheduling performances at ever more prestigious venues. On March 27, 1948, Holiday performed at Carnegie Hall in a recital setting. "Billie Ducats Like Hotcakes," *Down Beat* reported, hyping her ticket sales. The concert was a huge success; Carnegie Hall's 3,000 seats sold out, and standing-room ticket holders were seated onstage with Holiday herself. "They rocked and shouted, chanted and sang with her from all corners of the staid old auditorium when that enchanting voice again came to life after . . . months of silence," *The American Weekly* reported. The article portrayed Holiday as a wholly reformed drug addict, a story of one woman's triumph over adversity. They were right about the concert, if not the addict: it was a phenomenal show.[68]

"Lady Day made her entrance to one of the most thunderous ovations ever given a performer in this or any other concert hall," reported *Down Beat*. "Towards the end of the second half there were a few yells from an upper tier box in left field and spotted calls from the orchestra floor, similar to those heard from the congregation at a revival meeting." Like Bessie Smith's concerts, Billie Holiday's got to the heart of her listeners, pulling their emotions to the foreground as she sang. "Torrid" described the audience's reaction, *Down Beat* insisted, "and even that is inadequate." Holiday began her singing career as a means of escaping the seamier side of life: prostitution, petty crime. But now, because of her connection to the drug underworld, she was gaining acclaim from those associations. She was a rebel—a full-fledged felon now—and that set her apart from the rest of the crowd, even more than her one-in-a-million voice. The audience responded to her as a fallen woman. Her arrests had merely proved her hipster status. Here was a woman who didn't just flirt with danger; she seduced it and took it home. Being a wild woman had been a big part of Bessie Smith's appeal, and now Holiday was following that path herself.[69]

She was still singing well—it wasn't until the 1950s that her voice began to deteriorate—but her singing was no longer the only draw. She was now infamous, and magazine accounts of her rehabilitation weren't fooling anyone. Most of her audience knew, or at least suspected, that she was still using drugs. People were coming just to see her, up close: would she make it to the stage? How long would she stay up there? Would she fall apart? Rumors spread about her inconsistency. At an important concert at Carnegie Hall in 1954, Holiday was sharing the bill with Ella Fitzgerald. Holiday performed well at first, but during an intermission she disappeared into her dressing room, emerging almost totally incapacitated. "I took one look at her, and she was like the sphinx, like a graven image," said Oscar Peterson, who played piano for her that night. Holiday made it to the stage but was unable to find her vocal cue—a shocking gaffe for Billie Holiday, the acknowledged master of musical timing—and had to be led off the stage. This was as bad as it got. Still, both old and new fans accepted the obviously unreformed Billie Holiday, and she continued performing.[70]

In the late 1940s, Holiday had opted to record a few Bessie Smith tunes for Decca, including "Do Your Duty," "Gimme a Pigfoot," and, of course, "'Tain't Nobody's Business if I Do," a song whose message of defiance was convincing when either singer performed it. Smith's torch had indeed been passed on that day long ago in 1933, but Holiday was living a version of the blueswoman's life that Smith could never have imagined and would never have lived—Smith was never a victim. Bessie Smith was a musical genius, a woman who changed the music and made it better nearly every time she sang. So, too, was Holiday. But while Smith's fans basked in her great, rich voice, letting her unchecked emotions carry them away, Holiday's fans learned to wait for every hard-wrung drop of emotion occasionally squeezed out of the singer's tremulous rasp. Bessie Smith, Holiday's musical godmother, had been celebrated for the sheer power of her sound; it was indestructible. "When she was in a room her vitality flowed out like a cloud and stuffed the air till the walls bulged. . . . she felt everything and swayed just a little with the glory of being alive and feeling."[71]

Billie Holiday's fans got something else: a ringside seat at a slow-motion suicide, the flip side of Bessie Smith's journey. Holiday, who became ever more spectral as the years passed—flesh wasting from bone, voice wasting away—began to be celebrated for surviving at all. Smith's death had shocked her fans; Holiday's death was remarkable for its epic postponement, as her fans wondered how much longer she could go on.

Billie Holiday continued to record in the 1950s. She was much better known now, after several rounds of drug busts, comebacks, and assorted scandals, but her high points as an artist and as a recording star were behind her. She was not pathetic, however. Although her already limited range was narrowed even further due to the ravages of alcohol, drugs, and general poor health, she used her halting, higher-pitched voice to dramatic effect on songs such as "I Thought About You" (1954) and "What's New" (1955). She performed constantly. Though still unable to work in the nightclubs of New York City, she toured the United States and Europe, making a substantial salary that paid for her drug habit. And she had achieved an ironic personal milestone, for she was now featured in the very same gossip magazines she had read since she was a teenager. The January 1957 issue of *Rave* featured Holiday on its cover—head bowed, cigarette in hand, a picture of melodramatic despair. Her image was sandwiched between those of three other tragically flawed artists who defined their era: Jayne Mansfield, James Dean, and Elvis Presley—all subjects of the scandal sheet's "unafraid articles."[72]

The European press took a less sensationalist approach. As they had done with Bessie Smith, and in fact every other American jazz artist, they treated Billie Holiday with a kind of respect that she had given up expecting in her own country. "To see her—*and* to hear her sing those songs which we have all of us played so often on our gramophones—was something not to be forgotten," read the English review of Holiday's 1954 performance at London's Albert Hall. "To sit near and watch as she sings is pure delight. She feels what she sings and the words are mirrored in the ever-changing expressions of her beautiful face." In England, Holiday could do no wrong. "The almost unbelievable had happened," wrote Max Jones in *Melody Maker*. "Lady Day was behind a Manchester microphone. . . . This was really it—for me and, I'm sure, most of the 2,000 people there. I had gone into the hall with the conviction that Billie was the best lady singer still on the jazz scene. So the performance was a confirmation rather than a discovery." In France, she was known as the "Princess of Harlem," and she was celebrated as a great artist there, despite the fact that her "singing was well below standard." She told a reporter in Paris, "I do not want to stay in the States. . . . In Britain they do not just call me a singer, they call me an artist and I like that." But of course she did return to the States. It was everything she knew. Some people even started calling her an artist there, toward the end.[73]

~

Billie Holiday had left Baltimore with dreams fueled by Hollywood (Billie Dove) and the blues (Bessie Smith). She had achieved more than even she realized; it was only as she lay dying that the cult surrounding Holiday blossomed into a full-blown phenomenon. She had always craved success, as measured by the usual American yardsticks: money, glamour, fame. And as she began to die in 1959, the latter finally caught up with her. *Jet*, a fluffy gossip magazine targeted at middle-class black women, began running what essentially became an episodic deathwatch. Beginning in April, Holiday appeared in almost every issue.

At first, the clips were short and sweetly euphemistic. "Singer Billie Holiday, suffering from a liver condition, has been warned by her physician to avoid strong drinks." This was softball gossip: it sounded chaste but it wasn't hard to read between the lines. A liver condition? Avoid strong drinks? Anyone who had ever heard of Billie Holiday knew those kinds of "physician's warnings" were well behind her. The next article was more blunt: "Billie Holiday, Jazz Great, Critically Ill in

New York." As is traditional in the history of human endeavor, the nearer she got to death, the greater her reputation became: she progressed from mere "singer" to "jazz great" in two short months.[74]

Then the excitement began. Holiday, formerly snubbed by the media of aspirational African-Americans, was now referred to as "the exotic 'Lady Day,'" in the pages of *Jet*. The magazine gushed over Holiday, the "world-famous singer, idolized by millions and revered by musicians the world over," and carefully glossed over her sordid history with a perky reference to her "colorful personality." The article described her collapse after her last performance at the Phoenix Theatre, a "superhuman effort." It ended with a vision of noble courage that rivals the Bronte sisters: "The Lady whose songs have stirred a nation now lies on a sofa in her apartment wearing a white peignoir, smoking cigarets and coughing incessantly. 'I'll be alright,' she says hoarsely"—and at this point, the gloves came off. Holiday was obviously dying—cirrhosis of the liver was the immediate cause, but life itself had been the culprit. Holiday had grown up in a world of make-believe, as one young woman of her generation put it, possessing "a vague awareness that though one may be 'bad' the adults who live this way are contented and seemingly rewarded, at least in movies and magazines." Holiday wanted to be "bad" in just the same way, the way that involved no consequences. That had seemed more possible in the 1920s, when Bessie Smith and the vamps had given life to a Flaming Youth that seemed like it would never burn out. And the 1930s had had their share of tough dames, too. It was in the 1940s, though, that Billie Holiday had really hit her stride, standing onstage like the femme fatale she had always wanted to be. But film noir endings were never happy.[75]

Holiday was dying and she was being hounded by police, desperate to get her on one last charge. Why? Charlie Parker was much more flagrant with his heroin use, and he never served any jail time. Why Holiday? Perhaps because she was the rare woman to suffer addiction publicly. By June 18, *Jet* was running articles from her bedside: "Billie

Holiday Continues Life Struggle in N.Y. Hospital." " 'She is definitely not under treatment for narcotics addiction,' her attorney, Earle W. Zaidins, said." It got worse. The following week featured three stories on Holiday—an uplifting one to begin with, highlighting her strength of character. "Some damn body is always trying to embalm me," Holiday is quoted as saying. "They'll call this another comeback, and I've been nowhere but across town."[76]

The second article was more serious: "Arrest Billie Holiday in Bed on Dope Charges." It was true: police officers had shown up in her hospital room and charged her with using heroin even as she lay encased in an oxygen tent. At this point, she weighed under 100 pounds. "Police said she would be arraigned at bedside when she is well enough." The New York Police Department couldn't have dreamed up worse press if they'd tried, but it was all true. The final Holiday story in that week's issue foreshadowed her all-but-certain death: the debut of Sam Cooke's "Tribute to a Lady," an album of covers of songs Holiday had made famous. No mention made here of her problems with the law, though. Cooke was just about to visit the Dick Clark show, and it just wouldn't have seemed right.[77]

The next two weeks provided more of the same: a brief rally by "the great blues singer" ("I didn't know they could be this cruel to nobody, Daddy . . .") and a show of support the next week as members of the "Mid-Harlem Narcotic Committee" picketed the hospital. But then, three weeks later, the inevitable headline: "Billie Holiday Loses Battle, Dies in New York Hospital." How long had the editors of *Jet* struggled over their coup de grâce? They'd certainly had enough lead time.[78]

"She died like she sang," her (estranged) husband Louis McKay was quoted as saying, "beautifully and bravely." Yet McKay was not in the hospital when she died, according to the article. And so it went: half-truths and outright lies; the fabric of her life inevitably enfolded her death, as well. Then the encomiums began. The tributes poured forth, Sam Cooke being only the most prescient of many singers who started doing their own versions of Lady Day, the woman whom Frank Sinatra called "the most important influence on American popular singing in the last 20 years." To his credit, Sinatra made the comment a year before she died.[79]

~

Holiday lived on—and lived better—long after her demise. After death, Billie Holiday became all the things she wanted to be when she was alive: perpetually beautiful and glamorous. She became a kind of movie star when her autobiography, *Lady Sings the Blues*, was made into a film in 1972, starring the black diva of the day, Diana Ross. The Motown princess may have been miscast, but her popularity helped introduce many young fans to Holiday for the first time. Some were initially confused by the film's title: had Billie Holiday been a blues singer or a jazz singer? But learning the story of her life cleared up any lingering doubts, for here was a life—and a death—that defined the "blues." Musical categories aside, Eleanora Fagan was born into a world best described by the blues, and Billie Holiday died as a consummate blueswoman, someone who had seen the worst of life yet strove to live through it with dignity and grace.

Like the legend of Bessie Smith's final car accident, the many tragedies of Holiday's life transformed her death into a martyrdom. "Every time I sing," claimed British singer Marianne Faithfull, "I pray to Billie Holiday to help me: the singer's saint." Critics have often complained about the public's fascination with the darkness of Holiday's life. It is shallow and morbid, they insist, to dwell on those details rather than on the living sound of her voice. But her fans don't separate the two things, life and art. For Holiday, as for her audience, each gave the other meaning. "Music was invented to confirm human loneliness," Lawrence Durrell wrote just a year after her death. And so the music of Billie Holiday reaches out, expressing that loneliness in a beautiful, unending confirmation.[80]

Chapter Four

THE DEVIL AND THE DEEP BLUE SEA: ETTA JAMES AND ARETHA FRANKLIN

Cool Blue

> Actually, I think we wanted to be black. Being black was being great. The best musicians in the world were black, and black people had a better time. As far as we were concerned the worlds that we came from were drab by comparison.
>
> —Mike Leiber, ca. 1950s[1]

Like Carl Van Vechten, Mezz Mezzrow, and many other white Americans in the twentieth century, Mike Leiber and Jerry Stoller—the writing team responsible for such pop classics as "Hound Dog," "There Goes My Baby," and "Stand By Me"—looked to black culture for something they could not find in their own white one. Like Leiber, Jerry Stoller "felt alienated from my white peers. I felt there was something more special about not only the music I heard, that came from black people, but the black people themselves who made the music." In the post–World War II era, black culture was acquiring new power, extending itself into the American mainstream with a success that black artists and intellectuals in the 1920s and 1930s had only aspired to. The "Double V" campaign waged by the NAACP during World War II—"Victory at home and abroad"—had raised the expectations of all African-Americans: things would be different when the soldiers came home.[2]

In some respects, they were. In 1941 African-Americans, led by the NAACP, succeeded in their demand that the armed services desegregate, constituting a belated yet huge step forward for interracial relations. Wartime jobs had benefited black men and women who had stayed on the home front, and many experienced a degree of financial stability never known before. The postwar economic boom had positive consequences, as well. The demand for new cars and appliances from newly suburbanized white families led to high employment of blacks in Northern factories. The present and the immediate future seemed bright for African-Americans immediately following the war, but as the years passed and their hope for greater equality remained unfulfilled, the Double V campaign started to look like a failure.

As the 1950s began, black Americans were starting to express that anger with more force and less fear than ever before. The sheer number of blacks living in the North had forever changed the racial balance of the United States; their frustration was much more public than it had been in the tradition-bound South. Black people raised in Chicago, Detroit, and Los Angeles had never experienced the overt Jim Crow policies of the South (though they knew the less-flagrant Northern version), and when confronted with it, they revolted. When Emmett Till, a fourteen-year-old black teenager from Chicago was lynched by whites while visiting relatives in Mississippi in 1955, African-Americans protested like never before. Black soldiers had fought overseas against Hitler's policies of racial hatred, so why should they tolerate it at home?

This was a new era—or it was supposed to be—and in the 1950s, black Americans were determined to make it so.

While institutions of uplift such as the NAACP and the Southern Baptist Convention would become major players in the civil rights wars of the 1950s, the African-American community expressed its sense of righteous anger in other, darker ways. The figure of the black hipster had been an important part of the American cultural landscape since the 1920s. After World War II, the hipster became less of a dilettante and more of a militant; the reefer-smoking, anti-establishment pose that had first distinguished him was wearing thin. Several decades on, hipsters—male and female—were getting impatient for real change. They now felt more comfortable expressing that frustration, and events like the lynching of Emmett Till drove their simmering rage to a boil. In his 1947 novel *Invisible Man*, Ralph Ellison captured this growing resentment in the depiction of a black man whose demands on society were forever unacknowledged. "You're constantly being bumped against by those of poor vision," the eponymous hero explains. "It's when you feel like this, that out of resentment you begin to bump people back. And, let me confess, you feel that way most of the time."[3]

In 1955, the Swiss-born photographer Robert Frank traveled across the United States, creating an album of photographs that he called *The Americans*. When it was published in 1956, public reaction was harsh. *Popular Photography*'s review was representative: "They are images of an America seen by a joyless man. . . . [Frank] is also a liar, perversely basking in the kind of world and the kind of misery he is perpetually seeking and persistently creating." In the Introduction to the book, however, Beat writer Jack Kerouac disagreed, saying simply: "You got eyes."[4]

Frank's camera caught people in moments of unguarded emotion. Many of the white faces were tight with anger or slack with boredom, or simply seized in a mask of distrust. There were many black faces there, too; nearly one out of seven of Frank's photographs featured African-Americans, a percentage that took reviewers by surprise. And

Frank captured something new in them; something different shone from their eyes. Patience and pride in the face of a nursemaid holding a tiny white infant ("a picture that should have been blown up and hung in the streets of Little Rock," said Kerouac) and plaintive questioning in the gaze of a man seated at the back of a segregated trolley in New Orleans. And in one image, a premonition of the faces of African-Americans to come.

In a crowded frame, a hulking, gleaming Harley-Davidson motorcycle dominates the lowest third of the image. Astride it sit a mustached black man dressed entirely in black leather and a black woman, also in black leather and dark jeans, with a fitted, soft-leather helmet on her head, like the headgear of a latter-day Amelia Earhart. Physically, they are a striking couple—gorgeous, in fact—but it is their expressions that make the image vibrate. He, leaning forward and gripping the handlebars, looks back over his left shoulder as if waiting for a sign from his partner before roaring off. His expression is serious, intense. Yet it is the woman who commands the viewer's attention. Her back is straight, shoulders thrown back, her eyes are half-lidded with the composure of a saint or a psychopath. She is haughty, beautiful, dangerous, and proud of it. These are not Invisible Men—they flaunt their power and style. "The faces don't editorialize or criticize or say anything but 'This is the way we are in real life and if you don't like it I don't know anything about it 'cause I'm living my own life my way,'" Kerouac wrote. This was the face of the new, "New Negro." In *The Americans*, the photographs of black people had the most impact. Their faces communicated a moral gravity that the whites could not match.[5]

It was this integrity that attracted white teenagers like Mike Leiber and Jerry Stoller in the 1950s. While black Americans were beginning their own revolution, with its causes obvious and important, Hollywood dithered over white delinquency in *Rebel Without a Cause* (1955). When asked what he was rebelling against, for example, Marlon Brando (playing the leader of a marauding motorcycle gang) in *The Wild One* (1953), famously responded, "Whaddaya got?" Brando's impudence was easy to enjoy, but his remark illustrated the difference between white and black American culture at the time. White rebels impotently cast around for a reason to fight, while black Americans ruminated on centuries of racial injustice and expectations left unfulfilled. In the 1950s, it was black hipsters—like Miles Davis, whose albums *Birth of the Cool* (1949) and *Kind of Blue* (1959) bracketed and helped to define the decade; like *The Americans'* motorcycle toughs; like the spitfire singer Etta James—who made the imminently threatening side of black culture more visible. As the civil rights movement gained strength in the 1950s and 1960s, the hipsters' legacy would grow even stronger, eventually contributing to the glamour of Black Power by the early 1970s. Twelve years after the publication of *The Americans*, Aretha Franklin finally belted out "Respect." By 1968, it was a demand, not a plea.[6]

1938

> Woman's basic role . . . is to bring strength, security and serenity to those about her and to do her share to help develop these same qualities in the life of the community.
> —Dorothy Barclay, "On Becoming a Woman," *New York Times*, 1953[7]

> I think I was looking to do something wrong.
> —Etta James, ca. 1956[8]

Etta James

Etta James became a teenager just as teenagers began to get a bad reputation—no coincidence there. As a matter of fact, James's music set the tone for scandalous behavior, starting with her first single

Etta James (b. 1938) flanked by her first group, the Peaches (from left, sisters Jean and Abye Mitchell), in 1955.
THE SHOWTIME MUSIC ARCHIVE

(recorded when she was sixteen). "I guess I was a juvenile delinquent," she admitted cheerfully. Born in 1938 in the Los Angeles neighborhood of Watts and christened Jamesetta Hawkins, she was the product of a one-night stand. Her mother, the sixteen-year-old Dorothy Hawkins, gave her daughter various versions of her parentage, but eventually a family friend told the girl that the legendary white pool shark, Minnesota Fats, was her father, and that's what Jamesetta chose to believe; she certainly had the light coloring of a biracial union. Like her idol, Billie Holiday, the young Jamesetta was a child raised by a child.

Dorothy Hawkins was always a shadowy figure in her daughter's life. "I called her the Mystery Lady," James remembered. "She was Miss Hip, a jazz chick, a let-the-good-times-roller who wore midnight cologne. . . . I saw Dorothy as a distant goddess, a starlet I couldn't touch, couldn't understand, couldn't even call by the name of mother." Dorothy was sent to reform school shortly after Jamesetta's birth, and she left her baby with her older sister, Cozetta, for safekeeping. Aunt Cozie wasn't thrilled with the responsibility. As a madam at one of Central Avenue's busiest brothels, she figured the presence of a baby would be bad for business. Eventually, Jamesetta ended up in the care of Dorothy's landlords, Lula and Jesse Rogers, a childless couple who virtually adopted the baby. It was a lucky break for Jamesetta, for the Rogerses were doting parents who provided her with love and stability and nurtured her early interest in music. Lula—called "Mama Lu," or just "Mama," by Jamesetta—also made a point of reassuring her that her biological mother loved her and would have cared for her if she could. This was a generous interpretation. Dorothy showed up sporadically to whisk Jamesetta off to cheap hotel rooms for the weekend, and she would then leave her alone while she disappeared on dates. While Jamesetta loved and depended upon the Rogerses, the virtual loss of her real parents left deep emotional scars.[9]

A quick overview of Etta James's early childhood reveals that, despite the many changes in American society since the 1920s, many

African-Americans still struggled to survive in a kind of underworld invisible to most of white America. The classic image of 1950s domesticity—white-collar dad, homemaking mom, a few kids, and a few cars parked out in the quiet suburbs—did not include African-Americans. The young Etta James lived in South Central Los Angeles, an urban neighborhood with a then-thriving nightlife and jazz scene but not much to offer young children. One of the few bright spots in her life was St. Paul Baptist Church—more specifically, the Echoes of Eden choir that sang there—and its talented choirmaster, James Earle Hines, a giant figure in the world of gospel music. Jamesetta was lucky to find him; he recognized her vocal talent and molded her voice from the time she was five.

Like Bessie Smith before her, the mature Etta James constantly drew on the power of gospel phrasing and delivery in her performances. The young Jamesetta was thrilled by James Earle Hines and his "go-tell-it-on-the-mountain voice . . . all that force. All that spill-your-guts-out power. . . . Women in the choir were cool," she recalled, "but it was a man who brought down the sky and shook the earth." Hines gave her private lessons and encouraged her to sing confidently—to *be* confident. Hines's influence on her singing and personality was profound, but it never extended beyond that, for Jamesetta was not stirred by the sermons in the same way she was moved by the songs. Like Bessie Smith, Etta James found strength in the black church—vocal strength that recalled the great African-American tradition of sacred singing and preaching—and both women brought that aesthetic into the popular music they created.[10]

By the time of Billie Holiday's death in 1959, popular music had undergone a radical revolution. While Benny Goodman still had a contingent of older fans, the new sound of rock 'n' roll had eclipsed older, jazz-based musical forms and had taken over the *Billboard* charts. Even the charts were changing. In 1945, *Billboard* had begun classifying all recordings by black artists under the title "Race Records," alluding to the contemporary use of the term *race*, as when a black man who was proud of his ethnicity called himself a "race man." In 1949, then–staff writer Jerry Wexler succeeded in changing the chart's name to "Rhythm and Blues," arguing that it was "a label more appropriate to more enlightened times." Wexler had defined a new genre of music. Eventually, Wexler's own work as a record producer with Wilson Pickett, Otis Redding, and Aretha Franklin (and, much later, Etta James) would push the limits of the genre, creating a wholly new term for the music: "Soul."[11]

~

The young Jamesetta Hawkins had grown up on rhythm and blues. Aunt Cozie claimed that, as a toddler, Jamesetta would make her way to the jukebox and "holler until someone put a nickel in that box" and played her song: "Honky Tonk Train Blues," by the legendary boogie-woogie pianist Meade Lux Lewis. As a girl, Jamesetta had been exposed to a wide variety of music. Aunt Cozie worked on Central Avenue, at the heart of LA's jazz scene, and Dorothy was a well-known denizen of the city's jazz clubs, where she occasionally took her daughter to hear Stan Kenton's jazz orchestra, featuring the great singer June Christy, as well as rhythm and blues artists like Amos Milburn, bluesman T-Bone Walker, and even a special appearance by the great Josephine Baker. She probably heard Bessie Smith, whose records were common in African-American households, and Billie Holiday was Dorothy's favorite singer as well as her style icon—Dorothy wore platform shoes and red lipstick and cultivated a cool, mysterious air. As her mother played Holiday's records "on a cheapie little record player . . . [in] one of her dingy furnished rooms," the young Jamesetta instantly recognized in Holiday's voice "a world of glamour and grace and easy sin. . . . the life I secretly dreamed of living myself." Jamesetta was attracted to Holiday's style, but as an adolescent in the 1950s, rock 'n' roll demanded her immediate attention. Its popularity was causing hysteria among both teenagers and their parents.[12]

"Going to a rock 'n' roll show is like attending the rites of some obscure tribe, whose means of communication are incomprehensible," declared the widely read *Look* magazine. "An adult can actually be frightened." The article noted that rock 'n' roll "echoes classic blues shouters of past times, such as Bessie Smith. Music similar to rock 'n' roll has been recorded for decades, but under 'race' or 'rhythm and blues' labels, intended for a Negro market"—implying that this "insistent, brutal" music was appropriate for blacks, but not whites.[13]

Perhaps it was the lack of adult supervision, but no one seemed to mind Jamesetta Hawkins's fixation on rock 'n' roll. Mama Lu died in 1951, and the sad and bewildered thirteen-year-old Jamesetta was abruptly moved to San Francisco to live with Dorothy. Her mother's chaotic lifestyle and detached emotional style forced Jamesetta to grow up all at once. As she put it, "I left the little church girl back in L.A." Dressed in her "blackboard jungle outfit" of baggy blue jeans, an oversize man's dress shirt, white socks, and tennis shoes, she joined several girl gangs in the city and shoplifted costume jewelry, which they pawned to buy records: Guitar Slim and Ray Charles were early favorites. She hated singing in the school choir but found a comfortable outlet in the streetcorner doo-wop bands that were popular among black teenagers at the time. She and two girlfriends, sisters Abysinia (Abye) and Jean Mitchell started their own group, the Creolettes.

Jamesetta was back into singing. Just like her days with the Echoes of Eden, music once again became the one positive thing in her life. This time, however, it was all about rhythm and blues, and the Creolettes developed a twenty-minute stage show that became increasingly popular in San Francisco's amateur contests and teen dances. The Creolettes were big fans of Hank Ballard and the Midnighters, an R&B group known for its suggestive lyrics and bluesy rock. Their hit single, "Work with Me, Annie," was a sensation; "work" was understood to be a sexual euphemism, and the song was one of the Creolettes' favorites. "All the kids were crazy for that tune," recalled Etta James, "a nasty tune for grinding. Some of the parents wouldn't even let us play the record at home, which naturally made us play it even more." The girls were thrilled when Ballard and his band showed up unannounced at one of the Creolettes' regular bookings at a sock hop. Ballard performed his hit and encouraged the girls to keep singing. When he came back the following week, the girls had something to show him. Jamesetta had written an "answer" to "Work with Me, Annie": "Roll with Me, Henry." "Cool," said Hank.[14]

A week later, Abye was down at the Primaline Ballroom to see Johnny Otis, an R&B bandleader, musician, and talent scout for Modern Records. As LA's "Godfather of Rhythm and Blues," Otis was "much more than a promoter," according to Etta James; he was "a guru, a man with an encyclopedic knowledge and appreciation of black music." Like John Hammond, Leiber and Stoller, and Jerry Wexler, Otis was a white man who made black culture his exclusive domain. Not a "pretender" or a "voyeur," according to Wexler, who became his friend, Otis "opted to leave the white world . . . [this guy] converted." Etta James would later agree: "His soul was blacker than the blackest black in Compton," she liked to say.[15]

That night at the Primaline, however, Jamesetta was skeptical. Abye had called the girls, telling them that she had met Otis ("[Abye] was a groupie girl," James said) and that he wanted to hear them sing. Abye called again from a hotel, asking them to come over. "If he wants us at the hotel," Jamesetta figured, "it sure as hell isn't to hear us sing. He had three or four band boys with him and I thought—'Oh-oh—one for each of us, y'know.' I thought it was a trick." Abye was insistent and Jean was willing, so Jamesetta decided to go. "I was a tough teenager so I went anyway. . . . I thought if one of these guys tries to take advantage I'll just pop him."[16]

She didn't have to. Jamesetta was persuaded to sing for Otis ("[I]n the bathroom . . . everyone sounds good singing in the bathroom. Tile makes for great acoustics"), and he was impressed. The next morning, the Creolettes returned to the hotel with their bags packed. Jamesetta held a note from her mother, giving her fifteen-year-old daughter permission to travel back to LA with Johnny Otis and his all-male band.

Jamesetta had forged the note—Dorothy was in jail and Jamesetta didn't bother to contact her. "[F]uck Dorothy," she thought. This was an opportunity to escape life with her mother, not to mention school, where she was on the verge of expulsion for lack of attendance: "This was one adventure I was not about to miss." Abye and Jean Mitchell were orphans who had taken care of themselves for years. A job with Johnny Otis was the closest thing to a future the three of them had ever seen.

Once in LA, Johnny Otis masterminded the girls' nascent career, setting them up with a band, a recording date, and a marketing concept. Otis put "Roll with Me, Henry" on wax and started playing it out of his record store and on his local radio show to spark interest. "What should we call her?" he asked his listeners, capitalizing on her down-and-dirty sound as well as the erotic appeal of this underage girl. "She's got big ol' jaws, a hefty backside, and she's only fifteen." Otis had begun by calling her Miss Peaches, in reference to her fair skin, but that soon changed, and he decided that Abye and Jean Mitchell would be the Peaches, and Jamesetta Hawkins would be known as Etta James.[17]

"Roll with Me, Henry" hit big. Released around Thanksgiving in 1953, it was #2 on *Billboard*'s R&B chart by early 1954. The song still swings, nearly fifty years later. It starts out with a rough man's voice shouting, then a boogie-woogie piano and bassline ease in, and then a girl's shriek, "Hey!" before Etta James tears in, her fifteen-year-old voice gritty with experience beyond her years: "You got to roll with me, Henry, you better roll it while the rollin' is on!" The Peaches chime in with "awooh's" in the background, precursors to the famous "aa-woop's" that would be heard fourteen years later on Aretha Franklin's "Natural Woman."[18]

Although Hank Ballard's original song, "Work with Me, Annie," was acknowledged to refer to sex (much like his subsequent 1958 hit, "The Twist," later popularized by Chubby Checker), James insisted that her song was about dancing: "It's just that the word *roll* had a sexual suggestiveness prudes couldn't handle." Well, it was suggestive; James's sweet-but-rough voice promised much more than just a dance. Whatever it was really about, some radio stations refused to play it because of the sexual connotations, and it was soon renamed "The Wallflower," alluding to Henry's apparent reluctance to dance—and an inoffensive title that allowed radio stations to put the record back in rotation. "Young Etta James," as she was called, had a huge hit. Hank Ballard's music publisher reacted quickly—the song's musical structure was identical to Ballard's original—and a deal was worked out among Ballard, Modern Records, and Etta James. Though she was the sole lyricist, James initially wanted to give Abye and Jean Mitchell a writing credit, too, as writing and publishing royalties have always been the most lucrative aspect of the music business. Otis refused or simply ignored her request, and in the end they split the writing credit four ways—listing James, Hank Ballard, Johnny Otis, and his wife, Phyllis. The Otises, who had contributed nothing to the song's composition, ended up reaping half the publishing royalties. As a minor, James's take was paid directly to the court, to be claimed by her when she reached twenty-one. At that time, she split her share again, giving a third each to Abye and Jean Mitchell, in a move highly unusual in its decency. Generosity like this was rare in the music business.[19]

Back in 1954, however, when the record was still hot, it was covered by a white singer, Georgia Gibbs, whose toned-down version of the song, now called "Dance with Me, Henry," went to #1 on the national (i.e., white) pop chart. "My version went underground and continued to sell," James remembered, "while Georgia's whitewash went through the roof. . . . I was enraged to see Georgia singing the song on *The Ed Sullivan Show* while I was singing it in some funky dive in Watts." James was, to put it mildly, new to the music business. It took Johnny Otis to make her understand the significance of Gibbs's cover. "You better hope she sells six million," he told her, "because you're the writer!" Otis profited, too, of course. "We ended up splitting it and I guess overall I must have gotten 14 or 15 thousand dollars,"

James said—a small amount, especially once she gave a third each to Abye and Jean. This was a small payoff for a song that, by some estimations, sold more than four million copies.[20]

Unfortunately, Etta James's first rip-off was the beginning of a trend. Like many musicians, James was focused on the music and totally unprepared to deal with the complicated financial structure of the music industry. Song royalties are always split two ways: half goes to the credited writer(s), and the other half goes to the "publisher." Both halves belong to the writer—as long as she has her own publishing company, something that can be done in a few minutes by drawing up legal papers. Record companies know this, but seventeen-year-old first-time singers generally don't. For the five years Etta James was at Modern Records, the Bihari brothers who owned the company routinely paid her between $25 and $30 dollars for the publishing rights to every song she wrote. In effect, James sold half her future royalties for less than $40 a pop. As a minor who was just a phone call away from juvenile court, James was in a compromised position: "If Johnny Otis wanted a piece of my song, who was I to argue? Johnny Otis, after all, was the reason I got to quit school and make a record."[21]

"Like almost all the other artists in this era, [I] was hoodwinked," James later said. "[F]or practically nothing, we gave away half of the ownership of material that turned out to be incredibly valuable." Variations on this theme litter the history of the recording industry. Many of Bessie Smith's songs were erroneously credited to her ne'er-do-well husband, while the authorship of some of Billie Holiday's originals is still debated. As far as day-to-day survival went, artists on the Modern Records label, including James and guitar virtuoso B. B. King, had an unofficial agreement with the Biharis. If she needed money, she could go in and ask for it—$100 here or there to cover the rent or buy costumes. Sometimes these expenses would be deducted from future earnings, without the artists' being aware that they had received an "advance." Years later, Etta James refused to blame Otis for taking advantage of her inexperience. "Thinking back, I can see why Johnny

[Otis] felt like he deserved a piece of the song; he'd discovered me," she said. "With as many people that Johnny has been instrumental in . . . making them a big star, he's not in the position he should be in, if he was stealing that much—he'd be in a better position than he is. So, he got fucked, too, somewhere."[22]

Etta James went on earning money for Johnny Otis and the Bihari brothers for the rest of the decade as she toured with Otis's R&B revue throughout the country, returning to LA every so often to do another record. With James's potential as a solo star becoming more apparent, the Peaches accompanied her less and less, though Abye occasionally joined the tours as James's personal assistant. "There were some bad feelings—I didn't blame the girls for being pissed—but it was about survival, and I was surviving as Miss Etta James." James was paid a flat fee for her performances, starting at $10 per night—a fee that eventually was increased as she became more savvy about her own value to the show. Her subsequent singles for Modern continued to sell well. "Good Rockin' Daddy" went to the R&B top twelve in 1955, and a bluesy, bump-and-grind number called "W-O-M-A-N" was also released that year.[23]

A reinterpretation of "Mannish Boy" (1955), Muddy Waters's tribute to male sexual prowess, "W-O-M-A-N" was just as ferocious as the original. "I'm man, I'm a full grown man!" Waters shouts in his song. James's female version confronts Muddy Waters on his own ground. In the best blues-queen tradition, she asserts herself, using the same values as Waters used: physical allure, sexual stamina, and the power of her own charisma. "Talkin' 'bout you a maaaiinnn?" James growls as the song begins, enunciating "man" in just the same, drawn-out way that Waters did in "Mannish Boy," "always ready to go?" she challenges him. "Now when it comes to movin', boy you're awful slow."[24]

For a seventeen-year-old, she certainly sounded like a woman. Just as the early blues queens such as Ma Rainey, Bessie Smith, and Victoria Spivey had brought sexuality, humor, and sass to the new world of blues recording, Etta James was bringing the same qualities to early rock 'n' roll. Sex was always one of James's favorite topics, from "Roll with Me, Henry" on. Like Bessie Smith's "I'm Wild About That Thing" (1929), James's songs were evidence that women enjoyed sex and were comfortable asking for what they wanted. They also depicted sex as an integral part of the romantic experience, something to be approached with humor and passion, as opposed to something a "good girl" denied her partner, a concept popular among mainstream moralists that had been sold to women since the nineteenth century. Up until the feminist movement of the 1960s, women's blues were one of the few sources providing a counter-argument to the idea that sexual enjoyment was reserved for men only. Etta James and other inheritors to Smith's legacy adapted both the content of women's blues and their sound, singing in a deep, throaty voice whose power underlined the message in her songs. Like those early blueswomen, James was a pioneer in a brand-new musical form, and her successes set an example for those who followed her in R&B and rock 'n' roll.

It was not only her voice that set her apart. From her first days of touring, James began experimenting with new, wild looks. With her almond-shaped eyes, tawny skin, and ripe, sensual physique, James had always stood out in a crowd. "First Dorothy lightened up my hair to a carrot red and put it in spit curls," James explained of her mother's early attempts to effect a new stage persona for her. "But in Detroit, a gay guy bleached it until it was practically white and took out the curls. I was glad. To me the curls were Shirley Temple. . . . I didn't want to look innocent." This was the beginning of James's notorious, outrageous aesthetic. "I wanted to be noticed, I wanted to be glamorous," she declared. Now, it was no new thing for black women to be perceived as sexy; in fact, the hypersexualization of black women was one of the most destructive side effects of American racism, leaving a centuries-long legacy of black women brutalized by rape and black men victimized by their inability to avenge the crimes in a whites-only judicial system. But as the Bad Women of American music began creating their own personas, they had gradually become bolder and bolder in their proud assertion of their own sexuality. It took confidence to assert oneself as a minority woman in a white society. It was significant that James "wanted to be noticed," for the safest course for African-Americans in the 1950s was to blend in with the crowd, to avoid standing out. As James said, "There was also a defiance to my look."[25]

It was a look that was largely influenced by the "secret angels," James's term for gay men. She had long benefited from their support, beginning with some of the male members of the Echoes of Eden choir, and it continued throughout her career. Like Ma Rainey, Bessie Smith, and Billie Holiday, Etta James refused to subscribe to bourgeois ideas about sexuality, and her music and personality seemed to speak for those who felt left out of the American mainstream. The gay men and drag queens with whom she surrounded herself "offered me a kindness and sensitivity," she said, "—and a different sort of intelligence, a lighthearted view of life—I didn't find in the macho men who, in spite of myself, I'd often end up with." They also helped shape her image, remaking the "blackboard jungle" delinquent into "a sepia femme . . . [a] cigar-shaped drugstore-haired blonde" with high, dark, arching eyebrows, long false lashes, Cleopatra eyeliner, and frosted white lipstick. She wore only the tightest skirts and no stockings, so "the cats could see the sweat on my legs"—this in an era when female pop stars generally performed in elegant ball gowns and gloves. "I didn't think about how normal girls my age were still in high school wearing bobby socks and dating football players . . . dreaming of getting married and making apple pies," she said. "I'm glad I didn't go that way—trapped in some kitchen, I'd surely have a nervous breakdown."[26]

In many ways, gay men were role models for the young Etta James; she certainly thought more of them than she did of her own mother, who by this time was living off her daughter's earnings, acting as her nominal "manager." The "secret angels," on the other hand, lived by their own rules, outside the boundaries of respectable society. They encouraged James to express her wild side, and she in turn spent the 1950s earning a reputation as a hell-raising belter.

In 1960, she finally left Modern Records (when she was stranded in Chicago and the Bihari brothers refused to pay for a hotel) and signed on with a new pair of brothers: Leonard and Phil Chess, owners of the legendary Chess Records, the Chicago-based R&B label that had struck gold with Muddy Waters, Howlin' Wolf, Chuck Berry, Bo Diddley, and Ahmad Jamal, among others. While it seemed like a step up from the smaller, regional Modern label, James's years at Chess (1960–1975) were marked by outstanding performances and an almost uncanny failure to get her songs heard beyond the black audience. Although she had big hits with songs such as "I'd Rather Go Blind" (later covered by Rod Stewart) and "Tell Mama" (later covered by Janis Joplin), it was "At Last"—a slow, beautiful, jazzy ballad with lush orchestration—that remains a requested song today, and that made the biggest impact at the time.[27]

Despite her successes, Chess couldn't seem to organize a comprehensive plan for Etta James's career. The label never seemed able or willing to branch out to white audiences, where the serious money was to be found. One critic at the rock magazine *Crawdaddy* observed that her "erratic" career only "survived at all by the sheer momentum of the prodigious talent she commands." For her part, James was distracted from tending to the business of her career for most of the decade as she began a heroin addiction that lasted through the mid-1970s.[28]

James was familiar with heroin and its consequences; in the mid-1950s, in fact, she had met one of her idols, Billie Holiday, just as Holiday began her slide toward death. James's career was soaring, and she was invited to perform on an NBC radio show called "Jazz Plus Blues Equals Soul," featuring Count Basie, Holiday, and James. Though the term was not yet in wide use, James figured she was responsible for the "Soul" part, and she prepared to sing "Roll with Me, Henry." Still a teenager, James was excited and nervous. "I sat up straight out of respect for Miss Holiday. . . . Hell, I was on the verge of meeting royalty," she explained. Her feelings about Holiday were complicated. She loved her music and although she could not imitate Holiday's cool style, she aspired to the dangerous glamour Holiday projected. In James's imagination, Holiday was intimately linked to her mother, Dorothy, who idolized Lady Day, imitated her look, and listened to her records constantly. It was a "lifelong conflict," said James. Once Dorothy discovered her daughter's musical talent, she "so badly wanted me to be jazz, while my rebellious spirit ran to hot-and-nasty rhythm and blues." Despite her admiration for Lady Day, James could only be herself.

Now she was finally meeting the legend herself, an opportunity her mother could only dream of, so she tried not to stare. "I had to get a good look at Billie Holiday. I wanted to say, 'Hi, I'm Etta James and you're Billie Holiday and my mother loves you and I love you, too,' but I didn't want to seem like some crazy groupie." It was hard to look away, however, as Holiday walked slowly into the room, supported by a man on either side. "Her lipstick looked greasy and her eyes looked tired . . . swollen feet. Terribly swollen. My eyes went from her feet to her hands, which were so puffy they looked like boxing gloves." James was shocked and embarrassed by the sight of her fallen idol. "Are you looking at me?" Holiday demanded. When James responded in the affirmative, Holiday "looked down at her own swollen hands and rubbed them together as if in pain. 'Just don't ever let this happen to you,'" she told James, and walked away. Yet Holiday remained a huge influence on James, who later recorded an album of songs made famous by Holiday. *Mystery Lady* (1994) won James her first Grammy award. "The Mystery Lady" is "my mother," James said. "And Billie Holiday. And when all is said and done, the Mystery Lady is also me."[29]

Despite the shock of seeing the heroin-ravaged Holiday, James continued using heroin. She had started for the same reasons everyone else did: "It was a way of keeping the world at bay," she admitted. "I'd seen it. I knew what it could do but I did it to be hip." James's tough image had helped her to exorcise her emotions, but it also hid a great deal of inner pain, the result of her chaotic upbringing and increasingly unstable life.[30]

Touring became a way of life. James traveled throughout the country from the mid-1950s to the mid-1960s, and she spent much of that time in the South, where her earthy style was especially appreciated. She worked small clubs as a supporting act for numerous blues, R&B and rock 'n' roll acts, among them Zydeco King Clifton Chenier, Little Richard, and Bo Diddley. The audiences and the bills were sometimes segregated, sometimes not—a significant testament to the dismantling of racial barriers brought on by rock 'n' roll. Outside Memphis one night, James shared a booking with the young Elvis Presley, whose "gentlemanly manners" impressed James. This was a good night, but on other nights, the reality of segregation was hammered home.

James was confronted numerous times by angry white Southerners when she used the "white" instead of the "colored" facilities, though often they had to ask her to identify herself first. Her light skin and bleached blonde hair drew attention in the South, especially since she was usually traveling with a car- or busload of black musicians. On several occasions, the vehicle was stopped by a police officer alarmed by the sight (as they interpreted it) of a lone white woman among so many black men. Since the days of Reconstruction, segregationists had bred a hysterical fear of black male sexuality as a justification for the policies of Jim Crow. Subsequently, the notion that white women were constantly in danger of being raped by black men fueled white racism. James was angered by the harassment and often tried to avoid identifying herself by race, just to antagonize the cops. She refused to respond to insinuations that there was something amiss, only capitulating when asked a direct question: "You a white woman? You a nigger?" they asked. Not until the black men accompanying her—her friends and fellow musicians—began to get nervous did she relent. "No, I ain't no damn white woman," she would say. "The experience left a bad taste in my mouth." Although she identified herself as a black woman when pressed, like virtually all African-Americans, James's racial identity was mixed. Her Jim Crow experiences merely reinforced something she already knew: that racial identity is forced upon people by society, not biology. Bleaching her hair, powdering her face, and talking back to racist cops, James resisted society's rules as much as she could without endangering those around her.[31]

While on tour, James was always outnumbered by men. She had more freedom than most teenaged girls, but she usually refrained from getting sexually involved with her fellow musicians or men she met in clubs. Perhaps it was the teenager in her, but for the young Etta James, life on the road was full of crushes rather than one-night stands. Her sexually aggressive performance style and prostitute-inspired look belied her tender heart. She befriended many of the men she met, keeping her relationships with Sam Cooke and Marvin Gaye platonic, and many of her closest "girlfriends" continued to be homosexual men. There were a few boyfriends, though. Harvey Fuqua, leader of the legendary doo-wop group the Moonglows, was one of her first loves, and though the romance was brief, they continued to work together as Fuqua became a respected record producer for Chess, Motown, and other labels. In truth, James's main romance through the 1950s and 1960s was with heroin. Scoring the drug and working out how to pay for it increasingly consumed most of her offstage energy.

Like American women of the 1930s and 1940s who sought an inner refuge from their emotions, women in the subsequent decades felt a similar desire and often turned to drugs for relief. White middle- and upper-class women were able to obtain prescriptions for legal tranquilizers such as Wyeth Laboratories' Miltown, released in 1955—the infamous "Mother's Little Helper" that eased white housewives' anxiety and depression. Expensive prescription drugs were not as accessible to poorer and darker women, who tended to use other remedies: alcohol, marijuana, and heroin.

The expressive forms of American popular culture continued to expand, providing another outlet for stifled emotions. In 1958, when asked why she attended rock concerts, one fifteen-year-old girl replied, "It's just instinct, that's all. . . . I come to hear it because I can sing and scream here. Because it's not like at home where your parents are watching TV and you can't. Here you can scream all you like." Etta James was drawn to performing by a similar desire to "release what's bottled up inside me. . . . On stage I even shock myself," she told an interviewer. "I feel so vicious up there sometimes I just want to reach down and yank somebody up and wham! . . . like something inside me was clawing to get out."[32]

American women (and men) were looking for acceptable ways to express their emotions in a society that increasingly valued keeping emotions in check—at home, at work, and in public spaces. "A state of tension is inseparable from active intelligence but it is socially unpermissible [sic] in women," complained one woman in 1960, arguing that American society valued only "relaxed and compliant women" rather than the "one who makes demands"—emotional, intellectual, or otherwise.[33]

In response, leisure activities quickly provided the venues of choice for venting unruly feelings: large sporting events and rock concerts grew in tandem from the 1950s on, emerging as culturally meaningful events that either outraged or enraptured the American public, depending on one's personal preferences. One psychiatrist suggested that teenage rock 'n' roll fans were "infected with a 'communicable disease,'" while others simply concluded that "this generation of teenagers [is] going to hell." "Most of life is so constricted," explained one teenage rock 'n' roll fan in the mid-1960s. "This music . . . helps you to let yourself go."[34]

Rock and R&B concerts were cathartic for the audience, and they would seem to be especially so for the performer. Yet despite Etta James's relative position of emotional freedom as a cut-loose onstage presence, singing apparently did not provide enough of an outlet for her emotional needs. "Depression and crying are valid emotional feelings," she said, "but I've been stuffin' them inside me all these years. Mad? Hostile? Stuff it and withdraw, and heroin was the cap on the bottle."[35]

Heroin provided a temporary fix for her emotional distress, but it wreaked destruction on her career. She took an increasingly passive attitude toward her professional life, leaving it to the Chess brothers to make important decisions related to her recordings, finances, and future plans. Just as with the Bihari brothers, Leonard Chess controlled all her money in a paternalistic arrangement—the only kind of financial management James had ever known. "Leonard Chess was like a father to me," she said. "He took care of my problems and bought me a new Cadillac. He'd give me a little money now and then. . . . It didn't matter about all the other monies due you, so long as you had your Cadillac and enough money to keep you going." James claimed to have learned something about working with record labels from the Soul superstar Sam Cooke, who told her that "record companies were banks, there to loan you money to make music." Perhaps that was why James always seemed to be indebted to Chess, despite the money she earned for the label. Regardless of the judgments of others, Etta James never blamed Chess for the financial difficulties she experienced as years passed. "A lot of people have little things to say about him. Leonard Chess really did me all right. I didn't get paid royalties. Because I was so young and crazy and wild, I didn't get those things, but it ended up working out that I do get 'em now." The last statement is probably a reference to Leonard Chess's gift of a house in the early 1970s, and perhaps the efforts of the Rhythm and Blues Foundation, a non-profit organization supported by contemporary musicians such as Bonnie Raitt, which has collected fees for early R&B artists who were cheated out of their due earnings.[36]

Distracted by her addiction, Etta James depended on others—Leonard Chess, her business managers, and various boyfriends and husbands—to keep her career on track throughout the 1960s and into the 1970s. Heroin is a complicated drug. Users often are able to live with the addiction for years—not necessarily a healthy or happy life, but a relatively long one nevertheless. James kicked heroin numerous times but eventually fell back, always at war with herself and her conflicting feelings about her identity, torn between the light and dark sides of life. In contrast to Bessie Smith and Billie Holiday, James had a strong maternal urge. "I wasn't yearning for a husband," she said, "[but] I've always wanted babies." For all her sexy outfits and her low-down style, James merely played at promiscuity and was always attracted to the idea of living the straight life. She had a brief stint as a Black Muslim in the early 1960s, intrigued by the mix of danger and discipline they represented. "I picked up on the anger and rebellious vibe of the teaching. The messages were strong—let's not eat pork, let's wear those headdresses and go to temple every night . . . and mostly, let's hang out with those fine-looking clean-cut Muslim brothers." Her irreverence and taste for the wild side of life prevented her from ever fully adopting the Muslim life.[37]

She was a woman at war with herself, and her life was chaotic, a series of events designed merely to help her survive from one day to the next—whether recording a song (or occasionally a full album) for Chess to pay the bills, or concocting a phony check-cashing scheme to pay off the drug dealers (a crime that sent her to prison twice in the 1960s). This was not a career, it was mere survival. She remained popular among black audiences throughout the 1960s, playing regular gigs at Harlem's Apollo Theater as well as touring the South in a mobile home. During this time, Etta James was part of the R&B circuit, a life of nonstop touring and hustling that included gigs with Otis Redding, Sam Cooke, and James Brown. It was hard work and, given the cost of James's drug habit, it did not provide rainy-day security. The most she hoped for was continuing interest from the audience so that she could sell a few more records, play a few more shows.

The men she took up with only complicated things. Like Billie Holiday, James was attracted to strong men, and strength was often confused with violence. James's two most significant relationships in the 1960s were unhappy; one used her so badly that she refused to name him in her autobiography. "I don't want to give him that much dignity," she claimed. The other man, Billy Foster, she described as a "wannabe pimp," but perhaps because he was the father of her first son, she called him by name. In contrast to Holiday, James wrestled with her attraction to bad men. She recognized it as a pattern of behavior among women singers and acknowledged herself as part of that tradition of fellow "blues singers [and] black divas" who fell for abusive men. James speculated that the problem was fear:

> I wanted to look one way to the world. I painted myself over with a cool veneer. I acted like I had it all under control. I gave off this don't-fuck-with-me vibe. But underneath I was scared shitless. I have a feeling that was true of Billie Holiday, even true of my tough-talking mother. We're so frightened inside that when a pretty-faced sweet-talking man comes along, he nails us in no time. . . . Fear locks us in and holds us prisoner. Sometimes we never escape that prison. Sometimes we do.[38]

From childhood on, James had lived with a basic fear for her own survival: would her mother take care of her, would she be tough enough to make it in a new city, would she be good enough to make a career in music, and if so, could she sustain it? Looking at James's life, one is struck by the insistent, endless struggle to stay afloat: "When I look back, I see my life like a deck of cards I'm flipping through. . . . But it happened so quickly, and I was racing so fast, it looks like a big blur." The men she chose took advantage of the chaos and James's deeply rooted anxiety, manipulating her into believing that she needed to rely upon them to survive. The miracle was that she survived them.

Yet she did survive, from day to day mostly, continuing to perform and record. Her expectations were minimal and her attitude remained positive. Unlike Billie Holiday, James didn't focus much on the trappings of stardom or make an effort to maintain a glamorous image. She had more in common with Bessie Smith, a star by virtue of her talent and accomplishments but a woman uninterested in the politics of fame. "I was a people person," James said. "Didn't care about any of that star shit." It came through in her music—her voice natural, almost conversational until it soars on a high note of emotion. The "blues" in her music are found here, as she makes every love song sound like a personal confession. It's the sound of a real woman with real problems who just happens to have an incredible voice.[39]

James had diehard fans from the beginning, those who saw her as more authentic than the increasingly smooth products of the Soul and R&B industry. "Why haven't there been lavish anniversary albums, triumphant European tours, tributes on the *Ed Sullivan Show?*" critic Robert Palmer asked in *Rolling Stone* in 1971. "Why is Etta James still performing in ghetto clubs and one-nighter packages? Could it be 'cause she's got so much soul, and it shows?" She was certainly rougher—in sound and in personal style—than such peers as Ruth Brown and Aretha Franklin. Motown and its stable of artists domi-nated the black music scene for much of the 1960s, and the Motown sound was much softer than James's or any other of the Chess artists. Motown's stars were also much more polished in their appearance and demeanor, more "presentable" in the traditional sense. Etta James would never fit this mold.[40]

But even as black music got wilder in the later 1960s and early 1970s, with artists such as Otis Redding, the Ronettes, and James Brown achieving mainstream success, Etta James was not among those at the head of the pack. She remained popular, and songs such as "I'd Rather Go Blind" (1967) continued to make the charts, but she was never anointed a star in the way that Aretha Franklin was. Some of this was due to the logistics of her career—or, better put, the lack of any organization on the part of James or her (often nonexistent) man-agement. Popular music is an industry, and it's difficult to succeed without a business plan.

No doubt her attitude toward "playing the game" of celebrity was also responsible. Unlike, say, Diana Ross, James wasn't driven by a desire to be world famous. She loved to sing and simply wanted to con-tinue to do so. And despite her brief stint in the Black Muslim world, she wasn't interested in politics or in using the Black Power movement to further her career. She was supportive of the civil rights and feminist movements, as well, but her day-to-day focus was on her family and, for many years, her drug habit. There was no time to develop a long-term path to stardom.

In the end, though, time proved to be a friend to Etta James. After decades of struggling with addiction, abuse, and industry neglect, she demonstrated what, along with her voice, proved to be her greatest talent: sheer survival. Continuing to tour in the 1970s and 1980s, she began to be recognized for her contributions to rock 'n' roll. In the late 1970s, she was asked to tour with the Rolling Stones, who, unbeknownst to her, had been lifelong fans. "We were in awe of all you Chess artists," Mick Jagger told her, and guitarist Keith Richards became a close friend, often showing up unannounced to play with James in small clubs in the early 1980s as her performing career gained new momentum.[41]

After forty years in music and finally free of her addictions to drugs and the wrong men, in 1993 James was inducted into the Rock and Roll Hall of Fame and won her first Grammy award for her jazz album *Mystery Lady*, inspired by Billie Holiday. She continues to tour and record successfully today.

In the early 1970s, those familiar with the legacy of so many blueswomen feared for James's future. "Etta James, who lit up so many of those southern radio nights . . . is shining bright, right up there with Bessie, Billie and Aretha," Robert Palmer wrote, but he feared that it would take "a spectacularly tragic demise" to make her a household name. Bucking the trend of the women who had influenced her most, Etta James has lived to enjoy her legend.[42]

From her earliest days of singing in St. Paul Baptist Church, Etta James brought a gospel-based power to popular music, infusing even the most seductive, secular songs with all the intensity of a heavenly choir. But as with many who break new ground, her successors reaped the harvest. And no successor was better positioned than a Detroit preacher's daughter—Aretha Franklin.

1942

> Our household was superactive. Music was in the air.
> —Aretha Franklin[43]

The Rough Side of the Mountain

It would be difficult to conceive of a better preparation for the job of "Queen of Soul" than the childhood environment of Aretha Franklin. Imagine all the things lacking in the young Jamesetta Hawkins's life—strong parenting, a stable home life, musical education, emotional support—and Franklin enjoyed them. She grew up in Detroit when the city was a thriving, safe place to raise a family and its black population was reaching an apex of cultural energy. The young Aretha Franklin lived a few doors down from Smokey Robinson, in a home where visitors included jazz pianists Art Tatum and Dorothy Donegan, singer Sam Cooke, and gospel legends Clara Ward and James Cleveland. Franklin's two sisters, Erma and Carolyn, were also accomplished musicians and singers. Music was a big part of the girls' lives, whether it was the singing and playing of their talented family and friends or listening to records by R&B artists such as Ray Charles, Clyde McPhatter, and Ruth Brown as well as jazz musicians such as Billie Holiday. Whether Aretha listened to Bessie Smith is not known, but one of her favorite gospel singers was the great Mahalia Jackson, who herself was greatly influenced by Smith. Musicians aside, it was Aretha's father, Clarence LaVaughn—"C. L."—Franklin who had the greatest influence on her. "I didn't teach her," he said, "but she *heard* me."[44]

"Daddy was a minister," Aretha once said, "and he was also a man." Indeed, the Reverend C. L. Franklin excelled in both roles. As the minister of Detroit's New Temple Missionary Baptist Church, Franklin was known not just throughout the city but throughout the country for

The always polished Aretha Franklin (b. 1942) in 1967.
BETTMANN/CORBIS

his dramatic, inspirational sermons, which were broadcast on the radio and released as best-selling records on the Chess label. Tall and handsome, the Reverend acquired a reputation as a ladies' man (Aretha's parents separated when she was six; her mother died when she was ten) and as a flashy dresser—his nicknames included "Black Beauty." As one parishioner put it, he was "stinky sharp." Although C. L. Franklin's career was always rooted in his religious community, he created a public persona that was much flashier and more outrageous than his world-famous daughter would ever achieve, or aspire to.[45]

Aretha resembled her mother, Barbara, both physically and in personality. She had her mother's fairer skin and wide-set eyes and a much quieter disposition than C. L. Like Etta James's mother, Aretha's mother left her daughter in the care of others, but her father and siblings provided Aretha with the kind of stable, middle-class home life that Jamesetta Hawkins had seen only on television. Aretha's childhood and teenage years were the picture of postwar domestic aspiration, complete with roller skating, horseshoe pitching, pedal pushers, and cherry Cokes. "We were so innocent," Aretha recalled, "young black America at its best." C. L. had achieved what so many African-Americans had dreamed of: providing a safe and nurturing environment for his family. Aretha was one of the few blueswomen to enjoy a happy childhood.[46]

It was C. L. who recognized his daughter's musical gifts early on and actively guided her career—guiding her, in fact, away from the world of gospel singing (she made her first record—also for Chess—at age fourteen, singing the hymn "Precious Lord") and firmly in the direction of commercial music. With her father's permission, Aretha left school at fourteen and began touring with his gospel revue, singing and accompanying herself on piano. She was growing up quickly; she had her first child at age fourteen and her second at sixteen, both the result of brief love affairs with boys she met at the usual teenage hangouts: dances and roller-skating rinks. Unlike the proverbial preacher's daughters, the Franklin girls did not live cloistered lives. C. L. wasn't happy about the pregnancies—Aretha's sister Erma was also a teenage mother—but he accepted them and supported his daughters and grandchildren emotionally and financially. The strength of the Franklin family was its togetherness, and C. L.'s mother, known as Big Mama, agreed to take care of Aretha's children while she toured with her father and continued her singing career.

After four years of performing with the gospel revue, the Reverend removed Aretha from the religious sphere and took her to the avowedly secular center of the recording world, New York City, leaving her there at age eighteen to record a demo, perfect her skills, and acquire a recording contract with a major label. "[O]ne should make his own life and take care of his own business," C. L. said. Aretha's introduction to the record industry and adult independence was a far cry from the adventures of Etta James and the Peaches. Living in hotel suites and constantly accompanied by female chaperones selected by her father, Franklin embarked upon a metropolitan finishing school of sorts—taking dance classes and vocal lessons and even working with a fashion model who made her walk with a book balanced on top of her head. Unlike Etta James, Aretha Franklin was being introduced to professional life on a completely different level. There were no Southern cops accosting Aretha Franklin on drawn-out tours of the deep South or late-night gigs in juke joints for little or no pay. The greatest indignity Franklin faced was being locked out of her room in the Chelsea Hotel when C. L. forgot to send the rent. "I didn't mind that as much as the fact that they took my portable forty-five collection, including all my Sam Cooke singles and Billie Holiday records."[47]

Holiday's presence hovered around Franklin's early career as record producer John Hammond struck again. With an uncanny knack for recognizing significant women artists (and men—he also signed Count Basie, Bob Dylan, and Bruce Springsteen), Hammond heard Franklin's demo and was gripped with the same interest that had led him to record Bessie Smith and Billie Holiday. "It's the best voice I've heard in 20 years," he said. Franklin was well aware of Hammond's role in the careers of Smith and Holiday and was excited to enter the big time. (Franklin's hometown, black-owned label Motown had previously expressed interest, but as Aretha put it, "Daddy and I had our sights set on something bigger," a move that later irritated many African-Americans in Detroit. Aretha defended her decision, expressing her pride in all that Motown had achieved and her intuition that she might not have developed her own style there.) She was immediately signed to Columbia Records, in an almost-unprecedented agreement that afforded Franklin a substantial royalty rate. This was a professional arrangement that Etta James—and most other black artists—could never have imagined.[48]

Franklin's five years at Columbia hinted at her future power, especially on bluesier songs such as the classic "Trouble in Mind" and in her own composition, "Without the One You Love." Her voice is full and strong, yet she was often backed by lush orchestration that watered down the music's emotional punch. Jazz critics liked her, and in 1961 she won the prestigious *Down Beat* award for "New Star Female Vocalist," but it wasn't the kind of success she sought. She frankly told *Down Beat* that she didn't consider herself a jazz artist. "Her own personal preference—and bear in mind that she is still a teenager with more-or-less typical teenage musical tastes—is for the commercially successful pap. . . . If she has her way," *Down Beat* reported with amused disdain, "this is the direction in which she'll move." Perhaps Aretha had inherited some of her father's taste for glamour; she certainly knew where her future lay. A music journalist would later explain: the *Down Beat* honor was "the kiss of death. . . . If you get the approval of that mag . . . your chances of being heard again by anyone but a hard core jazz nut are very slim."[49]

In fact, Franklin moved between musical genres both on her albums and in her performing, which took her to jazz nightclubs like New York's Village Vanguard as well as on R&B tours with Sam Cooke and Jackie Wilson. As a young single woman living in New York City (her children remained at home with Big Mama in Detroit), Franklin experienced a tame, genteel world of romance and city life. Although she and Etta James knew some of the same people—Harvey Fuqua, James's first serious boyfriend, was a family friend of the Franklins, as was Hank Ballard, whose "Work with Me, Annie" first inspired the Peaches' "Roll with Me, Henry"—Franklin was protected from the wilder side of their lives by the influence of her famous father. The Franklins were part of the African-American elite, and despite her teenage motherhood, Aretha still saw herself as a sheltered, innocent daughter. A bohemian life could be found in early 1960s New York in the form of beatniks, political activists, and the burgeoning civil rights movement, but the city was also in many ways still the destination of the man in the gray-flannel suit, the home of American finance and leftover Eisenhower-era values. Even after several years of living on her own in Manhattan, Aretha was genuinely "shocked and in a quandary" when forced to share a dressing room with her fellow male and female performers while on tour with Sam Cooke and Jackie Wilson. "I just stood there . . . holding my gown, my eyes getting bigger by the moment," she said, and she remained frozen in fear until Cooke gallantly constructed an ad hoc partition for her. Some young women in the early 1960s were beginning to experiment with less-conservative attitudes toward life, but not Aretha Franklin. She was not a virgin, but neither did she see herself as a woman in need of sexual liberation: "I was not boy crazy, and I was definitely a one-man young woman."[50]

Although Franklin's personal life was relatively calm, her performances were exciting and soulful. Like Billie Holiday, Franklin brought a bluesy quality to her jazz performances that was unusual and compelling. While Holiday had been influenced by the blues of Bessie Smith, Franklin drew on Holiday's singing as well as her own gospel roots for her signature sound. Her performances made a "dimly-lit, smoke-filled jazz club [take] on the aspect of a revival tent," wrote *Down Beat* in 1961. Although her recordings for Columbia were mostly jazz standards such as "Skylark," she also covered bluesy songs such as Dinah Washington's "Soulville," and it was here that she seemed most at home. Her ease with the blues was noted by critics, who praised her " 'blues feeling' that comes—if we are to believe the jazz writers—only after long years of suffering, of being kicked around, of losing a lot of good lovers. Aretha has experienced none of this, yet she sings as if she were an amalgam of all the tragedy-haunted blues singers of the past." Aretha shrugged it off, crediting the influence of her father's soulful sermons for her sound.[51]

For Franklin, the early 1960s were years of experimenting with her style, gaining valuable stage experience, and becoming an adult. The bigger world was finally creeping into her consciousness, and as America's post–World War II innocence was challenged by the unfolding chaos of the 1960s, Aretha's was, too. C. L. Franklin was a close friend of national civil rights leaders, including Adam Clayton Powell and Dr. Martin Luther King, Jr., and Aretha got involved in politics for the first time, singing at fund-raisers and other events in support of the movement. In 1964, she met Ted White, a charismatic Detroit-based music promoter and manager who helped her form a new backing band. Within a few months, he became both her manager and her husband, and she soon gave birth to her third child.

With White's support, Franklin was becoming tougher and more secure in her career, confident enough to replace her booking agents because, as she saw it, they were "serving two or three different gods: I want them to serve me and my interests." She was also growing dissatisfied with Columbia's marketing approach, which changed from album to album in an attempt to chase a fickle audience. Her material was selected by the record company, and although Franklin approved the songs, only occasionally was she encouraged to compose her own music or accompany herself on piano. She was not only a gifted singer but also an accomplished and innovative pianist and arranger, and her gospel background endowed her with a talent for complicated harmonies. Little of this was reflected in her Columbia recordings, however. Junior executives at Columbia continued to control her career the way they would that of any other female singer, concentrating on pre-existing formulas. John Hammond worked with her only sporadically, due to company politics and an assumption that his taste was out of step with the younger generation. Hammond became just as frustrated as Franklin. "The musical misuse and eventual loss of Aretha as a recording artist disturbed me greatly," he said as he watched her go on to make history in her recordings for Atlantic Records, where she displayed "every musicianly quality I thought she had. All she needed to do was hold on to her roots in the church."[52]

Though she had been discovered by John Hammond, she was not destined to become merely a cult favorite like Billie Holiday. And unlike Etta James, she would not linger in the R&B charts, segregated by genre to sell only to the black audience. When her Columbia contract expired in late 1966, word quickly spread and Atlantic Records co-owner and producer Jerry Wexler immediately contacted Franklin's husband and manager, Ted White, offering a relatively huge $30,000 signing bonus to sweeten the deal. Franklin was already interested in Atlantic because of its legendary roster of R&B talent, including Ray Charles and Ruth Brown, who had been among her childhood favorites, so the deal was quickly concluded. After a lifetime of preparation, Aretha was ready to rock. "It's the rough side of the mountain that's easiest to climb," she said, referring to her years under contract at Columbia. "The smooth side doesn't have anything for you to hang on to." It was all smooth from here on out.[53]

1967
Aretha-ized

Aretha Franklin's new contract with Atlantic Records could not have come at a better time. While she had been recording old jazz standards and sugar-sweet pop songs for Columbia, new and exciting black artists had expanded the boundaries of rhythm and blues, infusing it with the energy and soaring spirit of the movement for black civil rights. This was Soul music—in the words of Ray Charles, "the way black folk sing when they leave themselves alone." Finally freed of Columbia's staid aesthetics, Aretha was primed to join the new group of Soul innovators—singers such as Otis Redding, Wilson Pickett, and Isaac Hayes. All three had recorded for Atlantic, and all had enjoyed substantial success with white audiences. "It started in the South, everything starts in the South," Atlantic producer Jerry Wexler said, explaining the first crossover hits on the label, when "white Southern people started buying our records." Just as Perry Bradford had argued in 1920 when trying to convince New York record executives to take a chance on Mamie Smith's "Crazy Blues," white Southerners were the first to appreciate the newest sound in black music. Despite segregation, white Southerners still lived in closer contact with African-Americans than their smug neighbors in the North.[54]

Elvis had challenged the color lines in the 1950s by drawing white teenagers to hear music inspired by black artists. In the mid-1960s, young whites finally started seeking out the records and concerts of the black artists themselves. "Popular music pacemakers no longer have to be white," *Saturday Review* proclaimed in 1968. "The young audience, fortunately, is color blind; and though somewhat compromised by the Establishment of their time, older brother and sister—even mother and dad—seek redemption." Aretha was there to provide. And in Jerry Wexler, Franklin had found another important mentor, someone who fully understood what she could do.[55]

John Hammond had started out as an early idol of Wexler's and eventually ended up as a friend. Hammond was gracious in seeing Franklin leave for Atlantic. He told Wexler, "You'll do good things with Aretha . . . you understand her musically." Although he had loved Franklin's work, Hammond lamented that, ultimately, "Columbia was a white company who misunderstood her genius." Although Atlantic also was owned and operated by whites, it had made its reputation by focusing on the black market. Jerry Wexler and Ahmet Ertegun, the two people most directly responsible for Atlantic's aesthetic, were students of black culture in the mold of Mezz Mezzrow and Leiber and Stoller.[56]

By 1967, Wexler had devised a winning formula for Atlantic's stable of Soul singers. Through Atlantic's extensive network of Southern distributors, radio disc jockeys, and salesmen, Wexler connected with two recording studios—and, more important, their incredible in-house rhythm sections—that would leave their imprints on Soul music as decisively as Motown had with its smoother, cleaner version of rhythm and blues. Stax was based in Memphis and the Fame Studio was in Muscle Shoals, Alabama. Both were small, independently operated recording studios that drew on local talent for their unique sounds. The house band at Stax was Booker T. and the MG's—two black men and two white—while Fame had what Wexler described as "a rhythm section of Alabama white boys who took a left turn at the blues."[57]

Wexler's strategy was simple: "Put Aretha back on piano, and let the lady wail." Franklin was excited about the new direction; while the musicians at Columbia had been technically excellent, Franklin found them "somewhat impersonal. . . . Putting me back on piano helped Aretha-ize the new music," she said. Franklin also chose or wrote all the songs for the album, and she came up with the basic outlines of the songs at home on her Fender Rhodes keyboard, creating harmonies with her sisters Erma and Carolyn. After that, they headed down to Muscle Shoals.[58]

The humble appearance of the Fame Studio belied the talent within it. Twenty by seventy feet long, it was a small shack standing in the middle of farmland virtually unchanged since the Civil War. ("I couldn't believe it," Wilson Pickett said when he first saw the Fame Studio. "I don't want to get off here. . . . They still got black people picking cotton.") The setting may have been less than glamorous, but Franklin was immediately impressed by the studio musicians. "Great musicians who were good and funky," she said, "the enthusiasm and camaraderie in the studio were terrific. . . . This new Aretha music was raw and real and so much more myself. I *loved it!*" This "good and funky" sound was far removed from the polished perfection of the Columbia sessions and was, in fact, much closer to the loose, spontaneous feeling of Etta James's Chess recordings. It was a more modern sound and much more expressive.[59]

That first session at Muscle Shoals quickly became the stuff of legend. "It was beautiful, better than any session I've ever seen," claimed Fame owner Rick Hall. But, unlike most legends, an actual recording exists as proof of the musical perfection achieved that day. Franklin had worked out the basic rhythms, keys, and vocal patterns before arriving at the studio. She sat down at the piano and started to play "I Never Loved a Man (The Way I Love You)." "When she come in there and hit that first chord, everybody was just like little bees just buzzing around the queen. . . . This was the real thing." The studio keyboard player, Spooner Oldham, was on hand as a piano player, but as soon as he heard Franklin, he reconsidered. "I wish you'd let her play that thing," he told Wexler, and he sat down at the Hammond organ instead. Together they worked out the dramatic, gospel-influenced beginning to the song, and it was arranged, performed, and recorded in two hours.[60]

"The musicians started singing and dancing with each other, giddy on the pure joy of having something to do with this amazing record." Great music is almost always the product of collaboration, and for all her individual talent, Aretha Franklin had long been in search of the right ensemble of musicians. Just as Billie Holiday had found her musical counterpart in saxophonist Lester Young, Franklin had found her musical soulmates in the brilliant Fame Studio band. Jerrry Wexler loved the recording but tried to remain calm. "[I]t can't be this good," he told himself. "I'll cool out in the morning. It will sound different in daylight." In fact, it sounded better.

Within two weeks, Wexler had made copies of the session for R&B

disc jockeys, and the song took off before the rest of the album had even been completed. "I had to get used to that kind of greatness," Wexler said. "I knew she was going to be good, but nobody ever knows about great."[61]

The album became a phenomenon. Along with "I Never Loved a Man," it included "Soul Serenade," "Dr. Feelgood," "Do Right Woman—Do Right Man," and, of course, "Respect." Aretha Franklin may not have been a Bad Woman per se, but she was not innocent; she was a mature, experienced woman, and that came across in her music. Her marriage was rocky, and Ted White's temper and heavy drinking threatened to derail her session in Muscle Shoals. She persevered and finished the album, but the marriage ended within a year. "She was searching for herself," Wexler said, and at Atlantic she was finally producing songs that reflected her experience as a wife, a mother, a daughter, a professional, an African-American, and as a woman. These were songs "expressing adult emotions," and they struck a chord with the American public, black and white.[62]

~

"Respect" was an Otis Redding song, recorded by him in 1965. When he heard Franklin's version of it, however, he said, "That little girl done took my song away." And it was true. Aretha Franklin took a man's frustrated complaint against his woman and flipped it. In the process, the song became the personal war whoop for anyone who had ever felt wronged, and what was more—you could dance to it. Aretha and her sister Carolyn devised the unforgettable "sock it to me" chorus, which was catchy, feisty, and pleasingly raunchy. The sound of a black woman demanding respect—"Find out what it means to me!"— was a revelation. The song became "the new Negro national anthem" and was immediately adopted as the new theme song for the civil rights movement. It also became the soundtrack of choice for the burgeoning feminist movement. "Respect" was sexy and strong, energetic and confident—it was something people needed to hear in 1967, as the victories of the civil rights movement slowed, racial tension grew, and women began to awaken from their postwar slumber and demand more.[63]

Aretha Franklin was suddenly the most compelling face of the civil rights movement. She had been close to Martin Luther King, Jr., since the 1950s, through the civil rights activism of her father. Aretha had sung at King's rallies in the past, but now it was King's turn to pay homage to her. King surprised her by showing up unannounced when Detroit designated February 16, 1968, as "Aretha Franklin Day." At this late stage in his struggle for civil rights, the public was beginning to tire of his message of interracial harmony and unconditional forgiveness. Franklin's take-no-prisoners attitude was a refreshing change, and King was eager to capitalize on her now-prominent position in the culture. For her part, Franklin was a lifelong supporter of King and his movement and considered herself a devoted partner in his fight. But something interesting had changed in American culture: the entertainer was becoming just as powerful as the politician. "The song took on monumental significance," Franklin said; it proved that music—and music made by women—mattered.[64]

> Memo to the American Woman:
> You are spoiled. You won your "rights" 45 years ago, but you are like a new African nation: You don't know what to do with them. Has everyone forgotten how much women like to be bossed?
>
> —Look magazine, 1966[65]

This was what Aretha Franklin was up against. Didn't women have enough "rights" already? And blacks (so the implication went) . . . they couldn't be trusted with the very rights they were fighting for! "Respect" challenged all these ideas. "No matter how pained she is in the song," a fan explained, "she is never the victim. She can deal with it. And that's the way we are. We can deal with it." After slavery, Jim

Crow, police dogs, and Emmett Till, the refusal to be victimized was an idea whose time had come. Just as Franklin had flipped Otis Redding's song, so she flipped the message of so many women before her, refusing to play the rejected lover, unwilling to accept the limitations and conditional approval of others.[66]

Although blueswomen had been giving voice to these feelings since the early part of the twentieth century—beginning as early as 1925 in songs like Bessie Smith's "I Ain't Goin' to Play No Second Fiddle"—the dominant message in popular music remained a story of abject devotion: I love you, please come back to me, I'll do whatever it takes. Love songs never change, nor should they. But there was room on the charts for more, and it was to the blues—its attitude, its themes, and its sound—that listeners and singers turned when they wanted to express something more. Billie Holiday had taken a break from the standards and written her own blues, "Billie's Blues" in 1945; Etta James had chosen a classic twelve-bar blues format for her song of female empowerment, "W-O-M-A-N" (1968). Aretha Franklin's phenomenal Muscle Shoals recordings were in part responsible for James's new direction. The music industry was astounded by the quality of Franklin's first album for Atlantic, and Leonard Chess was among the first to try to replicate her success, sending Etta James down to record with virtually the same Fame Studio band later the same year. "He figured what was right for Re [Aretha] was right for me," James said, and she concurred. Several of the songs she recorded there, including "Tell Mama" and "I'd Rather Go Blind," became James classics. What Bessie Smith had begun, Aretha Franklin and Etta James were carrying on, singing their messages of defiance and strength into the 1970s. The message was getting through to their female fans. "Your records have been very good for me," a young woman told Franklin, "and have taught me a lot about how to handle life. And love."[67]

1968

> I remember that when Aretha shouted something about, "Every now and then you gotta sit down, cross your legs, cross your arms, and say, 'Yes, Lord,'" I had an image of a middle-aged black lady like Rosa Parks on that bus in Montgomery, Alabama . . . and figured that feeling like that would feel fine.
>
> —Michael Lydon, 1971[68]

Inside Every Woman

A great deal had changed in the decade since Robert Frank published *The Americans*. Black people no longer sat at the back of the trolley in New Orleans, and the proud, strong black woman on the motorcycle was no longer an exotic vision. Between 1950 and 1970, black women had come to embody strength, integrity, courage, and dignity through the actions of such civil rights leaders as Rosa Parks, Fannie Lou Hamer, and Ella Baker. In every aspect of American culture, black men and women exercised power as they never had done before, flaunting their passion and rage with abandon, daring white America to protest. "People think that tough thing I do is an act," said Etta James. "No, that's the way I am and the way I like to be."[69]

Aretha Franklin also exercised her power in the following decades, continuing to record hit albums that were popular with a wide audience even as she experimented with different genres. From albums such as *Live at Fillmore West* (1971), on which she covered songs by Simon and Garfunkel and the Beatles, to *Amazing Grace* (1972), which became the most popular gospel album in recording history, to her standout performance of "Think" in the now-classic film *The Blues Brothers* (1980), and her surprising performance of the Puccini aria

"Nessun dorma" as Luciano Pavarotti's replacement at the 1998 Grammy Awards ceremony, Franklin became an American icon. Although in the 1980s and 1990s she seemed to have a hard time finding material worthy of her talent, the voice of Aretha Franklin was by then considered a national treasure, and many of her public appearances were designed as occasions to honor her—whether as a Grammy winner (she has won fifteen Grammies, a Lifetime Achievement Award, and a Grammy Legend Award), as a 1994 Kennedy Center honoree, or as the Queen of the Divas on the music television channel VH1.

Being a diva is now Franklin's real career, and it is a role she enjoys and takes seriously: "I do accept it as the ultracompliment." A sense of entitlement is the defining characteristic of a diva, and it's a quality Franklin claimed from childhood, raised by a proud father to expect only the best from life. While earlier blues queens, such as Ma Rainey and Bessie Smith, professed a similar attitude, they were never able to achieve the material and professional heights of Aretha Franklin— almost no other American entertainer has (although Elvis comes to mind). But drawing on the cultural foundation laid by such predecessors as Rainey, Smith, and others, Franklin was able to use the power of the blues to give voice to new generations of American women. From "Respect" on, Franklin's voice became associated with the sound of civil rights and the new hopes of the feminist movement. Not every woman had the courage to be Etta James or Aretha Franklin, much less Rosa Parks or Gloria Steinem. But any woman—or man—could listen to Etta and Aretha sing and get a little bit closer to what it might be like to have that kind of courage. They communicated strength for those who felt weak. "Inside every woman," said Lena Horne, "there's an Aretha Franklin screaming to come out."[70]

Chapter Five

THE GREAT SATURDAY NIGHT SWINDLE: TINA TURNER AND JANIS JOPLIN

I never thought about getting into music. I always wanted to be a housewife, but I was thrown into it. At home I separate myself from the stage. When I go onstage I'm one person; when I come off, I'm another.

—Tina Turner[1]

I'll take a split-level bungalow with two kids any day.

—Janis Joplin[2]

Do these sound like the dreams of rock goddesses? Housewife, mother: these were not rockin' roles. Yes, Tina Turner and Janis Joplin stormed the barricades of respectable society in the 1960s, manifesting raw sexuality and bare emotion in the face of a nation still trying to comprehend the 1963 bombshell, Betty Friedan's *The*

Feminine Mystique. Their energy was real and so was their influence, but it wasn't the end of the story. Turner and Joplin couldn't will themselves to feel completely fulfilled by their stardom. This they came to understand later, only after the ride began. But their willingness to try to forge new realities for themselves—to believe that a woman could start to change her life simply by putting it into words and belting it out—this was the path of the blues woman. As Turner and Joplin brought the lessons of the blues into the wider world of rock 'n' roll, they opened the eyes of women everywhere, women who kept a mental image of Tina and Janis in their heads as they lived through the 1960s and beyond, cranking up the volume in an exciting, electric personal soundtrack.

~

"Women, to be in the music business," Janis Joplin explained in 1970, "give up more than you'd ever know. . . . You give up a home and friends, children and friends. You give up an old man and friends, you give up every constant in the world except music. That's·the only thing in the world you got, man. So for a woman to sing, she really needs to or wants to." Joplin was on a train traveling through Canada at the time, part of the "Festival Express" that carried her and several carloads of musicians, including the Grateful Dead, Traffic, The Band, Buddy Guy, and more. Joplin was talking to a fellow singer, Bonnie Bramlett (of the rock duo Bonnie and Delaney) about the unique pressures of being a woman singer. "This chick is really beautiful, man," Joplin told the reporter on board. "She's as fuckin' macho as me!"[3]

Bonnie Bramlett understood Joplin's lament. As rock singers, they shared a commitment to emotional self-confession in their respective performances. "You might as well just get nude," Bramlett said, "because you're completely exposing your inside feelings."

"Sometimes I wonder if they're worth it," Joplin mused, alluding to the audiences. "If they're worth all that fuckin' grief that they drag out of you?"

Bramlett concurred. "I'm standin' up there, I got three children and it's very hard for me to go off and leave them. . . . I'm giving up someone who really belongs to me, because this is something I have to do as a complete individual. . . . This is the only way I can get release from what I feel. You gotta talk. You gotta tell," she said. "I don't have to live in a plastic shell all my life."

While male blues singers also exposed their feelings onstage, there seemed to be fewer consequences involved, as if there were more of a division for them between their performance onstage and their private lives. "I put it right out on the street," Joplin said about the way she used her personal experience in her music. "Nobody talks about their private pain. . . . I used to think, maybe they just had better press agents than me and kept it quiet. But then I realized that it's me. . . . Eric Clapton don't talk about his old lady."[4]

For those who were fathers, there seemed to be less of a pull between their lives as parents and as performers than for their female counterparts. Bramlett and Joplin both noticed that male musicians seemed to have an easier time maintaining relationships—with their children, wives, girlfriends—while touring. Their bad behavior seemed to be expected, tolerated, and forgiven. "But what man," Bramlett asked, "would have you and let you do what you must do?"

Janis Joplin was impressed—by Bramlett's opinions and her voice. "Bonnie, she's a bitchin' singer," she told the reporter. "You know she ain't making up nothing. . . . I don't know what kind of dues she's paying, but she's paid them; she's still paying them. She's an honest-to-God real life woman, man, or she wouldn't be able to sound like that." It was rare that Joplin came across anyone whose experience approached her own.[5]

By 1970, Bonnie Bramlett had been paying her dues for more than a decade, singing at nightclubs and strip joints in St. Louis. As a fourteen-year-old white girl, she somehow got an audition with the already-notorious Ike Turner when he was passing through town and she briefly toured as the first and last white "Ikette," backing up the

Ike and Tina Turner Revue. Bramlett's mother granted her permission to go because, "if she said no, I would've run away from home. That's how bad I wanted to sing with them." Bramlett had first seen Tina Turner perform in the late 1950s. The effect was "devastating." "I thought she was the greatest thing I'd ever seen in my life," Bramlett said. "She made me cry—yeah: I stood there and cried like an idiot. I knew right away that that was what I wanted to do, too. And I wanted to do it just like her." Though Bramlett's stint with the Turners was short-lived, by the late 1960s she had made it onto the pages of *Rolling Stone*, in league with another of her role models, Janis Joplin.[6]

In the 1960s, lots of women wanted to be like Tina Turner and Janis Joplin. As singers, they embodied a raw, new sense of freedom that existed far outside the "plastic shell" of middle-class expectations. The sexual energy and unchecked emotion that Turner and Joplin brought to the stage excited their male and female fans alike. While earlier blueswomen had challenged erotic barriers, only a few performers, such as Etta James, had put themselves out there physically, embodying a more aggressive attitude in the way they moved. Turner and Joplin were excited themselves; for them, the stage was a sacred space where they could express aspects of their personalities that were otherwise inhibited.

Joplin knew that her audience expected something more than just a musical performance. "At my concerts, most of the chicks are looking for liberation," Joplin said. "They think I'm gonna show 'em how to do it, how to get down," and she tried as hard as she could—sweating, shouting, provoking—to make that happen. She also recognized Tina Turner as a comrade-in-arms. "Currently, Tina Turner is my biggest influence," she told a reporter in 1968. "I saw her a short while ago and I realized that this was what I'm trying to do. I mean, she just comes on stage and aaagh! She hits you right there."[7]

Though white artists like Janis Joplin and Bonnie Bramlett wanted to be "just like" Tina Turner, it was not clear until much later what that might really mean. It was only in the mid-1980s that Turner's fans began to learn of the abuse and self-sacrifice that existed behind her vixen-like façade. And when Joplin, who died in October 1970, revealed to reporters her inner conflicts—between stability and the wild life, between having a family and having a career—she was regarded as a pitiful disaster: "The Judy Garland of Rock 'n' Roll," as *Rolling Stone* put it in 1969. Like the mainstream culture that it professed to despise, rock 'n' roll seemed to welcome only winners.[8]

Janis Joplin and Tina Turner entered the music world well aware of the great women singers who had come before; the songs of Bessie Smith, Billie Holiday, and Aretha Franklin functioned as both guides and cautionary tales for Joplin and Turner, who strove to create meaningful music of their own. Both Joplin and Turner came to international prominence in the chaos of the 1960s, becoming powerful, anarchic symbols of a decade they would barely survive. By the early 1970s, the women's movement was gathering strength and beginning to effectively channel the energy of the frustrated women of the previous decade. It was too late for Janis Joplin and, in some respects, Tina Turner. By the end of the 1960s, Joplin and Turner had become more successful at liberating their fans than at liberating themselves.

1939
Anna Mae, Little Ann, and Tina

Growing up in Tennessee after World War II, Tina Turner (born Anna Mae Bullock in 1939) remained relatively sheltered from the worst of Jim Crow. Although she and her sisters were handed off from one family member to another during their childhood while their parents chased jobs around the state, they managed to land in responsible homes and in close-knit black communities. Anna Mae enjoyed a mostly happy, productive youth, active in school as well as in cheerleading, basketball, and the church choir. While she didn't like going to church, she loved singing. "I wasn't aware that I was singing about

The ferocious Tina Turner (b. 1939) performing in 1976, rebuilding her career post-Ike. CORBIS

God, and how good he was; I just liked the songs. And I would always take the lead on the very upbeat ones—you know, the real shouters. Even then." With a mixed heritage that was heavily African and Native American, Anna Mae was striking even as a child. Her high cheekbones, almond eyes, and wavy hair set her apart from her peers. She was a good girl who aspired to become a wife, mother, and nurse. It was not until she and her sister moved to St. Louis in the mid-1950s that the future Tina Turner got a taste of the wilder side of life.[9]

Like the young Jamesetta Hawkins, another girl with raw vocal talent, Anna Mae Bullock entered show business under the guidance of a powerful, charismatic older man; it was Hank ("Work with Me, Annie") Ballard and Johnny Otis who transformed Jamesetta into Etta James. In Anna Mae Bullock's case, that man was Ike Turner, who was already legendary in the Southern music scene. A self-taught piano player, he had led the Kings of Rhythm since 1948; in 1951, with sax player Jackie Brenston doubling on vocals, he recorded the seminal "Rocket 88"—considered by many to be the first recorded rock 'n' roll song—at Memphis's Sun Studios. Soon Carl Perkins, Jerry Lee Lewis, and Elvis Presley would make their pilgrimages to Sun Studios to play their own versions of rock 'n' roll, all influenced by Turner's unique sound: a heavy backbeat, fuzzed guitar, and driving energy.

By 1956, Ike Turner and his Kings of Rhythm were a regular draw at the black nightclubs in East St. Louis. Unable to follow up with another hit record on the scale of "Rocket 88" (which had been the second biggest song on the R&B charts in 1951), Turner had made his living as a talent scout for the Los Angeles–based Modern Records— the same label that had recently signed the newly christened Etta James—and as a ferocious live act that performed throughout the South. He was known for something else, too. "They had a pretty rough reputation," Tina Turner remembered. "[T]he idea of a teenager like me going to one of those clubs to see them was definitely a *don't*." Tina had recently reunited with her mother and sister Alline in St.

Louis—a relatively safe place compared to its counterpart, East St. Louis. Despite its reputation, the sight of two young, unchaperoned women going into the Club Manhattan in East St. Louis was not unusual: "The place was filled with women," Tina recalled. "Tons of girls, black and white—and that really wasn't allowed then, you know, the white ones being there. But they came anyway. . . . Ike's band drew women, hardly any men—when men came, they were usually looking for their women." The young Anna Mae Bullock was shocked and intrigued by the spectacle, and especially by Ike Turner. She found herself simultaneously attracted to his charisma and repulsed by his looks and swagger. If nothing else, he was interesting.[10]

Anna Mae and Alline Bullock were soon regulars at the Kings of Rhythm shows, part of the panting, sweating crowd of young women who were making local legends out of Ike and the band. "Before Ike," Tina Turner later explained, "I didn't—I never owned a record player. I listened to songs on the radio, but I never knew the artists went out and performed. I never connected the two. . . . I just thought I'd be singing in a church the rest of my life and marry."[11]

Those early ambitions were typical of many young black women in the 1950s. While their white counterparts coped with ennui and the existential crises of affluent suburbia, black women were still strug-gling to support their families through work in decidedly less delicate realms. Just as in Bessie Smith's day, the primary occupations for black women were as laundresses, cleaning women, and cooks. Although World War II had allowed many black women to learn greater voca-tional skills, few of them were offered the opportunity to use them in the postwar era, when jobs as technicians and factory workers were handed back to returning white male veterans. White women began to enter the workforce in greater numbers in the pink-collar sector, and black men and women were, by and large, back where they started. Anna Mae Bullock wanted the same thing that white house-wives did: respect. Yet respect meant something different to each.

In the 1950s and 1960s, middle-class white women began to look for a sense of self-worth outside the home. They began attending college in much greater numbers, their attendance doubling between 1950 and 1970. They wanted to use their college educations for meaningful work, to be respected by their peers in challenging careers. "White women, middle-class women have to look at their problem and it is their husbands," said the Black Nationalist Dara Abubakari. "He is the oppressor, because he is the system. It's a white male system." For black women, the problem was different. Work was always a given; black women had to work to support their families. "The black woman is not undergoing the same kind of oppression that white women have gone through in the homes," Abubakari explained. "Black women had to get in the labor force, because black men didn't have jobs. . . . The black woman is liberated in her own mind, because she has taken on responsibility for the family and she works." Black women wanted respect, but they wanted the kind of respect that white women took for granted—as upstanding members of their community and as good mothers and wives. As one black woman writer put it, "Radical white women feminists are striving for a different family structure, [while] many black women are trying to stabilize their families."[12]

"I felt that I was a good girl," Anna Mae said. "I went to school. I did all the housework at home." And while the Kings of Rhythm may have been a "don't," Anna Mae made an exception for the sake of music and excitement and kept on doing it, enjoying the scene and especially the magnetism of Ike Turner. Her experience in the church choir convinced her that she could really sing, and she finally got up her nerve to show Ike her stuff one night during intermission. "He stayed up there sometimes between sets to avoid troubles with all his women," Tina Turner later explained. "Ike had twenty. And sometimes maybe six of them would show up at the Club Manhattan all at once. So he would stay onstage to avoid getting into fights." While Ike played the organ, sixteen-year-old Anna Mae Bullock grabbed a stray microphone and began singing along with the B. B. King song Ike was playing, "You Know I Love You." Ike was impressed, and she was soon gigging with the band.[13]

Her mother was not pleased. "'So you been singin' with Ike Turner?'" she asked Anna Mae—"and the way she said it sounded like a banner headline: PISTOL-WHIPPING IKE TURNER." Ike's mean reputation had spread beyond the nightclubs of East St. Louis. Despite Mrs. Bullock's disapproval, "Little Ann" (so dubbed for her thin, supposedly unsexy figure) continued singing with the Kings of Rhythm. Her slenderness worked in her favor. In the mid-1950s, the ideal feminine physique was a voluptuous one, a distinctly female shape modeled on the hourglass. An appreciation for womanly curves was especially pronounced in African-American culture, so while Little Ann's athletic figure was attractive, it was not va-va-voom. This made the Kings of Rhythm's female fan base feel a little more secure—they could appreciate Little Ann's singing without seeing her as a threat. They may have envied her costumes, though. Ike was fastidious about his band's appearance and crafted a flashy, sharp look for every member: suits for the men and tailored pastel sequined dresses, seamed stockings, and strappy shoes for Little Ann, who had never before been groomed with such care.[14]

She loved the attention and, at first, she and Ike were just good friends. After recognizing her talent, he began a charm offensive on her, and soon seventeen-year-old Little Ann was on the road, touring with Ike as her chaperone. Shortly thereafter, she moved in with Ike after having a baby (fathered by Ike's saxophone player, who promptly left the scene) and having become distant from her family. Although it was not her first sexual experience, she was still naïve. Her reaction to the pregnancy and to the father's abandonment was one of acceptance: it was simply another responsibility, just as babies always had been the responsibility of the women in her family. And Ike was helpful, giving her and the baby a place to live, taking care of them, giving Little Ann "a kind of family love." Ike and his band were becoming her entire world. "Ike was very into taking care of people. The first thing he would do when he met you was buy you clothes. . . . He had to make you become his. He had to own you."[15]

Their first sexual encounter was a shock. "One night, when we were driving to a show somewhere . . . he tried to touch me," Tina said. "I felt awful. I thought he was my friend. I never thought he'd try to do something like that. . . . I had never thought of having sex with him. I thought, 'God, this is horrible. I can't do this.' But I went ahead and did it. And from there it just sort of went on and on and on. . . ." Ike corroborated her memory. "The first time I went with her, I felt like I'd screwed my sister or somethin.' I mean, I hope to die—we really had been like brother and sister." Despite this awkward beginning, Ike and Little Ann formed a close relationship, one built on mutual dependency. Ike needed her talent and she—a young, single mother—needed his financial and emotional support. Her mother was not willing to take in her daughter and grandchild, which left Ike as Little Ann's only option. Although she had considered a career in nursing in the past, now that she had experienced the joy of singing, she couldn't imagine going back. Ike offered her a home and a career, and she took it.[16]

This uncomfortable arrangement worked for a while. They continued working together, and soon she became pregnant with his child—as did another of the singers now working for him. They toured constantly, dragging along a chaotic ensemble of wives, girlfriends, babies, and hard feelings. It was confusing and exhausting, but it was a life. Little Ann's singing kept getting better. That same year, 1960, she stepped in to sing lead on a demo that Ike was recording, called "A Fool in Love." By the summer, the record was a hit—on the profitable (white) pop charts, rather than on the (black) R&B charts, to which Ike's music previously had been relegated. Their new record label, the independent Sue Records, advanced Ike $25,000 on the song, and the label owner convinced Ike that Little Ann was a star. It was the end of the road for the Kings of Rhythm: from that point on, the group came to be known as Ike and Tina Turner. Ike recognized her potential, but "Little Ann" was no name for a superstar. Without consulting Anna

Mae, Ike changed her professional name to Tina—after the exotic Sheena of the Jungle, one of Ike's favorite cartoons—and bestowed upon her his own surname, despite the fact that they were not married.

~

"A Fool in Love" was a raucous record. The sound of Tina's voice, a cappella: "WHOOOAH . . . there's something on my mind . . ." grabbed the listener from the very beginning. It was her first recording, but at twenty years old she sounded like a mature singer—and a mature woman. The sung/spoken intro was a classic blues lead-up, an attempt to pull the listener into the song as if being pulled into a personal conversation, to be followed by a personal confession. Tina's low, throaty, almost rasping voice harkened back to the classic blueswomen. Compared to the other women on the pop chart that year— morning-fresh singers such as Brenda Lee and Patti Page—Tina sounded exotic indeed.

Although Ike originally wrote "A Fool in Love" for a male singer, with Tina on lead vocals the lyrics took on new meaning. Three female backup singers functioned as a kind of Greek chorus on Ike's behalf, advising Tina on the new realities of her life with Ike:

You take the good along with the bad
Sometimes you're happy and sometimes you're sad
You know you love him, you can't understand
Why he treats you like he do when he's such a good man.

Tina responded to their words with verses that accurately described her own situation. "He's got me smiling when I should be ashamed/ Got me laughing when my heart is in pain." These lines, though written by Ike, mirrored Tina's own personal doubts about her relationship with him. Both the lyrics and Tina's vocals communicated an emotional intensity that flattened her pop-chart rivals. The other "Fool" song of 1960, Connie Francis's "Everybody's Somebody's Fool," was a lovely song, but it did not approach the Turners' three-minute blast of paint-peeling heartache. The success of "A Fool in Love" set Ike and his soon-to-be wife on a quest for more hits.[17]

While "A Fool in Love" seemed to give voice to the frustrations of an unhappy woman, there was no such outlet in Tina's private life. Tina had approached Ike after the initial success of the record, hoping to end their intimate relationship and focus on just working together as bandmates. That was the first time Ike beat her and forced her to have sex. "With a shoe stretcher—" she recalled, "one of those men's shoe trees with the metal rods in the middle? Just grabbed one of those and started beating me with it. And after that he made me go to bed, and he had sex with me. . . . And that was the beginning, the beginning of Ike instilling fear in me. He kept control of me with *fear*." Unlike the voice of "A Fool in Love," Tina was unable to express her fear and unhappiness—to anyone. "One time, early on, I was dumb enough to tell Ike how I felt. Still thought he was my friend, right? Wrong—*pow!* After that, I kept my feelings to myself. . . . I didn't say anything, not out loud." The stark realism of "A Fool in Love" may have helped other women listeners come to terms with their own pain, but for Tina Turner it just predicted more of what was to come.[18]

The conflict between Ike and Tina Turner remained private for years, masked by the tightly united front they presented onstage as the leaders of the Ike and Tina Turner Revue. They quickly became part of the new wave of R&B groups that dominated the pop and R&B charts in the early 1960s. Motown Records' groups were among the most successful, with talented, tidy, well-groomed acts such as the Marvelettes and the Supremes exemplifying a respectable and unthreatening image of African-Americans during this early stage of racial unrest. With songs like "Please, Mr. Postman" and "Baby Love," Motown's "girl groups" projected a vision of love that was entertaining enough to appeal even to mainstream white Americans without offending them. Although some Motown artists became linked with the civil rights movement, such as Stevie Wonder and Martha and the Vandellas (whose 1967 hit "Dancing in the Streets" served as an unintended soundtrack to the series of urban riots that year), Motown's image remained relatively conservative in comparison to the social chaos of the decade.

~

Yet Ike and Tina Turner were not the only musicians challenging the Motown girl groups' sugar-sweet style. Another kind of female ensemble appeared on the scene around the same time as the Turners, bands that looked and sounded more like girl gangs than girl groups. The Shangri-Las, the Ronettes, and the Crystals used their multipart harmonies to sing the praises of bad boys (the Shangri-Las' "Leader of the Pack") and passionate love affairs (the Ronettes' "Be My Baby"). Both the white Shangri-Las and the black Ronettes embodied a tough-girl look that distinguished them from the better-behaved female stars of the day. With thick Cleopatra eyeliner and teased and tormented beehive hairdos, these women walked onstage in tight matching skirts and heels and made a big impression. But it was the Crystals, a black group from Brooklyn, that truly pushed the limits of good taste for the genre.

In 1961, the Crystals released their notorious "He Hit Me (It Felt Like a Kiss)," a song written by Carole King and Jerry Goffin and produced by Phil Spector. Not even Ike and Tina's masochistic "Poor Fool" (1961), with its lyrics, "I'd work my fingers down to the bone/Doin' the things to please him, right or wrong," could compete. Yet both were examples of a new type of pop song, one that addressed the more sinister aspects of love, and Phil Spector, the Crystals' producer, took notice of Tina's voice and style. These dark themes were unusual for the pop charts, but of course it had been done before, most memorably by Bessie Smith in "Sweet Mistreater" (1927) and by Billie Holiday in "My Man" (1937).[19]

It had taken several decades, but the emotional drama of blues and jazz had begun to infiltrate the mainstream. Songs such as "He Hit Me (And It Felt Like a Kiss)" and "Tommy" (1965), by Reparata and the

Delrons, echoed the laments of the blues queens of the 1920s: I shouldn't love him, but I do. It was no mere coincidence that the theme had come back around, for the 1960s would be a decade of change in women's lives every bit as radical as the 1920s had been. While women had officially gotten the vote in 1920, many black women would begin to enjoy that right only after the passage of the 1965 Voting Rights Act. Pop songs depicting the abuse of women could be read two ways: as misogynistic or as part of a legacy of women's—particularly black women's—tradition of "speaking truth to power," in which the vocalization of pain and suffering transforms that experience into empowering personal testimony. These songs, in fact, could be interpreted both ways simultaneously, as in the case of Tina Turner's "A Fool in Love" and "Poor Fool," songs that often meant one thing to her female fans and another to Turner herself.

~

Whatever their intended message, Ike Turner's songs were the right sound at the right time. They were rough but not too rough (the more scandalous "He Hit Me" was quickly pulled from radio playlists after listeners complained), with energetic tempos and rocking vocals by Tina and the Ikettes. Ike wrote almost all of the songs during this period, and their themes continually reflected the warped state of affairs in the Turner household: "I Idolize You" (1960), "I'm Jealous" (1961), and "You Should'a Treated Me Right" (1962) were a few of their most popular songs. Their biggest hit, however, and one of the few songs with an optimistic theme, was not written by Ike. The #4 hit, "I Think It's Gonna Work Out Fine," was the product of famed R&B artists and producers Mickey Baker and Sylvia Robinson (the same "Mickey and Sylvia" who went on to record "Love Is Strange" as solo artists).[20]

For Ike, Tina, and the rest of the revue, the early 1960s involved endless touring, practicing, and recording. After years of struggling in the music industry's lower pools, Ike pursued success relentlessly, pushing himself and his band to extremes and often losing band members and backup singers along the way. Tina never left, though. She was now the de facto mother of four boys: one from her first pregnancy with Ike's saxophone player, another from her pregnancy with Ike, and two boys that Ike had previously fathered with his common-law wife.

The inner circle of Turner employees knew that Tina was essentially trapped in the relationship. "Nobody should treat another human being the way he treated her," said Ann Cain, Ike's personal assistant during that time. "I could hear him beating her up in their dressing room. . . . But Tina stayed—she stayed because of the children." The children meant a great deal to Tina, not only because she loved them and felt responsible for them, but also because it was important to her to be a mother and wife—it had been so since childhood. Tina Turner shared the dream of many young African-American women—to create a home and family. Ike was the farthest thing from a dutiful husband or father, yet he shared Tina's desire at least to appear to be a stable family man, and all their public appearances and utterances remained on message. When they moved to the View Park Hills neighborhood of Los Angeles in 1964, reporters often were invited to do interviews in their large, lavishly decorated home. The image of the materially successful husband-and-wife team was an important one to maintain. Typical magazine photo shoots depicted them standing in front of their Rolls-Royce in the driveway or showed Tina cooking in their well-appointed kitchen.[21]

Ike's violent behavior was well hidden from the Turners' fans, but when a story did leak out, Ike's ambition and his work ethic usually were cited as a justification. "Ike is a very hard worker," one of his friends told a reporter. "He's such a driver. Last winter Tina was sick with bronchial pneumonia, 104 temperature, in the hospital with her body icepacked to bring the temperature down. And Ike was visiting, and he was going, 'You get out and SING, or you get out of the house!'" Tina rarely commented on these stories, probably for her own safety, but when she did, she couched her responses in respectful tones. "I can't question Ike because everything that Ike has ever gotten me to do, that I didn't like, was successful."[22]

On the rare occasion when she did appear to complain about Ike, she quickly qualified her words. "He hurts your feelings onstage," she told one reporter. "He's really on my case." She spoke of the way Ike yelled at her onstage for changing keys at the wrong time or for "over-singing," then she abruptly tried to justify Ike's behavior. "The way we live is not from records," she explained, coming back around to the issue of Ike's ability to provide for his family, "but from Ike's hustling ability—writing songs, managing, producing other singers. . . ." The reporter got the hint. "Ike hovers behind his wife, calling signals like a quarterback. . . . But Tina knows that her Svengali delivers the goods." Once, Tina was asked whether she had any plans to write a memoir. While carefully guarded, her cryptic response revealed a great deal about the sadness and pain of her life with Ike:

> Oh, I plan to [write a memoir], but I don't want to do it now because it will damage my career. I'm going to go into my personal life as well, because the book will be about the whole thing. I've got such a fantastic memory that I always reach back and get all the little details that people forget about, you know, or want to forget about.[23]

She managed to live with those "little details," while never forgetting them, throughout the 1960s, a period in which her public performances helped to change the way women were expected to sound, to behave, and to feel. Tina Turner embodied a vision of the liberated woman and, eventually, came to realize that goal herself.

1966
The Turned-On Revolution

By the mid-1960s, Ike and Tina Turner were living in a whole new world. It was not just the fact that they had moved from the South to the West Coast, but that the rest of the world—and especially the West Coast—had changed so much.

"There is a new kind of woman in the world. She is found today mostly in California. . . . She is the first really free woman in history. . . . She can make her own living. She is politically free; above all, and newest of all she is sexually free." Nowhere in America was the changing role of women more obvious than in California, the new Mecca for youth in search of an alternative to the blandness of suburban prosperity and all its privileges. The mythologies of California and California women grew as the narrative of the 1960s looped back upon itself; rumors of utopia begat road trips begetting their own lovestruck letters home. Summer migrations turned into long-term moves as The Scene lured more and more young men and women onto the streets of San Francisco's Haight-Ashbury neighborhood and the druggy canyons of Los Angeles.[24]

Above all, California and its lifestyle were linked to music, because in California in the 1960s, popular music drew most of its meaning from the context in which it was created. California's popular music—rock 'n' roll—"has made a community of its audience," wrote Ellen Sander, a contemporary journalist and self-confessed rock "freak." "[It is a] community that responds and reacts to every beat of the music and every nuance of the style." Although some version of this cultural revolution was going on in other cities, the entire state of California (with San Francisco as its countercultural capital) was becoming associated with the younger generation's new lifestyle. The 1967 Monterey Pop Festival—the first festival devoted solely to the new music—drew musicians from LA and San Francisco and attracted an international audience. "The festival was a banquet of rock music and communal bliss," Sander wrote. "Some came and were so enchanted at the sight of all of . . . *us* . . . that they committed themselves to pop as a way of life; in effect, they never left the festival." Rock 'n' roll, once considered a 1950s bobby-soxer fad, was by the mid-1960s the sound of the present and the future, more than a style of music—"the communications network of the turned-on revolution." Never one to miss an opportunity, Ike Turner focused on that network and quickly found a way in. It was Tina, of course, who made it possible.[25]

While Etta James, the Shangri-Las, and the Ronettes affected bad-girl looks reminiscent of 1950s women's prison flicks, with their heavy eye makeup, pale frosted lipstick, and clothes with a sausage-casing fit, Tina Turner was something closer to a burlesque showgirl. Beneath sequined and tasseled short-short minidresses that swung and rippled with her every move, her long, bare legs stalked the stage in a separate show of their own. Rather than ratting her hair, Turner and the Ikettes wore long, straight wigs—this was Tina's idea—so the hair could swing around, too.

Apart from her clothes and that chainsaw voice, it was Tina's sleek, muscular body that set her apart from—well, from most human beings. Her performances elicited outrageous metaphors: "She springs out onstage like a lioness in heat," wrote *Look* magazine, "twisting like a rutting mink." The animal imagery here is striking. While Tina projected a sexual intensity that was inarguably fierce, it's difficult to imagine a white woman being described in such bestial terms. Of course, the image of Tina as a predatory sexual animal was one that Ike had crafted for her. Her relatively prim dresses of the 1950s were long gone, and while the band members (including Ike) continued to wear suits, Tina now shimmied in increasingly revealing costumes. No dance move was too risqué, no moan or sigh too erotic to be included in the act. As the decade turned, what were once cheerfully referred to as Tina's "physical pyrotechnics" began to dominate the show, becoming more and more graphic as time went on. Tina's infamous, totally choreographed (by Ike) fellation of the microphone in the lead-up to "I've Been Loving You Too Long" was captured on film in the Rolling Stones documentary *Gimme Shelter* (1970), by which time the press began asking, "Is Tina all sex and no soul?" Although the extent of Ike's control over Tina's life was still mostly hidden from the public, those who had followed her career over the years seemed to suspect that the nearly pornographic new image Tina enacted onstage was per-haps not entirely her own idea. In the *New York Times*, critic Mike Jahn dubbed the Turners' evolving style "Porno Soul." Jahn first praised Tina's singing, then reluctantly addressed her sexual theatrics, which he found more silly than sexy. Tina was "as fine a soul singer as heard in years," he wrote. "I would go anywhere to see Tina Turner, even if her performance was shown on 8-mm film, which Lord knows, may be next."[26]

Privately, Tina was humiliated by Ike's choreography. She wasn't against expressing her sexuality, but unlike Ike, she recognized the line between eroticism and vulgarity. So, despite Ike's detailed direction, Tina managed to communicate a sense of self-respect that filtered through even the most outlandish pantomimes. There was a regal, almost stiff manner to her body and to her voice that endowed her with a sense of self-containment. This was no hippie chick; there was no eager frolicking for the audience's affection in Tina's style. Her clipped, staccato speaking voice (heard during audience banter between songs and in spoken introductions to them) had a pleasingly haughty air. Her dancing was stiff, too: straight legs pacing and pounding the stage, straight arms thrown up in the air, straight spine supporting her voice as it climbed to an unholy scream. Tina Turner was sexy without stooping to coyness. As one reporter put it, "Tina *spits* sex out to you."[27] Although her raw sexuality blinded many in the audience, a few seemed to pick up on the complexity of her performances. Just a few months after the "Porno Soul" review, another *New York Times* reporter wrote, "The thing about Tina Turner is that she knows she's kidding, you know she's kidding, and it doesn't matter."[28] Some essential part of Tina's personality was strong enough to penetrate Ike's dictates even as she performed with him watching her every move.

～

Back in 1966, Tina's strong, brassy style was the perfect foil for the aggressive music of the young Phil Spector, who had already made millions from his hits with such other tough-girl groups as the Crystals and the Ronettes. Like them, Tina possessed both voice and personality strong enough to stand up to Spector's so-called Wall of Sound, a reverberating sonic backdrop that often included multiple pianos and a full orchestra. Spector hired Tina to record a new song he had co-written with songwriting duo Ellie Greenwich and Jeff Barry—already famous for such hits as "Da Do Ron Ron" and "Be My Baby." Spector wanted Tina to record "River Deep, Mountain High," but there was one stipulation: the infamously fussy, irascible, and controlling Ike Turner would not be allowed at the sessions—probably because they would have clashed with Spector's equally perfectionistic production style. Ike's ego was reportedly soothed by the $25,000 fee, and Tina drove herself to Spector's mansion to rehearse every day for a few weeks. It was one of the rare opportunities she had to go outside her house without Ike's supervision, and she reveled in it.[29]

"River Deep" got the classic Spector treatment: nearly a hundred musicians, grueling rehearsals; one witness estimated that the production costs alone ran to $20,000, an incredible expense for a single in 1966. The lyrics and mood of the song were also a departure for Tina—no more shouting about being mistreated. In "River Deep," she celebrated an epic love affair. "Do I love you, my oh my. . . . River Deep, Mountain High, Yeah! Yeah! Yeah!" The song's uncanny intro, "When I was a little girl I had a rag doll" set the tune even farther apart right away. But it was Tina's vocal performance that set the song apart. Bob Krasnow, the Turners' new manager and head of their record label, Loma Records, was present at the recording.

Tina's really working—she's there, she's sweating. . . . Finally she says, "Okay, Phil, one more time." And she ripped her blouse off and grabbed that microphone, and she gave a performance that . . . I mean, your hair was standing on end. It was like the whole room exploded. I'll never forget that as long as I live, man. It was a magic moment.[30]

Most people agreed that the song was a pop masterpiece, but for some reason "River Deep, Mountain High" only made it to the lowest rungs of the American pop charts—a huge disappointment not only to the Turners but also to Phil Spector. Its perceived failure was the turning point for Spector, ending an incredible string of Top Ten hits and marking his turn toward a darker personal life. The man who had temporarily liberated Tina from Ike began his own twisted relationship with Ronnie Bennett, lead singer of the Ronettes, and instituted many of the same restrictions on his new wife that Ike had placed upon his— dictating her appearance and her performances and keeping her under virtual house arrest. "River Deep" marked the beginning of Spector's seclusion from public life.[31]

Ike and Tina Turner loved the song, too, and while its reception in the United States was a great disappointment, its success in Europe opened new doors. The Ike and Tina Turner Revue had had a British fan base for years, and in 1966 they went to England as openers on the Rolling Stones tour. "River Deep, Mountain High" had stayed in the British Top 50 for more than three months, and the fans went berserk when they finally had a chance to see Tina perform live. "She sings with tremendous feeling and sends the whole show wild," a British paper reported. "After their tour in this country it's a certainty that the British public will be seizing the new Turner track—even if their own America snubs it!"[32]

Their biggest fans were the Rolling Stones themselves. Mick Jagger and Keith Richards had founded their band on a mutual love of American blues from the likes of Muddy Waters, Howlin' Wolf, and John Lee Hooker, and their appreciation of blues-based American sounds had grown along with the music, making them early and lifelong fans of Etta James and Tina Turner. The tour was a sensation. "I think we worked much harder after Ike and Tina had been on," Mick Jagger said, describing the experience of following the Turners onstage. "Because they would really work the audience very, very hard. But that's the reason we had them on." The Rolling Stones learned a lot about showmanship from Tina Turner—Jagger most of all. Said Tina, "I'd always see Mick in the wings. I thought, 'Wow, he must really be a fan.' " He was a fan—of her singing and her dancing. Tina remembered watching his performances on that tour. "They'd play music, and Mick'd beat the tambourine. He wasn't dancing. And lo and behold, when he came to America, he was doing everything! So then I knew what he was doing in the wings. He learned a lot of steps." No one had a greater impact on Mick Jagger's famous rooster-stepping, straight-backed, side-to-side slither than Tina Turner. He even learned to cock his hip and wag his finger at the audience in classic red-hot-mama style. In the end, both groups got something good from the collaboration, and the Rolling Stones would prove to be loyal supporters of Tina Turner in good times and bad.[33]

The 1966 Rolling Stones tour was a watershed moment for the Ike and Tina Turner Revue. Very few R&B groups got that kind of opportunity to cross over to white audiences, and it was not news to Ike that there was more money to be made there. Ike had been experiencing the pangs of that reality since his first recordings at Sun Studios, watching white artists such as Elvis Presley and Johnny Cash go on to lucrative careers in rock while he and other blacks were relegated to the segregated R&B bins. Ike came up with a clever twist on that old trick: he began covering white artists' tunes, using Tina's unique, rasping howl of a voice to give them a wholly new sound. The couple described the shift in an interview:

TINA: I guess way before the Stones asked us to tour with them, Ike started to get into the hard rock thing, dragging me out of bed to listen to this or that, and at 4 o'clock in the morning.

IKE: She didn't like rock.

TINA: Finally, he said, "You going to have to sing it, so you may as well like it." So I started to listen to rock.

At other times, Tina implied that she was the one attracted to the sound of rock, and that Ike had simply recognized its potential after that. As a teenager, Tina liked the songs on the radio that her mother listened to: "usually the blues, B. B. King and all." In any case, the band began to cover songs such as the Beatles' "Come Together," the Rolling Stones' "Honky Tonk Women," and Creedence Clearwater Revival's "Proud Mary"—all of which became huge hits.[34]

The Turners were not the only black artists to gain acceptance in the rock world. It was in 1967 that Aretha Franklin had her phenomenal breakout with the Muscle Shoals–produced "I Never Loved a Man (The Way That I Love You)," and that same year Otis Redding and Jimi Hendrix won the hearts of California's "love crowd" with their performances at the Monterey Pop Festival. While other black artists, such as the Motown groups and even James Brown, saw their audiences segregate and splinter as the decade wore on, Ike and Tina Turner managed to cross racial boundaries even as the United States erupted in race riots.

Ike and Tina Turner had succeeded in attaching themselves to the wave of sexual and social revolution that was rippling across the West Coast in the late 1960s, but neither of them fully embraced its ideology. Ike happily availed himself of the newly-available sex and drugs on the scene, but as with many men of that era, he was interested in women's liberation only insofar as it made young women less inhibited about having sex. Tina's recreational behavior remained restrained, due to a combination of her own sense of propriety and Ike's iron grip on her freedom. As a public couple, however, they appeared to have it all: family, careers, and a glamorous rock 'n' roll lifestyle. "We get it to look like we out having a good time," Tina told a reporter in 1970. And it did look like that, for a while.[35]

1943

DON'T:

+ Wise off bad enough to get sent to the principal or swear in
  public (girls only)
+ Give any evidence of knowledge concerning bodily functions
  or fluids. . . .
+ Collapse in tears in a public place even if your dog's been run
  over, or you got your period on the back of your dress and
  everybody says well gee, who wouldn't cry, it's okay, let
  it out.
+ Hit anybody unless you can fake it's accidental. . . .
+ Wear two kinds of plaid, red on Thursday (means you're
  queer), anything you can't feature a cheerleader wearing.

—Mary Karr, *Cherry*[36]

Turtle Blues

Poet and memoirist Mary Karr was born in 1954, eleven years after
Janis Joplin, and grew up in the same area of southwest Texas—Karr in
Leechfield, Joplin in the larger but hardly more cosmopolitan city of
Port Arthur. Despite a decade's gap between them, the lives of the two
adolescent girls were governed by many of the same rules and expectations. As Karr's homemade list demonstrates, self-containment was the
key to social acceptance, or at least a safety zone where a girl would be
protected from teasing, a bad reputation, or, worst of all, an obvious
state of exile: an outsider. "Basically, you're hoping to manufacture a
whole new bearing or being," Karr concluded.[37]

Janis Joplin, born in 1943, spent most of her youth trying to do just
that: relentlessly rejecting her own tastes and mores in order to fit in
better with the tidy, middle-class 1950s community that housed her.

Janis Joplin (1943–1970) sings the Kozmic Blues to half a million fans at Woodstock in 1969. HENRY DILTZ/CORBIS

Although almost half the population was African-American, middle-class girls like Joplin had virtually no contact with them, since the neighborhoods and schools were strictly (if not legally) segregated. There were also sizable Hispanic and Cajun communities in Port Arthur, but these worlds were visible to Joplin only when driving through their neighborhoods on the way to somewhere else. She had an intellectual streak and loved to read books and paint. And she loved to sing, which she did in a clear soprano that pleased her parents and the local church groups. It was at puberty that things started to go wrong. "Port Arthur is sort of a cheerleader culture," a childhood friend of Joplin's later explained. "It was the kind of town where if you were reading books, you didn't let anyone know it. . . . She wasn't what you'd call a pretty girl. You know, girls who aren't pretty have to find some other way of getting along." Photographs of Joplin as a teenager reveal a girl who was not unattractive, just a little plain. With her dark blonde hair, round face, small eyes, and blunt features, more than anything else she looks uncomfortable in the teased hairdos and tight Peter Pan collars she wore on school photo days. She dressed the part of a bobby-soxer, but it never looked like anything more than a costume.[38]

Joplin did not dispute her friend's memory. "They thought I was completely insane; they didn't like me. You know how small towns are: you're supposed to get married when you get out of high school, have a brood of children, and keep your mouth shut. I didn't do any of those things." As an adolescent, Janis Joplin wanted all the same things as Mary Karr—"to transform magically into one of those chipper, well-dressed girls whose name-box on student ballots is automatically checked"—but by the end of high school, she knew it was an unworthy goal. In the unlikely event that she ever became one of those girls, she would have to shut off her own emotional response to the world around her, but that would have meant erasing everything meaningful in her life.[39]

It wasn't that emotion was all good, but almost nothing about the "cheerleader culture" of her hometown left Joplin feeling good, any-way. She did have a few friends, however, a group of mostly boys who were obsessed with music. They rolled their eyes at Port Arthur's squareness and introduced Joplin to their collections of blues, jazz, and folk records. "They took music very seriously, it wasn't just background music," said Laura Joplin, Janis's younger sister. "They would have a party and would lie down on the floor with their eyes shut, then some-one would put on a cut and they would try to identify it." These new friends helped Janis understand that her love of music, her intellectual curiosity, and her passionate feelings about racial equality could be integrated.

Joplin had already gotten in trouble for speaking up in class in favor of integration, an experience in which "her feelings were trampled on totally because she couldn't believe no one agreed with her," said Laura. Now she had met a group of friends who not only shared her vision of social justice but also knew much more than she about black culture itself. In the emotionally sterile world of Port Arthur circa 1960, she suddenly found an outlet to a different, more expressive uni-verse through the blues recordings of Huddie "Leadbelly" Ledbetter and the potent Bessie Smith. "I listened to them and I liked them a lot better than what I heard on the radio. They seemed to have some sin-cerity to them. . . . [I] just really fell in love with [Bessie Smith]. For the first few years I sang, I sang just like Bessie Smith. I copped her a lot, sang all of her songs."[40]

For Joplin, "copping" Bessie Smith implied more than simply imi-tating her, although Joplin's choirgirl soprano did change into a throaty, husky voice modeled on the rougher sounds of the classic blues queens. Smith demonstrated a style of singing whose power derived not only from her vocal chops but also from her emotional ones, and this was the central lesson Joplin received.[41]

She and her few high school friends sometimes snuck away at night, driving thirty miles across the state line to Louisiana and its juke joints in search of alcohol and good blues music. It is significant that one of the few songs Joplin ever wrote while in Port Arthur was the autobiographical "Turtle Blues," a song she described as "just a lonely woman's song. . . . It's an eternal blues. About me tryin' to act tough, and nobody noticed I wasn't."[42]

> I guess I'm just like a turtle
> That's hidin' underneath its horny shell. . . .
> But you know I'm very well protected—
> I know this goddamn life too well.[43]

As "Turtle Blues" shows, Joplin embraced everything about Bessie Smith's style—from the classic blues structure of her songs to their tough-but-tender lyrical themes. And although she was sophisticated enough to know that a white woman singing in a black tradition inevitably raised political issues, her attitude toward singing the blues was uncomplicated. "There's no patent on soul," she said. "You know how that whole myth of black soul came up? Because white people don't allow themselves to feel things."[44]

Joplin was well aware of racism. As a teenager, she was known for befriending African-Americans and refused to participate in her peers' recreational practice of "nigger knocking"—going across the tracks to beat up blacks. Yet she had no pretensions of wanting to be black herself, or of needing to be black in order to sing the blues: "What I'm doing is a product of my own head, not of my own culture. I didn't grow up with bare feet listening to the black folks out in de cotton fields or any of that crap." Joplin believed that whites had the same deep emotional lives as blacks, but restrained themselves from expressing them. "Housewives in Nebraska have pain and joy; they've got soul if they give in to it," she said, and then offered a possible reason why they chose not to give in: "It's hard. And it isn't all a ball when you do."[45]

By 1966, Janis Joplin had left Port Arthur but returned periodically, always seeking a community that would accept her on her own terms.

In the late 1950s, beatniks seemed to be that community. "I never heard about beatniks until I read about the integration movement and I thought, there are people out there, man. I've just got to go and find them." Joplin adopted the uniform—a man's workshirt worn untucked over blue jeans, much like Etta James's teenage gang style—and followed the beatnik crowd from the University of Texas at Austin, where she was briefly enrolled in 1962, to San Francisco in 1966, where a group of Texans had established a beachhead amid the ever-evolving Haight-Ashbury carnival of freaks. Joplin finally fit in. She wrote detailed letters to her family in Port Arthur, describing the scene and her affinity for it. The place she depicted was chaotic and electric and probably frightened her parents, but to her it was wonderful, a place where misfits ruled and cheerleaders did not exist. "[I]t's really amazing. . . . The society seems to be leaning away from itself; straining for the periphery of hell, the edges, you know. At least in California . . . (because there really is something going on here that's *not* going on anywhere else). . . . Really fantastic—a social phenomena [*sic*], really." No longer forced to protect herself under a turtle's shell, Janis Joplin made San Francisco her home.[46]

1966

> **Mother and Dad,**
> **With a great deal of trepidation, I bring the news. I'm in San Francisco. Now let me explain. . . . Seems Chet Helms, old friend, now is Mr. Big in S.F. . . . He encouraged me to come out—seems the whole city had gone rock & roll (and it has!) and assured me fame & fortune. I told him I was worried about being hung up out here w/no way back & he agreed to furnish me w/a bus ticket back home if I did just come and try. So I came.**
> **—Letter from Janis Joplin to her parents (June 6, 1966)[47]**

"There are only three significant pieces of data in the world today" . . . Chet Helms told me one night. We were at the Avalon [Ballroom] and the big strobe was going and the colored lights and the Day-Glo painting and the place was full of high-school kids trying to look turned on. . . . "The first is," he said, "God died last year and was obited by the press. The second is, fifty percent of the population is or will be under twenty-five. . . . The third," he said, "is that they got twenty billion irresponsible dollars to spend."

—Joan Didion, *Slouching Towards Bethlehem* (1967)[48]

Kozmic Blues

The year 1966 was not the first time Janis Joplin had gone to San Francisco. She had tried living there in 1963, made some friends, and even developed a reputation as a vocalist in the local coffeehouse scene, singing the songs of Bessie Smith and Ma Rainey. But her quest to embrace the beatnik lifestyle had progressed too quickly, and a dangerous methamphetamine addiction forced Joplin to return to the safety of her family home in Port Arthur to get off the drug. Once she recovered, it was only a matter of time before she was pulled west again, lured by the chance to audition for a new band, Big Brother and the Holding Company, which was managed by Chet Helms, her old friend from Austin. Joplin was fearful of making the same mistakes, but she was excited, too. "I really do think there's an awfully good chance I won't blow it this time," she told her parents. "Right now my position is ambivalent—I'm glad I came, nice to see the city, a few friends, but I'm not at all sold on the idea of becoming the poor man's Cher. So I guess we'll see." Joplin was afraid of scaring her parents by sounding too excited. (After she returned to Port Arthur weighing only eighty-eight pounds, they had insisted she see a psychiatrist, who prescribed tranquilizers—a common panacea for unhappy women in the 1960s.)

Beneath her cautious reserve, she was thrilled to be back in San Francisco.

The city to which she returned was a changed place. The jumpy, edgy beatnik scene that had flourished in North Beach—feeding itself on the Italian neighborhood's espressos and its cathedral of free verse, City Light Books—had shifted and grown. Alcohol and speed had given way to marijuana, LSD, and, gradually, heroin. The whole pageant had moved over the hill, into Golden Gate Park and the arteries leading to it: Haight Street, Ashbury Street, Page and Stanyan. Here were old, rundown Victorian mansions large enough to sleep twenty if no one minded crashing on the floor, and the neighborhood was well serviced by the streetcar that shuttled college kids between this leafy grotto and the San Francisco State University campus on the south side of town. The beatniks were fading out, and the hippies were taking their place.

The difference between beatniks and hippies was an important one to Janis. She had been attracted to beatniks because of their dark, existential attitude toward life. Their appreciation for poetry, jazz, and late-night intellectual debates appealed to her, too. Hippies, on the other hand, seemed to stand for something else entirely. While beatniks purported to engage themselves in opposition to the mainstream American reality, hippies preferred simply to escape it, forget it, or ignore it. Not that hippies were completely unaware of the world around them; they held a utopian vision of how the world might be if only it embraced love as a guiding force.

Janis Joplin was far too cynical to get behind the hippies' optimism. "Beatniks believe things aren't going to get better and say the hell with it, stay stoned and have a good time." This was Joplin's essential credo, and she stuck by it until the end of her life. Based on her own experience in Port Arthur, it was what got her through those difficult years. "The position I took a long time ago in Texas," she told a reporter in 1970, "was to be true to myself, to be the person that I felt was inside of me. . . . That's what I'm trying to do most in the world: not bullshit myself."[49]

The beatnik philosophy was the natural ideological counterpart to Joplin's love of black music and culture. The young white people of the 1950s and early 1960s who came to be known and associated with the Beats based their intellectual and aesthetic style on their perception of black hipsters. The figure of the black hipster was still a lonely antihero, living on the margins of mainstream society by choice, indulging in his passions for jazz and marijuana without guilt or apology. The tragedies of World War II and the resulting nuclear paranoia had given whites, for the first time, a sense of the existential fear with which African-Americans lived every day, as Norman Mailer argued in *The White Negro* (1957).

> The American existentialist knows that if our collective condition is to live with instant death by atomic war . . . or with a slow death by conformity with every creative and rebellious instinct stifled . . . why then the only life-giving answer is to accept the terms of death, to live with death as an immediate danger, to divorce oneself from society, to exist without roots, to set out on that uncharted journey with the rebellious imperatives of the self.

This was a philosophy of life that made perfect sense to a disillusioned young woman from Port Arthur, Texas, especially based as it was on the African-American experience, one of the few aspects of American culture that held some appeal for Joplin. "It was the Negro who brought the cultural dowry" to the world of white hipsters, wrote Mailer. "Any Negro who wishes to live must live with danger from his first day. . . . No Negro can saunter down a street with any real certainty that violence will not visit him on his walk." The threat of constant danger and the psychological attitude required to cope with it had informed African-American music, particularly the blues, from the beginning. That's what the blues were all about.[50]

Like Bessie Smith and Billie Holiday before her, Janis Joplin adopted this outlook quite naturally. Perhaps, as Mailer argued, it was the fact of her cold war childhood that allowed her to understand this kind of paranoia and simultaneous, humorous resolve. Or perhaps it was the social ostracism she faced as a shy, artistically inclined teenager that gave her a glimpse of that kind of pain. In any case, Joplin recognized the racial differences but refused to believe that the feeling was race-specific. "Black people have the blues because they can't have this and they can't have that," she said. "Me, I was brought up in a white middle-class family—I could have had anything, but you need something more in your gut, man. . . . Cats who feel it go hitch-hiking around," she explained, referring to beatnik heroes such as Jack Kerouac, "and chicks start singing," she said, referring to herself. "Inherently in life . . . you're gonna get let down. I call it the Kozmic Blues. . . . It's such a down concept you can't really wallow in it. . . . It's why you have to laugh at it."[51]

The impulse to laugh at the worst life had to offer was still abundant in San Francisco in 1966, particularly among newer groups of post-Beat writers, artists, and professional partyers like the Merry Pranksters and the Yippies, who sought to marry the insolence of the Beats with the fun-loving chaos of the hippies. Despite its many splinter groups, the San Francisco Scene was relatively small, and there was a great deal of overlapping among its various communities. After the Texan torpor of her Port Arthur convalescence, Joplin's return to San Francisco felt like a rebirth.

She may have disdained the hippies, but it soon became apparent that they controlled most of the cultural leverage in the Haight-Ashbury district (Chet Helms was right about their spending power), and Joplin was quick to accept their aesthetic, if not their intellectual position. She had traveled out from Texas full of ambition and anxiety about her ability to fit in with the burgeoning rock and psychedelia scene. "I sang blues—Bessie Smith kind of blues. . . . I'd never sung with electric music," she told a friend. But her audition blew the band away. "From the moment I heard her I knew she was absolutely incredible," drummer Dave Getz said, and Joplin was hired immediately. The band was managed by Chet Helms, who ran The Family Dog, a Haight-Ashbury–based capitalist endeavor that produced the Fillmore Auditorium and Avalon Ballroom concerts that essentially catalyzed the San Francisco Scene. "Big Brother and the Holding Company" alluded to both a beatnik-influenced cynicism ("Big Brother" came from George Orwell's dystopian novel, *1984*) and the hippie drug culture (in which *holding* was a term for the possession of marijuana, as in, "Are you holding?"). Joplin was able to appreciate the significance of both.[52]

Janis had found more than a singing gig; she had found a community. Big Brother and the Holding Company was the quintessential San Francisco band, made up of young men who were seekers in the broadest sense, looking for new experiences through drugs, philosophy, and music: Peter Albin on bass, Sam Andrew and James Gurley on guitar, and Dave Getz on drums. Though the newest member of the band, Joplin soon demonstrated her ability to keep up with their appetites for drugs, alcohol, and intellectual stimulation.[53]

Together they rented a house in Marin County, just north of San Francisco, where they could practice and get to know each other. It was just down the road from a house where the Grateful Dead were doing the same thing, and both bands traded gigs at the Fillmore and the Avalon, along with Jefferson Airplane, the Quicksilver Messenger Service, and other favorites of the hippie crowd. Grace Slick, the lead singer of Jefferson Airplane, was the only other prominent woman on the rock scene, and Joplin seemed to take a cue from her style at first, wearing ornate, psychedelic-inspired stage costumes that mirrored the taste of the acid-tripping audience members. True to her beatnik roots, Joplin never became a fan of LSD or of any of the psychedelics; she stayed faithful to the approved hipster inebriants: speed (occasionally), alcohol (constantly), and heroin (ultimately). She was smart and ambitious, though, and she soon realized that her Levis and workshirts would not make a very big impression on the flashy-looking crowd in the Haight. "Conforming to the style to the extent of my budget," she told her family, "I have a new pair of very wide-wale corduroy hip-hugger pants which I wear w/borrowed boots. Look very in."[54]

Joplin's experiments with fashion revealed her insecurity about her looks (she was constantly changing her style of dress according to the opinions of others) and her desire to succeed. She wanted people to believe that she didn't care about appearances, but she *did* care, and she rarely was happy with her looks. And as a woman in a rock band, she could not afford to disregard the importance of her appearance. Jerry Garcia might be able to succeed while looking like a caveman, but women in rock still had to conform to certain standards of beauty, even in the Haight. Joplin filled her letters home with fashion updates, describing the "young and beautiful" girls with "long straight hair" and "bare midriffs," while she struggled to straighten her hair and control her weight. "Still faced with the problem of what to wear on stage. . . . I'm pretty heavy again—so I want flattering things, plus they can't be too hot, plus I have to be able to move around a lot in them." She told her mother she would hire a "hippie girl" to make something for her.[55]

By 1966, women were beginning to challenge some of the restrictive social roles they were expected to fulfill, but many misogynist assumptions about women and their proper place were still in full effect. Even in groovy San Francisco, Janis Joplin still had to deal with stereotypes dating back to the sock-hop era. "The guys from the band are going to be in a movie," she told her family, "about 2 girls who fall in love w/a rock 'n' roll group. I can't be in it because I'm a girl & consequently no romantic figure for 2 girls." The concept for the film (which apparently was never produced) was clearly based on an outdated idea of what a rock band was—this was essentially the plot of an Elvis movie—when in fact the success of Big Brother was based almost entirely on the singing and charisma of Joplin, and not the spaced-out jam rock of the four men who backed her—a reality that became increasingly obvious as time went on.[56]

Despite her own insecurities, Janis Joplin was indeed a romantic figure—to men and women alike. Like Bessie Smith, Ma Rainey, and Billie Holiday, Janis Joplin had relationships with both men and women and was fairly open about it, at least within her community of friends and fellow musicians. While her wild hair, funky outfits, and gritty, sweaty performances distinguished her from more traditionally feminine women singers—such as her contemporaries Grace Slick (a former model) and the barely earthbound, saint-like Joan Baez—her rough style endowed her with an exciting sexuality that touched many of her fans. Although not as obviously striking as Tina Turner, the two women shared an erotic ferocity that was unusual for the time.

"Pogo," a young bisexual man, described his experience at a Big Brother and the Holding Company concert in 1968:

> Janis walked out, and everybody went wild. Her hair was so beautiful as it was thrown all over. She looked about 19. She dances around so beautifully that you can't stop from getting up and dancing yourself. I felt as though she were singing to me personally. She got me so sexually aroused—the way Mick Jagger and Jim Morrison do, but without the guilt. . . . We wrote all over the walls, "Janis is Sex," "Janis is Love," "Janis is Big Brother."[57]

Joplin's unorthodox sexuality appealed to men like Pogo, who were already interested in challenging sexual boundaries. Yet her appeal was broader than that. She may have had insecurities offstage, but once in front of a crowd, she lost all inhibition. The vitality of her performances allowed her full expression of her sensuality. She was confident in a way she could never be offstage. Her performing personality, plus her increasing fame, brought many sexual opportunities her way. Jimi Hendrix, Jim Morrison, Joe McDonald (of Country Joe and the Fish), Kris Kristofferson, and even, improbably, Joe Namath were among the famous men she slept with—or was rumored to have done so. Many of her lovers were also friends from the San Francisco crowd, where getting sex was relatively easy, famous or not. Joplin was, by all accounts, sexually voracious, but she also claimed to want to get married someday and have children. Male rock stars such as Mick Jagger and Keith Richards enjoyed free love and family life, but for a woman this combination seemed like pure fantasy. Joplin's sex drive was marveled at even as *Rolling Stone* magazine published an entire issue devoted to groupies, in which the insatiable sexual appetite of male rock stars was simply taken for granted while the sexual proclivities of the young women who serviced them were analyzed and critiqued.[58]

One of her steadiest relationships was with Peggy Caserta, a friend who was also a lover. Caserta was a successful boutique owner who embodied the Haight-Ashbury ideal Joplin so admired: she was tall, with long, straight and shiny brown hair and a slim yet curvaceous body, and she was full of confidence. Caserta and Joplin's relationship continued, on and off, from 1966 until Joplin's death, but Joplin never gave up her dream of marriage to a man. Whether because of the pervasive homophobia—even in San Francisco—at the time or some other reason, Joplin continued to wait for the proverbial knight in shining armor, a strong man to rescue her and make her feel beautiful all the time.[59]

She had trouble finding him. While fame won her admirers, it also scared off the type of man she liked—men like her, with big personalities and strong wills. Men like that usually weren't interested in sharing the spotlight with a rock-star girlfriend, though. "It's hard to find him, because the only cats that hang around dressing rooms are flunkies. . . . The men are out in some log cabin growing grass and chopping trees, and I never get to see them," she complained, then added: "But that gives you more soul, right?"[60]

The sexual energy that Joplin projected onstage could be intimidating. Critics were often surprised by how normal she looked offstage, once they had seen her perform. "This frail little Columbia Records artist, with the voice which makes amplifiers obsolete suddenly seemed to come alive," a concert reviewer wrote. "Girls fainted. Amorous males leaped to the stage to kiss their idol." The energy Joplin projected onstage transformed her into a rock goddess, despite her fairly unremarkable appearance. Even *Vogue* magazine, the cultural gatekeeper for mainstream standards of female beauty, featured Joplin in a Richard Avedon photo spread. They noted that despite the fact that her "lumpen extraordinary face has no makeup, her long brown hair doesn't shine [and] she screws her eyes up over constant cigarettes . . . when she gets out there and starts to sing, she is a magnetic moving fireball lighting up the whole auditorium."[61]

"Of course, she ain't beautiful, although she is to me." This quote about Bessie Smith from one of her fans could have applied to Janis Joplin as well. Like Bessie Smith in her day, Janis Joplin challenged prevailing ideas about female attractiveness and succeeded where the arbiters of beauty were convinced she would fail. In 1967, San Francisco photographer Bob Seidemann made a poster from his portrait of Joplin clothed only in love beads, and it quickly became a popular pinup in Haight-Ashbury. "Yes, folks, it's me," Joplin wrote to her family, thrilled to be the subject of such a sexy portrait. "Very dramatic photograph and I look really beautiful!! If it wouldn't embarrass you, I'll send you one." Joplin's enthusiasm was attractive in itself. "Janis is beautiful," one journalist wrote after Big Brother's triumphant New York City debut at the Anderson Theater in 1968. "In a business where popularity usually is accompanied by studied aloofness, she is a breath of fresh air. . . . In appearance she is a small, sexy doll. . . . She may become, since such distinctions are inevitable, the first major girl sex symbol in rock."[62]

But not everyone appreciated her style. "If she weren't so feminine, she might have become a lady wrestler," joked a reviewer at *Life* magazine, the chronicler of the American middle class. Joplin's tangled, wrinkled, hungover aesthetic communicated something less than ideal femininity to the average *Life* subscriber. Outside Haight-Ashbury and the world of rock fanatics, Joplin's looks branded her as a freak and opened her up to more criticism. In the late 1960s, respectable older, middle-class women were still wearing girdles, stockings, bras, and matching purses and shoes. Their hair was "done" at salons, which usually involved shellacking it into an impenetrable helmet that could not be moved for days. Women with problem skin were expected to cover it with thick pancake makeup. Younger women were experimenting with looser styles, but Joplin's look was intentionally wild, even by Haight-Ashbury standards.[63]

Janis Joplin had had enough of foundation garments, hairspray, and rollers in high school. Her refusal to play the role expected of her not only was shocking to some of her critics, it was actually offensive. Didn't this woman realize she couldn't get away with looking like this? One male critic was so irritated by her apparent disregard of female expectations that he dreamed of telling her: "You forget you have acne," as if that would silence her. His comment revealed more about his own sense of limitations than it did of hers. What her detractors couldn't understand was the fact that Joplin's fans didn't think she was flawless; they didn't need to think that in order to love and respect her. "[T]here were as many times when she looked truly homely as there were times when she looked beautiful," one of her female fans explained. "And that went for a lot of her sisters. I think she taught America that beauty didn't have to be a constant, it could ebb and flow and surprise you by being there one minute and not the next." Joplin's appearance simply made her more accessible to her fans, who had their own insecurities about their appearances, after all. Joplin's "natural" style was organic to who she was and what she represented. It was, in fact, the visual counterpart to the blueswoman aesthetic: the Ideal is always subservient to the Truth.[64]

1967
Cheap Thrills

Janis Joplin had transitioned from Beat junkie to hippie princess in a short year after returning to San Francisco in 1966. Hooking up with Big Brother and the Holding Company had been a godsend for both her and the band. Almost exactly a year to the day after joining forces, they stormed the 1967 Monterey Pop Festival, an event that expanded their horizons far beyond the San Francisco Bay.

It was, in fact, Joplin's performance that mattered. The sonic bombast of the boys in the band provided a medium for her singing but didn't add much to it. The combination of her howling/quivering/whispering/screaming voice and the way her entire body—especially her long, wild hair—moved along to it, stamping her feet, pointing, shaking her fist, shimmying her shoulders, head thrown back and sweat dripping down her neck, it all added up to a vision of emotional energy that nearly blinded the unsuspecting audience member. Caught on film during the performance, Cass Elliott of the Mamas and the Papas was obviously stunned, her mouth agape and her head slightly shaking from side to side as she marveled at her comrade-in-arms. "Wow," she appeared to be saying, "oh, wow."[65]

Three stars were born that weekend: Janis Joplin, Otis Redding, and Jimi Hendrix. All three stunned their audiences with the ferocity of their attacks. Joplin's emotional assault, Redding's sweaty, soulful power, and Hendrix's electrified art blazing to an end as he set his guitar afire—all these were signs of the roiling energy that the 1960s generation was only starting to unleash. Two years before Woodstock, Monterey was an early sounding bell transmitting from the West Coast. For Janis Joplin, it represented everything she had hoped her music could be. The cameras followed her as she left the stage . . . skipping with joy.

"It's so fulfilling," she said, explaining her love of singing before an audience, "because it's real, it's not just a veneer, it's not just a performance." The intensity that Joplin conveyed onstage was, like that of the blueswomen before her, fed by her own internal emotional reserves. Joplin's performances were inextricably tied to her most intimate feelings. When a reporter asked her how she went from being a "recluse" as a young woman to becoming a successful rock star, she answered, "I got liberated! No . . . I started to sing and singing makes you want to come out." The idea of self-liberation was always linked with singing for Joplin, no matter how she chose to delineate the exact sequence of events.[66]

Despite her use of personal emotions as fuel for her performances, Joplin found it difficult to connect her private self with the image she portrayed onstage. As with Billie Holiday and Tina Turner, the woman known and loved by the public was often more confident and commanding than the woman in the wings. Holiday and Turner adopted femme fatale personas that masked their passivity in the face of abusive men, and Turner's fiery onstage seductions often represented the tastes of her husband rather than her own. In Janis's case, the swaggering, bawdy broad that she channeled onstage evoked a woman who knew how to put a man in his place. Like her idol Bessie Smith, even when she was singing about a failed relationship, an essential core of strength permeated her voice. "I used to sing exactly like Bessie Smith," Joplin said, "and I used to wonder—especially when people would clap and tell me I was good—I used to wonder, 'is that real, or is that something I've learned to do with my voice?' . . . Is it really me, or am I putting on a show?"[67]

Joplin's public face was so convincing that reporters often were astonished to see the private Janis Joplin offstage with all her insecurities exposed. Most of them were charmed by her vulnerability. "She is straight-talking, hard-drinking, and very natural," Tony Wilson reported in *Melody Maker* in 1969, "a spontaneous person with a tough charm that comes like a breath of fresh air after the mechanical plastic-coated females so often encountered on the pop scene." *Down Beat* called her "a beautiful person, not only as a performer, but as a human being," after glimpsing the "child-like innocence that she keeps in reserve under her protective, hard exterior." At the end of this interview—a few months after her first album, *Cheap Thrills*, had gone platinum—Joplin asked the reporter to send her manager a copy of the interview: "You see, I'm keeping a scrapbook." These were moments when the inner Janis Joplin shone through, as a woman proud of her accomplishments but needy enough to rely on the approval of the outside world.[68]

It was that same neediness that alarmed other critics. They tended to justify their disgust with concern for her well-being, but it often sounded like Joplin was simply being criticized for having failed at her job as a rock star. Wasn't she living the dream? She was—and therefore she didn't deserve to have any doubts about her life and how she had gotten there. "Janis seems that rare kind of personality who lacks the essential self-protective distancing that a singer of her fame and stature would appear to need," Paul Nelson wrote in *Rolling Stone* in 1969, a comment that could have been interpreted as a friend's worry, were it not for the rest of the piece. This infamous article, entitled "Janis: The Judy Garland of Rock 'n' Roll?" portrayed Joplin as an emotional wreck whose insecurities were out of control. Describing her performance at San Francisco's Fillmore Auditorium as "incredibly nervous," Nelson wrote: "Janis doesn't so much sing a song as to strangle it to death right in front of you." Nelson ended the article with quotations from two men who hated the show. Joplin's performance that night may—or may not—have been subpar, but Nelson's review implied that Joplin the person was incapable of being Joplin the rock star.[69]

Joplin's insecurities were inescapable, but they also made her who she was; they made her capable of delivering her songs of pain and loss with real power. Hers was "the most powerful voice in the business," wrote a reviewer for *Jazz and Pop*. "I am not one to exaggerate—Miss Joplin is the best white blues singer I have ever heard." Being a blues singer ("It's blues–rock," Joplin once said. "If ya gotta call it anything, call it that.") meant *not* losing touch with life's great pain. Joplin knew this better than anyone. "Maybe my fans can enjoy my music more if they think I'm destroying myself," she said. Joplin internalized this odd logic and used it to her advantage in performance. As music journalist Ellen Willis wrote in the *New Yorker*, Joplin rose above the expectations of the music business, "screaming out the misery and confusion of being what others wanted her to be. But," the critic wrote, lamenting the unlikelihood that other women would follow in Joplin's footsteps, "she was a genius."[70]

Despite her insecurities, Joplin understood that she was talented, that she did have an effect on people. "Janis was excited by her talent and loved exploring what she could do, she loved being a part of the culture," her sister Laura said. She saw herself as an actress, and she knew what an actress had to do. "You're aware of the fact that you're standing on a stage and that people are looking at you, so what you do is, like, I suppose an actress; you put your head in a place where you recall all these emotions . . . an emotional place that is apt to that tune." This ability to access her emotions explained why she was able to connect with her audience, particularly her female fans. She enacted emotional liberation onstage, practically demonstrating how it was done. Joplin admitted that "you can't really feel [emotions] standing out on stage at the Avalon Ballroom, with a thousand spotlights on your face," but she could act as if she did, providing release for her audience and herself in the process. "I don't know whether I can act or not," Joplin once told an interviewer, "but I can act like *me*. I can act like me like a son of a bitch." The effect of her spectacle —acting as her most emotionally resonant self—was so great that, as with Billie Holiday in the 1940s and 1950s, the mere sight of her inspired an emotional reaction in her fans: "19-year-old Mimi . . . weeps with joy every time she hears Janis Joplin. . . . 'I don't know [what she's singing],' Mimi says, but tears have filled her eyes anyway."[71]

Joplin had a sense of her ability to touch people. "I know exactly what happens, man," Joplin said, referring to her ability to move a crowd. "If you can get them once, man, get them standing up when they should be sitting down, sweaty when they should be decorous . . . I think you sort of switch on their brain. . . . Whoooooo! It's life. That's what rock 'n' roll is for." She knew she could rock the house, but she was less sure of her ability to touch her fans with just her voice.

"Billie Holiday, Aretha Franklin, now they are so subtle," she said. "They can milk you with two notes. They can go no farther than from A to B and they can make you feel like they told you the whole universe. . . . All I've got now is strength. But I think maybe if I keep singing, maybe I'll get it." She was never satisfied with her own talent, or with her own success. When a reporter told her, "You're a star, Janis," she protested:

I know me, I've been around a long time. . . . I was the same chick, because I've been her forever, and I know her, and she ain't no star: she's lonely. . . . I have to get undressed after the show, my clothes are ruined, my heels are run through, my underwear is ripped, my body's stained from my clothes, my hair's stringy, I got a headache and I got to go home, and I'm lonely, and my clothes are all fucked up, my shoes have come apart, and I'm pleading with my road manager to please give me a ride home, please, please, just so I can take these fuckin' clothes off, and that ain't no star, man, that's just a person.[72]

1970

Dear Mother . . .
I don't think I can go back now. I don't know all the reasons, but I just feel that this has a truer feeling. True to me. A lot of the conflicts I was having. . . . I've resolved. Don't take my tranquilizers anymore. I don't feel like I'm lying now. . . . I somehow feel that I have to see this through first. . . . If I don't, I'd always think about singing & being good & known & feel like I'd cheated myself—you know?

—Letter from Janis Joplin to her mother
(September 1966)[73]

They Didn't Know the World
Would Change

"I don't think I'm a very special kind of person," Janis Joplin told a London audience, "but I don't think you'll find another person to try so hard." Joplin's decision to devote herself to being a singer was harder for her than many realized. Her numerous letters to her family demonstrated that she understood just how radical her choice was. She knew that the Joplin family, like most middle-class, "nice" American families, could hardly conceive of telling the neighbors that their child had gone off to San Francisco to become a rock singer—the fact that she was female just made it worse. "I apologize for being so just plain bad to the family. I realize that my shifting values don't make me very reliable and that I'm a disappointment and, well, I'm just sorry," she wrote to them.[74]

Once her family realized the depth of her commitment, they became fairly supportive of her goals. Like Aretha Franklin, Joplin's closest family relationship was with her father, Seth. Janis thought of him as "a secret intellectual" trapped like she had been by the small-town values of Port Arthur. Seth had gone to college, loved to read books and discuss ideas, and valued the life of the mind. Unlike most of the practically minded adults in Janis's childhood, Seth was a dreamer. He saw these same qualities in Janis, and he encouraged her to look beyond Port Arthur for her future. With well-meaning parents and a stable family life, Janis's childhood was idyllic by comparison with that of Bessie Smith, Billie Holiday, or Etta James. Nevertheless, it was unsatisfying, and a desire to escape the confines of quasi-suburban domesticity fueled her drive to sing. "She was never alienated from the family," said Seth Joplin. "Although we disagreed with the way she lived, she liked us and we liked her." "They always had faith in me," Janis said. "They just thought I was . . . misguided. They didn't know the world would change."[75]

As her letter suggests, once Joplin made her decision to remain in San Francisco and pursue her dream—"singing & being good & known"—she was able to stop taking the tranquilizers her doctor in Port Arthur had prescribed. She didn't want to smother her ambition with drugs; she wanted to feel everything for herself and funnel that emotion into her music. Like many of her generation, she began to see that instead of bringing her in closer contact with her friends, the universe, and herself, drugs were profoundly isolating. Yet once she got off the tranquilizers, she found others—Southern Comfort and, increasingly, heroin, which she had begun using in 1967—to ease her stage fright and her loneliness. Unlike most of her peers in the San Francisco Scene, Joplin preferred alcohol to marijuana and LSD. Drinking was part of the culture in the Louisiana juke joints she had frequented as a teen, and psychedelics probably were too prone to sparking Joplin's paranoia to be enjoyable. "I got the Dead drunk," Joplin crowed after cajoling Jerry Garcia and his fellow Grateful Dead bandmates to swill tequila with her instead of indulging in their usual marijuana. Yet Joplin often drank alone.[76]

Like Billie Holiday and her heroin, and Bessie Smith with her gin, Joplin became known for her devotion to Southern Comfort, frequently posing with a bottle in photographs and on stage. In this, a more innocent era of American marketing, Joplin had to persuade the company to compensate *her* for the product placement (they sent her a fur coat). Drinking bourbon was an essential part of her brassy, roadhouse persona, and it set her apart from the hippies she continued to disdain. Drinking was one of the few bits of her Texan roots to survive the trip to California, one of the only things about her Southern heritage that she held onto and claimed as her own.

Although Joplin had taken a personal vow as a teenager "to be righteous to myself," it wasn't easy simply to become a new, self-fulfilled Janis Joplin, rock star. Bessie Smith was an orphan, Billie Holiday was practically one herself, and they were able to invent themselves sui generis, with virtually no old friends or families to call their bluffs. Like Aretha Franklin, Janis Joplin came from a solid family. Aretha, though expressive and soulful on stage, never challenged the respectability of the Franklin family reputation. But Janis's parents and siblings bore witness to her metamorphosis from choirgirl to rock 'n' roll temptress. Their very existence was a constant reminder, especially to Joplin, that the "San Francisco Janis" was a wholly new creation, and that the "Port Arthur Janis" still existed in the minds of many. Many of those Port Arthur residents refused to let her forget the days of shame in the hallways of Jefferson High School, and they resented her success. Whenever she appeared on national television in the late 1960s, her parents would receive obscene phone calls; after her death, they called to laugh.[77]

Janis Joplin attempted to settle the score in 1970 by returning to Port Arthur for her ten-year high school reunion. It seemed like a safe bet: by 1970, she had released three albums: *Big Brother and the Holding Company* (1966), *Cheap Thrills* (1968), and *I Got Dem Ol' Kozmic Blues Again Mama!* (1969). She had performed at the two biggest rock festivals of her generation, Monterey Pop and Woodstock, and she had appeared on television, in films, and on magazine covers, even making it to the cover of *Newsweek*, a publication that meant something even to conservative, small-town Port Arthur. Appearing on *The Dick Cavett Show* a few weeks before the reunion, she told Cavett that her classmates had "laughed her out of class, out of town and out of the state, man. . . . That's why I'm going back." She delivered the last line with a wicked chuckle, and the studio audience cheered in approval. At last, the swan was going home to confront anyone who had ever hurt the ugly duckling.[78]

The reunion was a disaster. The hint of vulnerability that had surfaced in Joplin's *Dick Cavett* appearance came into bloom at the reunion. Surrounded by local reporters, former classmates, and her little sister, Laura, Joplin—her emotions roiling—appeared to come close to tears at several points during her pre-reunion press conference. She had made sure that her San Francisco entourage was with her, which was a wise move, as their presence buffered the reality of being surrounded by the straight population of Port Arthur, all gawking at the California freak show in its midst.

Today we look back on the sixties and imagine an era of free love and flowing hair, but the reality was different. Most Americans in the 1960s disapproved of the clothing, hairstyles, and certainly the lifestyles of the beatniks, hippies, and flower children who made up a tiny minority of the population, especially away from the coasts and the larger college towns. "The sixties have a reputation for being open and free and cool," said Ronnie Cutrone, a member of Andy Warhol's Factory group in the late 1960s, "but the reality was that everyone was straight. . . . We had long hair and we'd get chased down the block. . . . Nobody had long hair—you were a fucking freak, you were a fruit, you were not like the rest of the world." This was certainly how Janis Joplin was received in Port Arthur in September 1970. Women were allowed to have long hair, of course, but not like hers, with colored feather boas attached to long, frizzy hair that was "positively triangular in its electricity." Wearing oversize granny glasses and mutlilayered colorful clothing, Joplin appeared like a vision from outer space to her hometown community.[79]

Reporters razzed her about not being asked to the prom as a teenager, about being an outcast, and when she was finally asked why she was treated so poorly by her schoolmates, she lost her cool and snapped, "I don't know, why don't you ask them?" The interview was recorded on film, and it captures her pain in terrifying detail as she avoids eye contact, tries to smile, licks her lips and then bites them, trying to control her humiliation. She looked to her sister for support—Laura was still living in Port Arthur—but that failed when Laura told the press that her family had lost two of Janis's records (and presumably had not replaced them). Janis stayed around for the whole reunion and was embarrassed when the class awarded her with a rubber tire for having come the farthest distance to attend.[80]

Nothing had changed. In the eyes of her hometown, Janis Joplin was still a weirdo, a freak. Dorothy Joplin, Janis's mother, had predicted as much in a letter to the rest of the Joplin family before the reunion, in a tone suggesting that she had her own reservations about her daughter's new image. "It's a strange scene to read of one's eldest as 'the Queen,' 'the Goddess,' 'the Superstar.' She calls now and then, but never writes anymore. Perhaps the home folks [will] bring this halo down to polishing distance."[81]

1970
The Great Saturday Night Swindle

Both Tina Turner and Janis Joplin entered the 1970s as stars. Ike and Tina Turner spent the end of 1969 on a second tour with the Rolling Stones, this time playing in America to stadiums packed with fans cheering their covers of such white bands' songs, as the Rolling Stones' "Honky Tonk Women." The Turners' soulful versions of these tunes (which also rocked harder than the originals) were aural history lessons for the Stones' largely white audience. B. B. King's presence as a second act was another reminder of the African-American foundations of the British Invasion. The Rolling Stones were happy to admit as much. Including the Turners and King on their tour was a symbolic and financially remunerative way of thanking the American artists who had made their act possible. Yet this was no gesture of charity, for many artists would shrink at the prospect of performing with their idols.

American critics appreciated the spectacle. *San Francisco Chronicle* rock critic Ralph Gleason called the double bill "the best rock show ever presented" and gave Tina Turner most of the credit. "Tina Turner must be the most sensational performer on stage," he wrote. "Jagger ought to get a medal for courage in following B. B. King and Tina Turner." In a scene from *Gimme Shelter*, the documentary film made during the tour, Tina's effect on the Rolling Stones is evident. Backstage, the Stones are surrounded by fans and hangers-on and the band members seem to be trying to ignore the people around them. Suddenly, Tina Turner walks in, and the surly Jagger and soporific Keith Richards spring to life, smiling and chatting as she arranges a dinner date. As she leaves, Jagger and Richards look at each other like two lucky schoolboys who've just been anointed by the prettiest girl in school. For Tina, moments like these were a sweet release from the daily grind of life on the road with Ike. Though they had never been more successful, Tina was reaching her limit—physically and emotionally—in dealing with Ike's constant abuse.[82]

~

For Janis Joplin, touring and recording were often the happiest times. After her demoralizing confrontation with reality in Port Arthur in September 1970, Joplin returned to California—now, unquestionably, her spiritual home—to begin recording her second album with her new band, Full Tilt Boogie. Unlike Big Brother and the Holding Company, into which she had been inserted as lead singer after the instrumentalists had already bonded as a group, Full Tilt Boogie existed to serve Joplin's vision, and the album reflected it. Songs such as the a cappella "Mercedes Benz" and the country-influenced "Me and Bobby McGee" (co-written by her friend and former lover, Kris Kristofferson) revealed a less bombastic yet no less powerful voice, uncluttered by indulgent guitar solos and blaring horn riffs. The album was to be entitled *Pearl*. "Pearl" was a nickname Joplin had acquired in San Francisco among her friends. She described it as "a private name for my friends to call me so they won't have to call me Janis Joplin." Her explanation was telling: "Janis Joplin" was a name now associated with an image, one that had grown bigger than the woman herself. Joplin was now looking to bring the two sides of herself, public and private, into greater harmony.[83]

Before starting to record *Pearl* in Los Angeles, Joplin's producer asked her how she saw herself in the future, as a middle-aged woman.

"I want to be the greatest blues singer in the world," Joplin replied. As mentioned earlier, it was a phrase with which she had become familiar that fall, for it had been carved into Bessie Smith's recently installed headstone in Philadelphia, a monument made possible by Joplin's financial support: "The Greatest Blues Singer in the World Will Never Stop Singing—Bessie Smith." Like her fellow white blues-rockers, the Rolling Stones, Joplin was grateful for the opportunity to honor her artistic forebears. She had, in fact, joined the Stones/Turner/King tour for one show in Madison Square Garden on Thanksgiving night, 1969, singing a duet with her idol, Tina Turner, for the first and last time. B. B. King, who had played with Joplin before at the Fillmore, said, "Janis Joplin sings the blues as hard as any black person." The opinion of King, a legend in modern blues, meant more to Joplin than that of the Rolling Stones. She was unquestionably a rock star, but she still thought of herself as essentially a blues singer, and blues singers like Bessie Smith remained her greatest idols.[84]

During the recording of *Pearl*, Joplin was in a period of reassessing her life. As her comment suggested, she was still fully committed to singing as a career. Yet she was still trying to imagine a way of making room in her life for the basic pleasures of a steady romantic relationship. All these ideas were filtered through her unique worldview, a cynical-but-hopeful perspective that had only deepened since her teenage experimentation with Beatnik philosophy; one could call it Blues Existentialism, or use Joplin's term: the Kozmic Blues. She liked to tell a story about herself, explaining how she came to understand the world and her place in it.

It started with her father, Seth Joplin, the only person in Port Arthur who "made her think." When she was twenty years old and still struggling with her desire to become a singer, she wrote him a long letter about her frustrations and unmet expectations:

[You] always told me it was going to get better, and I always thought it was an incline up, that one day would level off. And you know, you motherfucker, it ain't leveling off. . . . People used to tell me, when you grow up, it'll be okay, or when you get the right man, it'll be okay. I did all those things and it wasn't okay. . . . I felt burned.[85]

She mailed her father the letter. Seth Joplin had a best friend, "the only other intellectual in town," she explained. "This guy also dug me a lot and thought a lot of me. And my father showed him the letter." The next time she returned home to Port Arthur, her father's best friend walked in, "with a sly smile on his face and he reached out his hand and said, 'Well, Janis, I hear ya heard about the Great Saturday Night Swindle." She had never heard the phrase before, but she understood it immediately—this was the root of the Kozmic Blues. "I went whooooh! I mean, it's really true, huh? Here was a 50-year-old man telling [me] like it is. I was proud of that." In her reaction— laughter mixed with terror, followed by pride in the older generation's decision to bring her into the fold—Joplin entered the legacy of blueswomen and men who had likewise learned this truth. "I *think*," she told an interviewer, "unless I'm fooling myself on one more level . . . at the very bottom. . . . it's all a big joke [*laughs*] . . . on us." Understanding this truth was her rite of passage into the world and worldview of the blueswoman, and she never forgot it.[86]

Langston Hughes thought that the blues were sadder than the black spirituals for this very reason, "because their sadness is not softened with tears, but hardened with laughter, the absurd incongruous laughter of a sadness without even a god to appeal to." They captured the feeling of existential loneliness like no other music, "the worthless lovers with hands full of gimme . . . the eternal unsatisfied longings." These feelings were not limited to African-Americans, they were fundamentally human. In Joplin's view:

the black man's blues is based on the "have-not"—I got the blues because I don't have this, I got the blues because I don't have my baby, I got the blues because I don't have the quarter for a bottle of wine, I got the blues because they won't let me in that bar. Well, you know, I'm a middle-class white chick from a family that would love to send me to college and I didn't wanna. I had a job, I didn't dig it. I had a car, I didn't dig it. I had it real easy . . . [but] it's the want of something that gives you the blues. It's not what isn't, it's what you wish *was* that makes unhappiness.

"Out of the jumble of my life," she said, "it's one of the few things I can remember clearly."[87]

~

Tina Turner struggled with her own version of the Kozmic Blues. For her, the sixties dissolved into a long string of days spent simply surviving, putting one foot in front of the other, recording and re-recording according to Ike's whim, performing to the point of exhaustion and hospitalization. Because of her incredible physical stamina and her own sense of professionalism, rarely did anyone outside the Turners' inner circle learn of her suffering. Barely three years older than Janis Joplin, Tina Turner had been working as a singer almost twice as long, had raised four children, and had personally experienced a brand of suffering that most people could not imagine. By 1973, Turner could not will herself to proceed any further. Tina was thirty-four years old. "I started thinking about my marriage. And I remembered what marriage had meant to me when I was a girl—the loving husband and wife, the happy children. My god, I thought, how had things gone so wrong? . . . So this was my life, and I was starting to see it real clearly now."

Like Joplin, Turner experienced a moment of clarity that reorganized her understanding of the world and of her life's path. In 1973, Ike casually introduced Tina to his new secretary, Valerie Bishop. Though she didn't work there long (unwilling to tolerate Ike's erratic behavior), it was long enough for her to introduce Tina to a chanting practice based on Nichiren Shoshu Buddhism. She left her with a book, some prayer beads, and a mantra that changed Tina's life. Tina had already been exploring alternative forms of religion—psychics and tarot card readers—as an escape from her reality, but something about the simplicity of chanting brought her a profound inner peace. She also noticed that her chanting made Ike scared, and though he forbade it, she continued to chant every time he left the house.

As with Joplin, Turner's new outlook did not solve any of her problems, but it did offer a kind of freedom—a freedom from self-delusion and fear. She began to stand up to Ike, calmly explaining that she would not tolerate being beaten by him anymore. The beatings did not stop, but they lessened. Ike was baffled. He had never expected Tina to complain; after all, she had put up with him for more than a decade. A friend of his, Bob Gruen, who also worked in the music business, tried to explain what was happening to Tina—and to women everywhere. "I was trying to explain this to Ike—about this new feminist movement, that you can't just boss a woman around and expect to be considered a powerful man." He told Ike about the changed relationship between his friends John Lennon and Yoko Ono, how Lennon had stopped drinking and using drugs to help raise their son. "Women today don't want to be a shadow to a man—they want to be their own individual person and pursue their own destiny," Gruen explained. "This was something that he had never heard before, and it didn't make much sense to him. . . . He just didn't get it."[88]

It was a noble effort, but it failed. Ike and Tina Turner lived in a bubble, one created and maintained by Ike, and neither of them had any concept of the burgeoning women's liberation movement that was changing the culture around them. Because of Bob Gruen, Ike probably knew more about feminism than Tina did, at least by name, but it still meant nothing to him. It was no women's movement that liberated Tina Turner from her marriage, but her realization of what her life had become and her newfound serenity, which gave her the courage to change it. This was her Great Saturday Night Swindle, her Kozmic Blues: she had a stellar career, a marriage, children, and money in the bank, but she could claim none of it as her own. In 1975, Tina Turner walked out on Ike with the clothes on her back and a pair of sunglasses to cover her blackened eyes. As she looked back at her husband, asleep on a hotel bed, she thought, "You just beat me for the last time, you sucker." Their divorce was finalized in 1978.[89]

~

Janis Joplin died on October 4, 1970. A lethal injection of heroin took her life, and she was found alone in a hotel room in West Hollywood shortly before finishing the recording of *Pearl*. Her band waited for hours for her to show up at the studio, but she never did. News of her death traveled fast. By that evening, most of San Francisco's music scene had heard about it. Many of her musician colleagues were determined to be philosophical about it. "It was the best possible time for her death," insisted Jerry Garcia, leader of the Grateful Dead. "She was on a real hard path. She picked it, she chose it." The Dead's guitarist, Bob Weir, said, "I can't bring myself to be in abject misery about it because, like I say, she drank herself to death, she lived up to her image." The hippies of Haight-Ashbury may have convinced themselves that Joplin's death at the age of twenty-seven was nothing to get upset about, but most of her fans—particularly her female fans—could not.[90]

"She represented me, who didn't go to the Senior Prom and was never elected to anything," a woman named Pamela Kane wrote in a letter to *Rolling Stone* after Joplin's death. "All the outcasts who didn't fit into the closed society that is the American high school knew she was one of us. Her beauty and creativity said 'no' to all those teachers who had ignored us, all those football heroes who wouldn't date us, all those cheerleaders who seemed to own the world." Rock critic Lester Bangs was upset not only by her death but by the reactions to it. "It's not just that this kind of early death has become a fact of life that is disturbing, but that it's been accepted as a given so quickly." Many people saw Joplin's death as a tragedy, not a forgone conclusion or a fitting end to her young life. In another letter to *Rolling Stone*, the writer complained, "When the geniuses of our culture waste their gifted lives, isn't it enough to make people see?"[91]

Joplin's close friends were also shocked by her death. True, Joplin had been known to abuse herself with drugs and alcohol, but she had been in much worse shape before. She seemed to be looking forward to the rest of her life, making plans for the future, and excited about her career. Joplin had gone through a lot in her brief life, but she seemed stronger for it. "I never saw so much life left in someone who had lived so much, I don't think anybody or anything could break that woman's spirit." This quote came from a friend of Bessie Smith's, shortly before her untimely death, but it expresses the same feelings Joplin's friends had about her. She was "happier and more turned on than anyone can remember," said one. "She was enthusiastic about the band and about her own singing. She said she 'felt like a woman.'"[92]

And the fact that she *was* a woman made a difference to her female fans, and made her absence from a culture dominated by men that much more significant. Janis was celebrated shortly after her death as "the world's first truly liberated woman"—an image that her female fans wanted desperately to believe. But overdosing from heroin, alone in a crummy hotel in Los Angeles, didn't seem very liberated at all. Yet, just as the young Janis Joplin had been inspired by the late Bessie Smith, the woman who "showed me the air and how to fill it," Joplin's own legacy offered some hope to her fans. "Janis was a comet, a life force, a light in our darkening world, a beautiful person, and she was Ours," one wrote. "Janis died physically," explained another. "Mostly the rest of us die as personalities and as integral human beings." But it didn't have to be that way; Janis's example offered an alternative. "It's all loud and clear for every sister to hear now even if the presence is gone. . . . All women can learn from Janis and if she couldn't get it together and get out of it, maybe we can."[93]

1973
The Blues Way of Life and Death

Janis had escaped her problems one way; Tina found another. Forced to hide from Ike during their separation and eventual divorce for fear of violence, Turner eventually walked away from legal negotiations, declining to fight for her share of the substantial joint property she and Ike had acquired over the course of their career. But she did fight for one thing: the rights to her professional name, Tina Turner. She knew she could try to rebuild her career as long as her fans knew who she was, and she was right.[94]

With sole custody of the four teenaged children (she was the biological mother of only two of them), Tina struggled to pay her bills and began appearing wherever she could get paid: Hollywood Squares, Canadian casinos, and other second-tier show-business venues. No matter how small the room, however, Tina continued to charm her audiences. She still had it. Eventually, with the help of her new manager, the tireless Roger Davies, she began to craft a new image for herself—one that reflected her taste, not Ike's. "I never tried to be anything else but what I was. . . . I sang rock 'n' roll, and R&B, and blues the whole time." Those who saw her shows had no doubt that Tina had survived the breakup, but she needed a bigger audience. Finally, in 1981, she managed to get a booking at the Ritz nightclub in New York, a city she hadn't played in ten years. Her three nights at the Ritz restarted her career, as the place filled to capacity with celebrities and record-industry executives who had heard the rumors of Tina's comeback. Rod Stewart saw the show and invited her to join him on *Saturday Night Live* that very weekend. Their duet on "Hot Legs" was a sensation, and it gave the American public a chance to see the new Tina: single, happy, hardrocking, and forty-one years old. She had never looked better.[95]

The New York shows were the beginning of Tina Turner's triumphant return to music, sparking a decade-long ascent to a career that eclipsed her achievements with Ike. She reunited with the Rolling Stones, opening this time as a solo act on their North American tour and performing with them in encores of "Honky Tonk Women," which she had covered years earlier. Each new triumph added momentum. Her 1984 album, *Private Dancer*, was a phenomenon, winning three Grammy Awards the following year for Best Female Pop Vocal Performance, Best Female Rock Vocal Performance, and, finally, Record of the Year. Many of her fans at this point were unaware of her dramatic past, but for those who knew what she had been through, her success was extra-sweet. *Private Dancer* stayed in the Top 100 for two years and sold eleven million copies worldwide. Since then, Tina has managed to create one of the biggest careers in entertainment history, appearing in films and continuing to sing and tour. The 1993 film based on her life with Ike, *What's Love Got to Do With It*, not only was a critical success but also revealed to the world the obstacles she had overcome. As Ike Turner faded to a footnote in music history, Tina remained a vital force in popular culture.

~

Both Tina Turner and Janis Joplin began their careers with simple dreams: happiness, some emotional security, and the chance to sing the music they loved. The primal themes of the blues became the soundtrack to their lives, accompanying them from anonymity to fame and through the turbulence of their lives in the spotlight. The blues is about the long way around, not the shortcuts. It's about facing life, not pretending there's no pain to face. Janis Joplin looked the Kozmic Blues in the eye and died a blues death anyway, but decades later, people are still telling her sister Laura that "Janis gave them the strength to speak their own voice, to make their own choices and I just find that an incredible legacy." Turner lived to look back on her blues and use it to infuse her life with greater meaning. "I never allowed myself to get lost," she said. "The whole thing is about earning your way, and you don't really get there until you earn it. That's the real truth."[96]

Chapter Six

BLUES
ATTITUDE

New Orleans, 1971. It's nearly seventy years since Mamie Desdoumes sang her blues to parlors full of sailors and street-walking women. Storyville is long since gone, but the blues remain. Bourbon Street is still there, too, and though prostitution is no longer legal, nor the drugs, the neighborhood has remained appealingly dissolute. In a bar called Andy's, pressed against the strip joints and other dark bars, another young woman only eighteen years old sings the blues . . . well, a version of them. "They're not technically blues songs, but they stem from the emotive quality of the blues," Lucinda Williams (born in 1953) will say later, trying to describe her music. She sings for tips and the gig is good enough for her to drop out of college, or so she feels. It's the beginning of a career, one that will span the next three decades (and counting), weaving its way through the genres of folk, blues, country, and rock 'n' roll. This is one way the blues goes on after Woodstock—as an attitude. Just as it was a hundred years ago, the blues is still a state of mind. "It's such an illusory thing," Williams says. Like the blues musicians before her, she finds it difficult to define the blues, trying to explain what she finds in it that makes it worth writing and singing. "It's so much a feeling," she says, finally.[1]

~

In the decades since Janis Joplin's death and Tina Turner's emergence as a solo phenomenon, the blues have changed. The folk revival of the 1960s had renewed interest in the blues musicians of the early twentieth century, many of whom were still alive. Musicians such as guitarists Skip James, Memphis Minnie, and Son House, and singer Alberta Hunter, were rediscovered by young, mostly white fans who were beginning to appreciate the musical roots of the rock 'n' roll they loved. A wave of British, blues-influenced rock artists—the Rolling Stones, Led Zeppelin, Eric Clapton, Van Morrison—stoked this interest in traditional blues as the young Englishmen paid homage to their elders, along with some American musicians such as Janis Joplin and the Paul Butterfield Blues Band. The rockers covered their songs (Led Zeppelin's version of Memphis Minnie's "When the Levee Breaks" and the Rolling Stones' remake of Robert Johnson's "Love in Vain" were standouts) and invited them on tour, which led to artists such as Lightnin' Hopkins and Muddy Waters playing to throngs of young hippies at San Francisco's Fillmore Auditorium in the 1960s. In 1971, a young, white Harvard graduate named Bonnie Raitt released her first album, on which she covered not only Robert Johnson but also three songs by the great country blueswoman Sippie Wallace. The album was well received, though Raitt would have to wait almost twenty years for her Grammy.

Despite their resurgence in popularity, traditional American blues artists never challenged the record sales of the rock stars who loved them. As the folk/blues revival faded in the 1970s, the blues retained its status as an important part of music history, but its relevance to the present seemed minimal. Blues music was increasingly segregated to its own clubs and music festivals, much like jazz and classical music, no longer part of the mainstream. The blues had become, if not intellectualized, then institutionalized—not a great place to be for a young musician.

The cultural bombshell of 1969's Woodstock festival proved that rock 'n' roll was now the overwhelming influence in mainstream music and the minds of American youth. But popular culture depends on change, and rock, though remaining a dominant cultural force, was challenged on radio airwaves by emerging new sounds: the sexy, strong rhythms of soul and funk, the four-on-the-floor bass thump of disco, the lo-fi whine of punk, techno-propelled New Wave, the crescendo of soft rock power ballads, and the growl of nineties grunge. They all seemed far from the blues music of Bessie Smith and Billie Holiday, but certain artists carried some blues flavor inside them, just as a drop of Mississippi River water dissolves into the Gulf of Mexico. The blues attitude abides.

~

The legacy of the early blueswomen became less clear from the 1970s on. The most obvious problem was the changing status of the blues itself. By the 1980s, blues was a special-interest category, a part of the record store populated by autodidact experts digging through crates of old 78s and newer recordings on small labels far from the engines of the increasingly conglomerated music-industry machines of Los Angeles and New York. Blues had become something one "was into," not simply something in the air. On some level, this had always been true for white blues fans—recall John Hammond sneaking into Harlem's nightclubs in the 1930s—but something strange had happened with the folk/blues revival of the 1960s: now all the blues fans were white. Well, never all. But the audiences for traditional blues in clubs and festivals in the 1980s and 1990s were overwhelmingly so. Which is not to say that the music was any less wonderful or legitimate than it had ever been, because the genius of the blues idiom is its structural purity, and it's hard to ruin something so simple and direct.

One could also argue without contradiction that African-Americans had never stopped listening to the blues, they simply found it somewhere else. When Amiri Baraka (formerly LeRoi Jones) called African-Americans "Blues People," he meant that the blues were simply a part of who they were, and vice versa. They heard the blues in all sorts of music: soul, funk, R&B, disco, hip-hop, and, yes, in rock, and they were right. Little bits of blues were everywhere, whether in the righteous wail of James Brown, the tuning of Jimi Hendrix's guitar or the tales of everyday life rapped over a breakbeat.

The fact was that, like other cultural styles—hipsterism, for example—the blues had simply infiltrated American society on a fundamental level and was now informing aspects of American culture from the ground up. Just as the figure of the 1920s hipster had morphed from a reefer-smoking jazz freak to a 1950s hep cat to a swinging single in the 1970s to a broad array of "hip" figures in the 1980s, 1990s, and beyond, the blues aesthetic and attitude had become a part of American culture, too. Its musical structure survived in rock and funk, as did its predilection for highly personalized vocal styles in music at large, its affirmation of the potentially epic quality of everyday living, and, of course, the bold, brassy, emotional performances of its singers, both women and men. Where would rock be without its *"Baby, baby, I love/miss/need/want you . . . ,"* wailed in a high-pitched singing scream? Nowhere. That's what rock is, and it can't happen without the blues.

Less obvious were the ways in which blues and the great blues-women influenced styles of music and areas of the culture whose roots were not easily traced to turn-of-the-twentieth-century New Orleans or the Mississippi Delta. This is where the blues attitude comes in. If it doesn't exactly sound like the blues, look like the blues, or call itself the blues, yet it still sort of feels like the blues or at least reminds you of it . . . is it the blues? The simple answer is yes. Because the legacy of

the blues and of the blueswomen fans out toward the end of the blues
century. The music may change, but the blues were always about much
more than just the sound of the songs. The blues encompassed a way of
life and worldview. It's here that the legacy of the blueswomen burns
brightest.

1971
Blue, songs are like tattoos.

—*Joni Mitchell*[2]

The blueswomen's musical inheritors have been those who kept pushing against the edges of songwriting and performance, reshaping the
contours of music to fit the changing patterns of women's lives. Joni
Mitchell was one. She was the very picture of a 1960s folk princess,
with her lilting soprano voice, corn-silk blonde hair, and face of a
Nordic angel—the aesthetic opposite, it's fair to say, of Ma Rainey.
Mitchell wasn't a blues singer, not by a long stretch, but with sharp,
surprising songs such as "Woman of Heart and Mind" and "Rainy
Night House," she brought to music the complex inner lives of so
many modern women "so busy being free." As her lyric suggests, the
new freedoms women were fighting for and winning brought their own
problems. As for the blueswomen before her, emotional freedom was a
necessity. "Freedom to me is the luxury of being able to follow the path
of the heart," she said. "Freedom is necessary for me in order to create
and if I cannot create I don't feel alive." Mitchell made public the
loneliness and confusion that faced many strong, idealistic women of
her generation: how can one be free and be loved, too?[3]

While the sound of Mitchell's music was most identifiably drawn
from the canons of folk, jazz, and rock, she returned to the idea of the
blues over and over again in her lyrics—so often, in fact, that she
titled her 1971 album simply *Blue*. Arguably her greatest record (her
passionate fans love to argue), the title captured the deep melancholy

of Mitchell's perspective. Like a great novel, the album could be experienced as a single work of art, each song a chapter in the story of a woman coming to terms with the contradictions and disappointments of love in the age of feminism. *Blue*'s songs—"All I Want," "California," "Blue," "A Case of You," and the others—were specific in their details: a love affair with a "redneck" in Greece, a map of Canada drawn on a coaster in a bar, an ex-boyfriend's marriage to a figure skater. As with the great blues songs of the 1920s, the naming of particulars was no obstacle to her fans as they tried to relate to the stories; the details merely made the singer's experience seem more authentic, as real as their own lives.

Joni Mitchell was already a star by the time *Blue* was released. Her first three albums had connected with an increasingly literate rock audience, and her well-publicized romances with some of rock's leading men contributed to a perception of her as a kind of celebrity girlfriend, albeit a talented one. But *Blue* established Mitchell as a genius in her own right, and in it she addressed the issues of her public image without resorting to the unbearable isn't-it-hard-to-be-a-rock-star line that was taken by some of her contemporaries. Mitchell dealt with the problem not by putting herself on a pedestal but by revealing her most intimate feelings, however unpleasant or ugly. "*Blue* was the first of my confessional albums," she said. "It was an attempt to say, 'You want to worship me? Well, okay, I'm just like you. I'm a lonely person.' Because that's all we have in common." Like Bessie Smith and Billie Holiday, Mitchell used her artistry to become more fully herself, not to hide behind a tune or a lyric. And also like Smith and Holiday, her self-portraiture was immediately understood by her fans. *Blue* was a new version of an old blues, new music for a new era.[4]

As Joni Mitchell's success proved, the blueswomen's goal of communicating the issues in women's lives through their music was just as potent and necessary as it had ever been, and in some ways it was needed even more. The early 1970s provided the stage for the full flowering of the feminist movement, as women who had been radicalized by the civil rights and antiwar movements began to apply their sense of justice to their own experiences as women. They made an effort to communicate explicitly about their frustrations and desires in feminist political meetings, consciousness-raising groups, and in the press, through books such as Kate Millett's *Sexual Politics* and Ms. magazine, both first published in 1971.

They were also becoming more comfortable with the idea of being difficult, as attested to in such documents as *The Bitch Manifesto* (1968), by Joreen (aka Jo Freedman). Bessie Smith's tough attitude found an audience in the 1920s when the first wave of feminism was in the air and women had just gotten the vote, and in the 1970s as second-wave feminists campaigned for abortion rights, state-subsidized child care, and equal pay for equal work. Along with the voices of the older blueswomen, the voices of new, equally tough women were welcomed.

"Jesus died for somebody's sins, but not mine." It doesn't get much tougher than that. From the suburban wilderness of New Jersey emerged a female voice with ten million new things to say. Patti Smith jumped on the stage of the St. Mark's Poetry Project in 1971 with her poem "Oath," her guitarist Lenny Kaye, and a blues attitude that took even New York City's downtown cynics by surprise. By the time she released her first album, *Horses*, in 1975, "Oath" had been transformed into a version of the blues-rock group Them's (fronted by Van Morrison) "Gloria," or perhaps it was the other way around. Morrison's song was itself an homage to traditional blues, the story of a man and his love and lust for a woman. Smith accepted the premise. The straightforward structure and chugging momentum of the song suited her needs, which were to convert this blues song into a vehicle for her own sexuality. In Smith's "Gloria," she takes on the male point of view and intensifies it, maximizing the eroticism of the encounter on her part and on Gloria's, and the song becomes a churning, speeding erotic spell, finally exploding and fading out, just like a night with Gloria herself.[5]

And "Gloria" was just the beginning, for in addition to other songs of lust and rage, there was Smith herself, this waif of a woman with her choppy black hair, skinny pants, and defiant expression to the camera (her lover, friend, and artistic collaborator was the photographer Robert Mapplethorpe). Smith embodied a new female attitude toward the world: she was tough and complicated but also vulnerable and sexy. Her charisma was a reminder that there was more to female beauty than an hourglass figure and long, shiny hair. Those who saw her first poetry performances recognized her power immediately. "[She had] real crowd magnetism," remembered poet Ed Friedman. "She was able to really BE this star presence as a poet—this mix of Rimbaud and Keith Richards and the Velvet Underground and Janis Joplin . . . sort of alternately female and male." Smith's courage to draw on both male and female energies also set her apart. She cited poets Walt Whitman and Arthur Rimbaud and musicians Bob Dylan and Mick Jagger as some of her primary artistic influences. Yet when she first started singing in earnest, she sang the songs of Billie Holiday and "little blues songs . . . I just did what I liked. So our set list would include a couple of Lotte Lenya songs, and a couple of old R&B songs, and [her poem] 'Piss Factory.'" To Smith, they were all of a piece, and she quoted Whitman as an explanation, saying, "We 'contain multitudes.'"[6]

Although she was clearly an independent, strong woman, Smith never hewed to any particular party line, feminist or otherwise, in her music. Like all great artists, she was merely concerned with communicating her personal vision, not the political agenda of any outside group. Yet her music and her personal style were perfectly in tune with the times. Women—and, increasingly, men—were open to a tougher sound that suited the revolutionary times. A blues attitude with its sad wisdom and wry humor came in handy as the seventies wore on: the feminist revolution won and lost its battles, the president lied, the troops died in Vietnam, college students were shot down on an Ohio campus, and the idealism of the sixties faded into a muggy haze.

The doldrums of the 1970s were interrupted from time to time by great music. Mitchell and Smith kept on releasing excellent work, while new forms of R&B and Soul contributed to the decade's sexy, funky soundtrack. Such singers as Chaka Khan and Carla Thomas explored the world of Soul that Aretha Franklin had opened up, and Franklin herself continued to sing, as did Tina Turner and Etta James. The newest sound was disco, and it proved to be a ripe medium for strong women singers, belters such as Gloria Gaynor, whose "I Will Survive" (1979) became a feminist anthem along the lines of Helen Reddy's "I Am Woman" (1972), though Gaynor's was catchier, bluesier, and a thousand times more fun.

~

Lucinda Williams, meanwhile, was meandering through the seventies, too, having traveled from Bourbon Street to Austin to Houston and eventually back to Fayetteville, Arkansas, where her father lived—all the while singing in bars and on the street, practicing her style, especially her songwriting. Just like everyone else that decade, Williams heard the voices of popular singers such as Linda Ronstadt, Dionne Warwick, Barbra Streisand, and Aretha Franklin playing over and over on the radio. "I was really inspired by [women] who could sing their asses off like that," she said, but it was a funny kind of inspiration. Williams's voice was pure in a deep Southern way, its drawl curling around the edges of lyrics like blotting paper on a hot, humid day, and it sounded nothing like Streisand or Franklin.

"That's why I started writing songs," she said, "because I knew I wasn't going to be a singer like that. I used to get real frustrated about it when I listened to Joan Baez, Joni Mitchell, and Judy Collins . . . so I thought I better write songs 'cause I'm gonna be limited vocally." Here she's underselling herself, because her voice is a treasure. Like Billie Holiday, who exploited her perfect timing and drew great soulfulness from her high, wavery voice, Williams made the most of her vocal limitations. She sang up to the raw edges of her range, extending syllables into high notes that dropped right back down again, bringing to mind such great male blues singers as Son House and Skip James. Her strong

Happy Woman's Blues: Lucinda Williams (b. 1953) onstage at the New Orleans Jazz and Heritage Festival in 2003.

Southern accent caressed each vowel like a seduction. All this gilded the lyrics themselves, which were brilliant miniatures of an often-heartbroken life, each song a short story.

The blues figured prominently in her music, from the song structure to its classic themes, but it was only one of many styles she practiced in the 1970s. "I didn't pay attention to whether I was a blues singer or country singer," she said. She was writing her own material but also singing others' songs, as many struggling songwriters do, reeling in an audience with a song they recognize and then presenting them with something brand new. "I did a lot of people's songs: Jimi Hendrix, Jefferson Airplane, Jesse Winchester, Hank Williams, Robert Johnson. I mixed it all. Then when I started writing it was all mixed up, and it kept me from getting a record deal 'cause I didn't know how to market myself. I didn't know, when I first started out, that that was going to be a problem." The music industry relies on music segregation, dividing its artists among various genres (Rock, Country, Blues, etc.) in order to market them more efficiently. Williams's multifaceted sound worried those who might have signed her to a recording deal, since she didn't quite fit the expectations of any one commercial niche. Too white for a blues market obsessed with misguided notions of "authenticity," too raw for the polished sound of contemporary country, and too rootsy for the rock market—or so the thinking went.

She finally found a home with Folkways Records, an independent label based in New York City and known for its recordings of traditional blues and folk music. Signing with Folkways was a quick way to earn credibility with folk and blues purists, since it was the recording home of such musical heroes as Woody Guthrie and Leadbelly. Folkways was (and still is) a terrific label, dedicated to preserving music that might otherwise go unrecorded, but in 1979, the year Williams released her first album, *Ramblin'*, she shared space in the Folkways catalog with such records as *Eugene V. Debs: Trade Unionist, Socialist, Revolutionary* and *The Magic of Belly Dancing*. This was not exactly the fast track to *Rolling Stone*.

Ramblin' was nearly all straight-ahead blues covers, including Memphis Minnie's "Me and My Chauffeur Blues," which belonged to the tradition of great erotic blues songs and told the story of a woman and her unusually close relationship with her driver. Although Williams had been writing songs for the previous decade, "there was the thing of being on Folkways, which was so purist I didn't think they'd take other kinds of stuff," so she didn't use any of her original songs.[7]

Ramblin' was a great album, but there was little hope for making a fulfilling career out of covering traditional blues, especially for a young white woman obsessed with the lyrics of Bob Dylan and the Southern gothic writing of Flannery O'Connor, two of her biggest artistic influences. So her next album for Folkways in 1980, *Happy Woman's Blues*, was blues-influenced but also incorporated folk and country sounds. Most significantly, it contained all her own compositions, exposing her incisive lyrics to the public for the first time. Songs such as "Maria" spoke for generations of blueswomen, describing the pull and the pain of living life on the wing: "Are the songs we sing worth the broken heart?"[8]

Happy Woman's Blues was full of the songwriting that would eventually define Williams's singular aesthetic. They were soulful, sexy, intelligent songs that dealt with the problems of loving the wrong man, or the right man at the wrong time, or some other love combination that added up to romantic disappointment and philosophical questioning about the meaning of it all. Williams loved the blues for its ability to evoke the emotional spectrum—from the thrill of first meeting someone to the agony of losing him years later—but she learned that not everyone interpreted the blues or her music the same way. "There's a kind of stereotype of what a blues singer is, particularly a female blues singer, miserable, crying in her beer," she said. "I don't think people understand that it's a joyful sort of thing." Williams was right, she was fighting a stereotype. More than that, she was up against a music industry that seemed to have no open slots for what she had to offer. She had moved to New York City's Greenwich Village in 1979 in hopes of tracking down its legendary folk scene, but "by the time I actually got there it was right after punk and people walking down the street . . . weren't really happy or romantic or anything like that. I was too late, and I didn't stay long." She did not release another album until 1988.[9]

The 1980s

Blueswomen such as Lucinda Williams and Bonnie Raitt languished in the 1980s, but the decade wasn't all bad news for women working in other genres of popular music. Female voices were a big part of the post-Disco era in the synthetic sounds of New Wave (Blondie, Siouxsie and the Banshees, the Go-Gos) and in dance music (Janet Jackson, Jody Watley). Women got a lot of attention, especially one woman: Madonna.

Madonna (born Madonna Ciccone) was a musical artist—songwriter and singer—whose actual music always seemed somewhat beside the point, overshadowed by her gigantic public persona. When discussing her career, it makes more sense to think of her as simply an entertainer or a pop-culture phenomenon. Working within the dance-pop genre for her entire career, Madonna made gender issues central to her work, always exploring the power and limitations of female stereotypes—from the come-hither dance hits of her 1983 debut, *Madonna* ("Physical Attraction," "Borderline"), to her breakout 1984 album with its erotic koan of a title, *Like a Virgin* ("Material Girl," "Into the Groove"), to virtually every other move she made in the following decades. Madonna was interested in some of the issues made famous by earlier blueswomen—and especially female sexuality—but her musical models came from the disco-dance floors, several times removed from American roots music.

This was true of many women in music in the 1980s. The rise of synthesizers and drum machines gave the decade's music a sharper, less funky sound. And rather than focusing on the drama of everyday life in their lyrics, as the blueswomen had done, the 1980s musicians sought escapism and fantasy—exemplified in the epic, imaginative songs of Kate Bush and Fleetwood Mac's lead singer and lyricist, Stevie Nicks. The punk movement of the 1970s had produced its own female stars, including a number of strong, intentionally abrasive female performers who continued to sing in the 1980s, such as Poly Styrene of X-Ray Spex, Siouxsie Sioux of Siouxsie and the Banshees, and Nina Hagen, none of whom sounded like any women performers who had come before.

There was, however, one area of popular music in which the legends of such singers as Etta James and Aretha Franklin still dominated, and that was in the balladry of R&B, where a new generation of women singers was primed to invade the dark corners of American proms and cineplexes. With mouths agape and lungs bellowing, the Whitney-Mariah-Celine juggernaut launched itself toward the hearts and minds—or, failing that, at least the radio airwaves and *Billboard* charts—of the nation.

Whitney Houston's eponymous 1985 debut was the music-industry equivalent of Columbus's "discovery" of the New World; in each case, something that had existed all along was suddenly exposed as fertile territory for making lots of money. In Houston's case, the tradition of the emotional, dramatic R&B love song, exemplified by Etta James's "At Last" (1961) and Aretha Franklin's "Do Right Woman—Do Right Man" (1967), was revisited and revamped in order to create a new version of an old idea: the power ballad. With her first hit single, "You Give Good Love," Houston reintroduced the concept, combining the smooth sound of contemporary Soul with the gospel-influenced style associated with Aretha Franklin, and working every possible melodic angle in order to emphasize the highs and lows (but especially the highs) of her vocal range. This was more than a #1 smash hit; this was an artistic and economic blueprint. The rest of the album's singles followed in the same format, including the inspirational epic "The Greatest Love of All," whose success finally made *Whitney Houston* the best-selling debut album by a female artist of all time (up to that point), at thirteen million copies.[10]

Houston (born in 1963) was a gifted singer with a rock-solid musical pedigree. Her mother, Cissy Houston, was a talented singer who had worked with Aretha Franklin as part of her backing vocal group, the Sweet Inspirations, and she had recorded well-regarded solo albums in the 1970s. Whitney's musical family also included cousin Dionne Warwick. Like Aretha Franklin and Etta James, Houston began singing in her church choir. She moved onto the stage as a teenager, accompanying her mother, and then launched herself into the bigger world of entertainment, modeling, and acting before being signed to Arista Records by its president, Clive Davis, in 1983. Davis was an industry rainmaker, an executive whose ability to find and support talent matched that of John Hammond and Jerry Wexler. Davis was unique, however, in the breadth of his taste. He was responsible for signing Janis Joplin (as part of Big Brother and the Holding Company) to CBS Records in 1967 and Patti Smith to Arista in 1974.

To Davis, Whitney Houston must have seemed like a gift sent from the industry gods. She had the voice and the ambition to be a huge star, plus she was exceptionally beautiful—a tall, slender vision of elegance. The photograph of Houston on the cover of her debut album could have been mistaken for a fashion layout from *Vogue*, as Houston sat with regal posture in a toga-like gown, pearls around her long neck and her makeup perfectly applied. Joplin and Smith may have earned Clive Davis industry credibility, but Houston was about to earn him a great deal more money and change the industry's expectations of how its singers needed to look and sound.

The music industry has always loved beautiful women—just think back to the "canaries" of Billie Holiday's era—but the advent of the Soul and Rock eras in the 1960s had created more space for women who didn't fit the mold—Etta James, Nina Simone, Aretha Franklin, Janis Joplin, and Carole King, among many others. The phenomenon that was Whitney Houston was the start of a new era in the recording industry. From this point on, *sounding* incredible was not enough—in fact, in some cases it hardly mattered—*looking* incredible was now a priority.

Which is not to say that Houston wasn't a talented singer. She could sing the hell out of any song offered to her, but that wasn't necessarily a good thing. Houston's success also signaled the beginning of another trend in popular music—singing as an expression of technical achievement, rather than as a credible expression of emotional depth. Houston's records were a triumph of production, relying on the work of numerous studio engineers, songwriters, arrangers, technical assistants, and backing vocalists to create a shiny, flawless sound. When Phil Spector used a 100-piece orchestra and three grand pianos in his 1960s recordings, he was considered extreme. By the time Whitney Houston recorded her first album, such practices were becoming much more commonplace, and the cost of record production kept rising. Partly due to increasingly complicated recording technology, there was also a keeping-up-with-the-Joneses element at work. Houston's magnificent voice needed (so the thinking went) an equally grandiose context. But the result, though technically perfect and commercially successful, was surprisingly bland. Yes, there were some thrilling moments in "The Greatest Love of All," but in general the listener was left merely impressed with her talent, not touched by her emotional intimacy—the way Aretha Franklin, or even Tina Turner in the Spector–produced "River Deep, Mountain High," could make one feel. The acknowledgments for Houston's 1985 debut cited some twenty-one people (musicians and backup singers) with performing credits and thirty-two with technical credits. Aretha Franklin's 1967 debut on Atlantic acknowledged only eleven performers (including herself) and just two technical credits. The sound of the eighties and nineties was bigger, but not necessarily better.

Houston became America's go-to girl for such Big Song moments as the Super Bowl and the Olympics; wherever "The Star-Spangled

Banner" needed singing, Houston was there. Her style was a perfect match for the Reagan era, full of the excess and superficial charm that characterized the decade's preferred aesthetic, from *Dallas* to crack cocaine. And, like Ronald Reagan, the "Teflon President," Houston was a smooth, slick paragon of musical achievement whose success made her impervious to criticism—not that there was very much. She had exposed and then immediately filled a previously overlooked niche in the mainstream music market, and other young, beautiful vocal gymnasts were eager to take her place. After Reagan stepped down and the 1990s began, Whitney wannabes such as the five-octave-voiced Mariah Carey and the future queen of the movie sound-tracks, Celine Dion, were humming their scales and watching their diets, preparing for their own National Anthem moments.

And of course they did succeed. Both Carey and Dion released their debuts in 1990. Carey followed Whitney Houston's template to the letter, from naming her debut album after herself to earning four #1 singles and winning that year's Grammy for Best Female Pop Vocal Performance, just as Houston had done in 1985. Dion's debut was a hit, but not as big as Carey's. Not until the mid-1990s did she get the Olympic (Atlanta, 1996) and *Titanic* moments toward which she had been working. Dion's rendition of "My Heart Will Go On (Love Theme from *Titanic*)" (1997), with its soaring crescendo, challenged Whitney Houston's "I Will Always Love You" (1993) for the decade's top prize for overachievement in singing. It established this ornate, dramatic style as the mainstream's idea of what a real singer should sound like, as was evidenced by the ascendance of similarly histrionic singers in other genres—Shania Twain and Faith Hill in country music and Christina Aguilera and Beyoncé Knowles in pop.

All of these drama queens were quick to cite earlier artists such as Aretha Franklin and Etta James as key influences, but they seemed to have misinterpreted their legacy. Blessed with vocal talent, this new generation of women singers was loath to hold back anything, prefer-ring to jump from one high point of the music to the next in an attempt to maintain the listener's attention. Franklin was often remembered for her swooping, gospel-influenced embellishments. The fact that these vocal elements were embellishments—used sparingly to emphasize the emotional intensity of key parts of specific songs—seemed to have been forgotten. Audiences witnessed this difference in action at a 1998 charity concert organized by the television channel VH1. Called "Divas Live," it brought together several of the younger-generation "divas" (Celine Dion, Mariah Carey, Gloria Estefan, and Shania Twain) with Carole King and Aretha Franklin. After an evening of young women attempting to outdo each other with vocal pyrotechnics, Franklin stepped in and "went to church," as the saying goes, demolishing any notion that her singing belonged to a bygone era. The "Divas" concert quickly became a VH1 franchise, and the following year Tina Turner played the part of "elder stateswoman" to younger singers such as Whitney Houston, Mary J. Blige, and Faith Hill.

Sadly, the presence of such blues-influenced singers as Franklin and Turner seemed to encourage their protégées to work even more baroque vocal curlicues into their songs, in a desperate attempt to keep up with their idols. The "Divas" concerts were good for the careers of the older singers who had first created the pop-diva genre, but they also cemented oversinging as the pop status quo. Proof of this can be found in each episode of television's *American Idol*, where every singer, male and female, apparently feels compelled to approach a song as if it were an ascent on Everest—and the result is just as exhausting.

The 1980s and 1990s
Alternatives and Anti-Divas

Not every woman singer followed the Whitney Houston approach to musical success. In fact, many women didn't sing at all. Hip-hop was born in the late 1970s in New York City, and by the mid-1980s, women MCs, or rappers, were making noise. Early hip-hop was basically party music, with a lyrical focus on having a good time with a dose of competition among fellow MCs as to whose lyrics were the best. One of the earliest women rappers started her career the same way Etta James had, by creating an "answer song" in response to an already established hit. In 1984, fourteen-year-old Roxanne Shanté recorded "Roxanne's Revenge" in response to the hit "Roxanne" by U.T.F.O. Shante's was just the first of a wave of more than a hundred "Roxanne"-inspired raps by women, each of whom claimed to be the "real" Roxanne. This avalanche of female hip-hop recordings unfortunately did not lead to a bigger role for women in the genre over the following years. Although many female rappers came and went (MC Lyte and Monie Love among them) in the late 1980s, none achieved the success of such male rappers as Kurtis Blow or LL Cool J.

By the end of the 1980s, rap lost its carefree patina when artists such as Public Enemy and Boogie Down Productions started to use the music as a platform for increasingly critical sociopolitical messages. This was protest music, and if Public Enemy's Chuck D was the movement's Bob Dylan, the LA–based rap group N.W.A. (Niggaz With Attitudes) was its Weather Underground, forever changing the hip-hop landscape with its violent aesthetic. One of the cornerstones of N.W.A.'s aesthetic was its misogyny, exemplified in such songs as "A Bitch Is a Bitch" and "Findum, Fuckum & Flee." Although the group's chaotic, energized, and aggressive sound was notable in its own right, N.W.A. became one of the most influential bands in hip-hop due to its focus on the glamour of crime and cruelty to women. N.W.A.'s 1988 debut album, *Straight Outta Compton*, became as significant a template for the next decade of rap as Whitney Houston's had been for the ballad, and subsequent groups such as 2 Live Crew and the Geto Boys were able to build entire careers around these themes, despite virtually no radio airplay. As hip-hop became a more mainstream musical form in the 1990s, violence and misogyny were simply accepted as basic features of the genre. Middle-class rappers endlessly tried to prove their "gangsta" credentials, and women usually were referred to as "bitches" or "hos."

This absurd posturing was at first offensive and eventually just bor-ing. Although Parental Advisory stickers began appearing on music in 1990, a more effective protest against hip-hop's sexism came from within the community, as women rappers began to make some noise. Salt 'n' Pepa, a trio made up of rappers Cheryl "Salt" James, Sandy "Pepa" Denton, and DJ Dee Dee "Spinderella" Roper, approached the issue in a way that harkened back to the early blueswomen, focusing their energy not on overtly political themes but on asserting the power of female sexuality. Their songs "Push It" (1987) and "Let's Talk About Sex" (1991) positioned women as strong sexual aggressors, emphasiz-ing not only female sexual pleasure but also the control that women needed to take over their own sexuality. Salt 'n' Pepa and other women rappers, such as MC Lyte, Monie Love, and Yo-Yo, used their songs as vehicles for criticizing men who mistreated them or were oth-erwise out of line.

Building on this tradition, Queen Latifah (born Dana Owens in New Jersey in 1970) emerged in the 1990s as the most prominent fem-inist hip-hop artist. Taking a cue from the black-is-beautiful ethos of Public Enemy, Latifah dressed in Afrocentric clothing and used the royal moniker of "Queen" in a purposeful attempt to distinguish her-self from other rappers (who usually went by the term "MC"). "I didn't want to wear gold chains and call myself MC Latifah. I threw a crown on." In doing so, Latifah drew on the legacy of early blueswomen who competed for the titles of "Queen" and "Empress" of the Blues: Ma Rainey, Bessie Smith, Ida Cox, Sippie Wallace, Koko Taylor, and numerous others. Like the royal blueswomen, Latifah created a public persona that was based on strength and demanded respect. "I estab-lished my attitude from the beginning," she said: "You can't push me over."[11]

Albums such as *All Hail the Queen* (1989) and *Black Reign* (1993), including such songs as "Ladies First" (featuring Monie Love) and

"U.N.I.T.Y.," established Queen Latifah as the preeminent feminist voice in hip-hop, as well as a successful entertainment-industry entrepreneur. By the mid-nineties, she had won a Grammy for Best Solo Rap Performance, started her own management company to guide the careers of other hip-hop artists, and launched an acting career that eventually would earn her an Oscar nomination for the hit movie *Chicago*, in which she played Big Mama Morton, a tough, sexy, blues-singing prison matron straight out of the Bessie Smith tradition. Her example also set the stage for a new wave of women hip-hop artists— Mary J. Blige, Lauryn Hill, Erykah Badu, and Missy Elliott.

This new generation of artists integrated the feminist messages of women's rap with the music of R&B and Soul, their vocals often switching, midsong, from rapping to singing. Mary J. Blige, Erykah Badu, and Lauryn Hill came of age in a hip-hop era and it informed all their work, but the influence of earlier musical forms, such as the Soul singing of Aretha Franklin and the 1970s R&B of Roberta Flack, was even stronger. Like Queen Latifah and the early blueswomen, Blige, Hill, and Badu assumed the stage with an air of confidence and a regal poise, uninterested in playing the coquette. Blige (born in 1971), who had grown up in the housing projects of Yonkers, New York, made a point of singing about the difficulties of living poor and of the struggle to succeed. As with all blueswomen, though, her main theme was love, and when faced with the choice of singing a perfect note or expressing a raw emotion, emotion always won.

Erykah Badu was much smoother than Blige, with a mystical, spiritual aesthetic more evocative of the imperious Nina Simone than of Bessie Smith. With her signature towering headwrap and flowing robes, the elegant Badu (born in 1972 in Texas as Erica Wright) was still down to earth in her attitudes toward human relationships. Her song "Tyrone," which appeared on her *Live* album in 1997, was a straight update of a blues queen's tough-talking song directed toward irresponsible men. From its opening line, "I'm gettin' tired of your shit," Badu lays down the law, singing her sexy, slow jam to an audience full of cheering, laughing women. The success of "Tyrone" proved not only that the problems between men and women were unchanging, but that the world still needed its blueswomen to point this out.[12]

But no other hip-hop artists invoked the power of the blueswomen with more style or success than Lauryn Hill, another New Jersey native (born in 1975), who began her career as the female member of the hip-hop trio The Fugees. After establishing herself as a performer on their update of Roberta Flack's "Killing Me Softly," Hill struck out on her own in 1998, releasing *The Miseducation of Lauryn Hill*, on which she performed, wrote, and produced almost every song. The album's title referred to a classic text in African-American history, Carter G. Woodson's *Miseducation of the Negro* (1933), a manifesto for black empowerment. Hill's choice of album title and her lyrical focus suggested that internalized oppression—for blacks and women, too—was still a problem. Hill tried to counter it with a strong blues attitude, and her lyrics focused on her own struggle to be a stronger, more conscious person. "I gave up my power, ceased being queen," she sings in "I Used to Love Him," a cautionary tale that ends with Hill's regaining control of her own life. Other songs lament prevailing Eurocentric notions of beauty and the way women allow themselves to be undervalued. Overall, the album's message is one of black female power and pride: "My emancipation don't fit your equation."[13]

The Miseducation of Lauryn Hill was a huge success, earning Hill the most Grammy awards ever for a woman artist (of the eleven for which she was nominated, she won five, including Album of the Year) and also solidifying hip-hop's place in the popular-music mainstream, since *Miseducation* was the first hip-hop album ever to win that accolade. The women artists of hip-hop had transformed the genre from a platform for misogynist one-upmanship into an art form capable of expressing a diverse range of experience. By the end of the 1990s, women often were creating the most interesting hip-hop music around and had made the title of "Queen" their own.

~

The blues attitude survived in other corners of the culture, as well. While women in hip-hop had appropriated the notion of royalty, focusing their energy on gaining the respect of their community, another group of women musicians thumbed its nose at the whole idea, adopting an attitude closer to that of Bessie Smith's classic, "'Tain't Nobody's Business If I Do." Following the path of Patti Smith, a whole generation of punk-rock girls came of age in the late 1980s and early 1990s, looking to the harsh, hard-rocking sounds of punk as a medium for their emotional and political imperatives.

The late 1980s saw the rise of college radio stations as an outlet for what would become known as alternative or indie rock—music that was too edgy, raw, or challenging to get on the Top 40 stations ("indie" referred to the record companies producing them, which were *independent* of the major-label recording industry). College radio championed some of the decade's most original and, ultimately, influential rock artists, from R.E.M. and U2 to such women artists as Throwing Muses and Sonic Youth's Kim Gordon. As diverse as they were, most alternative bands shared a DIY attitude taken from the early days of punk. In the early 1990s, this attitude became the organizing principle of one of the decade's most radical cultural movements, the "Stolen Sharpie Revolution" known as Riot Grrl.[14]

Riot Grrl was a feminist revolutionary phenomenon that incorporated music, visual art, political activism, and the making and distribution of " 'zines," homemade manifestos and newsletters that chronicled the frustrations and ecstasy of being a young woman in a patriarchal society. (The stolen Sharpie pens were part of the quasi-Marxist 'zine culture, which encouraged the petty theft of office supplies in the service of feminist empowerment as a legitimate form of co-opting the means of production. The Sharpies would then be used to draw cute flowers on one's arm or belly, with the word "SLUT" or "WHORE" underneath—very Riot Grrl.) Juxtaposing an "I Enjoy

Being a Girl" whimsy (baby-doll dresses, reclamation of the word *girl*) with hard-core feminist politics (combat boots, reclamation of the word *cunt*), bands such as Bikini Kill, Bratmobile, and Babes in Toyland were among the many groups that became associated with Riot Grrl—a movement that, in accordance with its DIY ethos, explicitly rejected defining itself. For some young women, Riot Grrl meant meeting up with other women to talk openly about rape; for others it was deciding to start a band on Friday and performing on Saturday night; and for many it was the experience of sitting alone in one's bedroom, creating collages of drawings, photos, and words to create a personal 'zine.

Kat Bjelland (born in 1963) was initially part of the latter group. "I'd listen to Billie Holiday, read Sylvia Plath, drink Kahlua from my dad's liquor cabinet, and fantasize how I was going to get the fuck out of here," she said of her teenage existence. While Billie Holiday was still a meaningful figure for strong-minded young women like Bjelland, there obviously was a bigger (or at least angrier) future in punk. Like many Riot Grrl musicians—and not unlike Billie Holiday's early employment in the sex-work trade—Bjelland worked for a while as a stripper, finding it an efficient if boring way to make money. (Bikini Kill lead singer Kathleen Hanna did, too. "I've been a waitress, and I hated that much more than taking my clothes off for money.") Bjelland and a fellow stripper named Courtney Love next formed a band called Sugar Baby Doll, and although that band eventually dissolved, both Bjelland and Love went on to influence the sound of 1990s rock—Bjelland as lead singer and guitarist of Babes in Toyland, Love as singer, guitarist, and songwriter for the band Hole.[15]

~

No chronicle of women with attitude would be complete without the mention of the fabulously self-contradicting Courtney Love. She was born in 1964 in San Francisco, right around the time Janis Joplin moved back there from Texas, and maybe there was something in the

Courtney Love (b. 1964), the bad girl's angel, performing at the 1999 Glastonbury Festival in England. RUNE HELLESTAD/CORBIS

water or the air, because no woman musician since Janis Joplin has outraged the mainstream music press as has Courtney Love. Just as male journalists felt compelled to put down Joplin for her bad skin or frizzy hair, so have many contemporary commentators enjoyed criticizing Love's often slatternly appearance. The fact that Love's provocative hair, makeup, and clothing have always been part of her publicity strategy seemed to escape most of them. Like a true Riot Grrl (although she protested any association with the movement and complained that it promoted unprofessional musicians), Love enjoyed subverting mainstream expectations of how women ought to look, act, and sound.

Hole's first album, *Pretty on the Inside* (1991), was a well-received blast of punk rock and established Love's favorite themes: sex, anger, and the eternal good girl/bad girl conflict that has been dogging women since Eve tasted the apple. Hole was just establishing itself as an up-and-coming part of the nascent Seattle-based grunge rock movement when Love married fellow rocker Kurt Cobain in 1992, a move that would change her life forever. Cobain was the lead singer and songwriter of Nirvana, a group on the verge of becoming the biggest rock band in America, thanks to their Zeitgeist-defining album *Nevermind* (1991) and its lead single, "Smells Like Teen Spirit." Suddenly, Love was no longer simply an angry punk rock girl but the lesser half of a rock couple, and Cobain's newfound recognition as the voice of his generation marked the beginning of Love's Yoko Ono phase.

The early 1990s saw its share of 1970s reruns: Iran-Contra was the new Watergate (without the consequences), underemployed post-college "slackers" were the latest manifestation of Nixon's despised "bums," and Courtney Love was the new black widow of rock. Just as Beatles fans had blamed Yoko Ono for breaking up the band and allegedly stealing John Lennon from the limelight, so Cobain's fans resented Courtney Love for distracting him from his public and for demanding to be taken seriously as an artist in her own right. She was publicly excoriated when rumors spread that she used heroin while pregnant with Cobain's child, and the news that Geffen Records had signed Hole to a contract rivaling Nirvana's was seen as proof of Love's parasitic relationship with Cobain. Although Cobain continuously protested the way his wife was treated by the press and the public, nothing he said seemed to make a difference. Like John Lennon, Cobain was a self-professed feminist who was disgusted by the public response to his wife, as his private diary (later published) revealed: "Courtney, when I say I love you I am not ashamed, nor will anyone ever come close to intimidating persuading, etc me into thinking otherwise. I wear you on my sleeve."[16]

And like Lennon and Ono, who shocked even their most liberal fans when Lennon retired from performing in order to be a full-time father to his son Sean, Cobain and Love subverted mainstream ideas about gender roles when he wore her dresses onstage and Love confidently acted the part of protector to her fragile, effeminate husband. The situation finally climaxed when Cobain was found dead of a self-inflicted shotgun wound in April 1994, and Love was forced into the position of public widowhood.

Americans tend to like their widows quiet, meek, and gracious. So when Love organized a memorial gathering for the public and then urged the crowd of young fans to join her in chanting obscenities at her dead husband, a new chapter opened in Love's public image. She read excerpts of his suicide note, in which Cobain complained that being a rock star had become a tiresome burden, but she omitted his description of her: "I have a goddess of a wife who sweats ambition and empathy. . . . I love you I love you." Was it just too personal, or did she fear that the mention of the word "ambition" would just stir up old controversies? It's hard to imagine that Love was worried about the latter, since she had built her career on provocation. So while Love's anguish over her husband's death was apparent to all, her subsequent behavior—drug overdoses leading to the temporary loss of custody of her daughter Frances, public romances with various rock stars, and her typically brash, opinionated interviews—combined with the success of Hole's next presciently titled album, *Live Through This* (released, according to previous schedule, just weeks after Cobain's death), made Courtney Love one of the most controversial women musicians of all time.[17]

Like Ma Rainey, Bessie Smith, Billie Holiday, and Etta James, Courtney Love never tried to hide the truth about her lifestyle from her fans. She took drugs, flirted with women and men, and struggled with the double standard women faced in the entertainment industry, choosing to confront the issue publicly rather than pretend it didn't exist. She had cosmetic surgery after Cobain's death and told a journalist she did it "so I would take better photographs and sell records and not be considered the way [former all-girl band] Frightwig was considered—'Oh, they're fat, they're ugly, no wonder they're screaming.' . . . I want my anger to be valid, and the only way to do that is to be fairly attractive." Janis Joplin had faced similar issues in her day, and always had longed to be more conventionally beautiful. It's hard to imagine Joplin getting a nose job, but if it had been more easily available in 1970, who knows? Love certainly didn't see it as a conflict with her feminism (though Cobain might have)—it was just a way to make her life easier as a woman in the public eye.[18]

Live Through This brought the intimate world of Riot Grrl–style female rage to the mainstream (though Love was still feuding with Riot Grrl and criticized the movement in "Rockstar," the album's final track), with songs such as "Miss World" and "Doll Parts," which reinterpreted traditionally feminine icons as symbols of self-loathing and disgust. The album was a critical and popular hit and earned Love a devoted following of young women who identified with her anger and defended her against the incessant sniping of Cobain's self-appointed legacy-keepers. Her fans—just like those of Rainey, Smith, Holiday, and Joplin—saw Love for what she was: a strong, complex, often troubled but talented woman willing to tell the truth about her experience and share it with her audience. She was a mess, but she was real.

Like the blueswomen before her, Love was hard to intimidate. It wasn't easy to understand where she found the courage to defend herself against constant rumors that her late husband was the real author of her songs, or that she herself had murdered Cobain. But not only did she continue to record and perform great songs, she also did something unprecedented in the history of popular music: she took the recording industry to court to protest its allegedly unfair labor practices, something musicians had been complaining about since the earliest days of recording. In an open letter to the Recording Industry Association of America (RIAA) in 2000, Love accused the industry of piracy and conspiring to steal artists' work and subsequent profits in a decades-long tradition of legal chicanery. Describing herself as a "defiant moody artist worth my salt," Love argued on behalf of all musicians trapped in the system and pressured to conform to a prepackaged marketing vision. "If you want some little obedient slave content provider, then fine. But I think most musicians don't want to be responsible for your clean-cut, wholesome, all-American, sugar corrosive cancer-causing, all white people, no women allowed sodapop images," she said. Although her decision to settle out of court with her record company in 2002 took the sting out of Love's righteous crusade, she vowed to continue lobbying and pushing for musicians' collective-bargaining rights on the issue.

Love may not have been a blueswoman in any traditional sense, but she was willing to live according to the blueswoman ethos of speaking truth to power. And she was well aware of the risks facing women who challenged the status quo, though her share of the Nirvana song catalog and inheritance of Cobain's multimillion-dollar fortune ensured her economic security. "Maybe my self-destructive streak will finally pay off and serve a community desperately in need of it," Love said at the time of her initial RIAA attack. "They can't torture me like they could Lucinda Williams."[19]

1988 . . .
World Without Tears

A lot had changed in Lucinda Williams's life, as Love's evocation suggested. Somehow she had gone from being just another struggling
singer/songwriter in the early 1980s to an icon of music industry mis-
fortune by the end of the 1990s. Love's interpretation—that Williams
had been "tortured" by the music industry—was not as exaggerated as
it sounded. After releasing her second and final album with Folkways
in 1980, *Happy Woman's Blues*, she went eight years before signing
another record deal, finally getting a reprieve as the indie rock world
caught up to her sound. Rough Trade, a label previously known for its
punk records, in 1988 released the album *Lucinda Williams*, full of
carefully written, poignant songs, each one containing the small but
truth-telling details of a life, and it was easy to imagine they were
autobiographical. *Lucinda Williams* was a good title for her third
album—not just because it was so intimate, but because it served to
introduce her to a wider audience than the blues and folk fans who
had bought her first two albums almost a decade earlier. Her sound
was a little more rock 'n' roll now, though it still retained the rootsy
sound of the blues. But not many rock songs in 1988 dealt with the
issues Williams did. "Change the Locks" was a relentless dark groove
of a song, either dedicated to a stalker or simply the expression of
someone who really, really wants to get over her last breakup. "Side
of the Road" described the feeling so many women have experienced of
wanting to connect with a part of themselves that often gets abandoned when they enter a relationship: "I wanna know you're there,
but I wanna be alone." The album was a critical success and sold
respectably for an indie label, but its greatest success came when other
artists covered its songs, most notably Mary Chapin-Carpenter's 1994
Grammy-winning version of "Passionate Kisses."[20]

It wasn't good enough—living between songwriting royalty checks, playing small clubs, getting lots of praise from fellow musicians and even record executives, yet still working day jobs to pay the bills (praise is cheap). What was her alternative? She had dropped out of college in 1970 to play songs for tips in a bar on Bourbon Street, and somehow, eighteen years later, she was living in Los Angeles and still looking for a break. "I had to keep doing it, I thought sort of by default. I'd made the choice, and I was so deep into it that I had to keep going." She had shopped her demo tapes to executives at the major labels, most of whom agreed that her songs were wonderful yet unmarketable, their sounds too uncategorizable to fit into the preordained marketing matrix. Before Rough Trade came along, Williams had been briefly signed to RCA, but the man who hired her was fired, so she was left to the wolves again, listening to "other people, who have always been men, telling me what I should sound like." She got tired of listening and walked out on the deal.[21]

Williams knew that "you always end up giving some things up and compromising along the way," but by the early 1990s, she had almost nothing substantial to her name except the songs she had written, so she refused to compromise there. "You can't be a good artist without vision," she said. "The only thing that lasts is your art and principles and staying true to them." Her next album, four years later, was *Sweet Old World*; it was on a new label, which quickly folded. Once again, Williams's songs were praised and eventually covered by her peers but rarely heard on FM radio. *Sweet Old World* contained some of her greatest songs, including the title track (later covered by Emmylou Harris and Steve Earle), a song sung for a dead friend, and the poignant "Little Angel, Little Brother." The pitiless lyrics of "Pineola" sounded like something her hero Flannery O'Connor might have written. The song begins, "When Daddy told me what happened I couldn't believe what he just said/Sonny shot himself with a .44 and they found him lyin' on his bed."[22]

Songs like these were easily misinterpreted as the sound of a woman coming unhinged. The darkness in her music, combined with the long lapses between albums, started to earn Williams a reputation for being a difficult artist and a troubled woman. To Williams, this was all a misunderstanding—but of course the industry and the public had always misunderstood her. Still, she was puzzled by the way people reacted to her songs: "They seem to always bring up that my music is so dark, that there's a kind of darkness or sadness to it, and I'm always kind of amazed by that. I mean, why mine more than anyone else's—Bob Dylan, Leonard Cohen, Joni Mitchell—they all wrote dark songs." But their songs, though sad, were rarely as emotionally raw as Williams's, and this she attributed to the blues. "It occurred to me that maybe that's what people are picking up from my songs even though they're not blues songs per se, like a song like 'Side of the Road' which is not technically a blues song, but because I started out with the blues, it was steeped in it." Williams's father had introduced her to the blues as a teenager, playing his favorite Bessie Smith and Dinah Washington records in the house. But when one of his students brought over Bob Dylan's *Highway 61 Revisited* (1965), the then-twelve-year-old Lucinda had what she described as "a huge awakening. . . . I didn't understand it all at the time. . . . but I made a mental note."

It was Dylan who showed her that the literary tradition she loved (her father, Miller Williams, is a poet, and Lucinda wrote poetry from early childhood on) could be wedded to the music that moved her—whether the folk songs of Pete Seeger and Joan Baez, the country of Hank Williams or the blues of Robert Johnson and Bessie Smith. "When I discovered the blues I just ate it up, every bone in my body was soaked in the blues and I kind of discovered myself in it," she said. "But at the same time I think I made a conscious decision that I wasn't going to be a blues artist necessarily, just limited to that idiom, simply because I wanted to write about other things too. If I sang blues then I was going to be singing other people's songs, 'cause to me there's no point in writing *new* blues songs that sound like old blues songs."

Decades later, at the age of forty, she was doing just that, writing and singing blues songs that didn't sound like the old ones yet still communicated the same emotional punch. But the blues in her songs made people wonder: why did she have to sound so sad? For Williams, it all came down to the question of musical genres, the tendency to categorize music as a shortcut to understanding it. "That emotive quality seems to be more readily accepted in blues and jazz," she said. "My stuff still stems from that blues thing, emotionally, the emotive quality of the blues, and maybe that might be what people might be responding to subliminally." The constant critique of her "sad" songs felt "like a put-down" at times. And, truly, she would have had an easier time of it had she stuck to playing the traditional blues and the blues festivals, where audiences expected a certain level of emotional honesty. "I wouldn't imagine someone going up to [blues legend] Howlin' Wolf: 'God, Howlin', your songs are so dark, why do you write such dark, sad songs?' and yet they come up to me. Maybe it's a female thing, they just can't handle that a woman can express herself to that extent." For most of her career, Lucinda Williams had been a blueswoman trapped out of time.

Six long years passed between *Sweet Old World* and the 1998 release of Williams's next album, *Car Wheels on a Gravel Road*, but they were important years despite her lack of presence in the public sphere. Certain country and blues artists—Emmylou Harris, Bonnie Raitt, Shawn Colvin, and others—were making successful transitions to the mainstream rock world, and the public's acceptance of their work made Williams's future look a little brighter. This time, instead of the delay between albums resulting in public amnesia, tension and rumors grew surrounding Williams's supposedly obsessive recording demands. It's true that she recorded *Car Wheels* from scratch three separate times with three different producers, but when an artist is hitting middle age without even one album that the industry will acknowledge as a hit, could anyone blame her for wanting to make a success—just once?

The time lag also had something to do with Williams's other ongoing problem, the mergers-and-acquisitions game within the record industry, which had sabotaged her attempts to plot out a career so many times before. Two labels dissolved beneath her while she worked on *Car Wheels*—this was the "torture" to which Courtney Love referred. For an established musician, losing one's record label is a form of homelessness. "It's always a constant uphill struggle," Williams admitted. As a fan of older music, she knew something about the history of the industry and she knew it didn't have to be this way. "In the past, you had the John Hammonds at Columbia who had tenure and stature. These guys had great vision and passion." But Hammond was gone and Williams had to function as her own industry champion.[23]

Thankfully, the country label Mercury stepped in at the last minute and released the album—and won the Williams jackpot. Finally, the sound of Lucinda Williams had intersected with the Zeitgeist. *Car Wheels on a Gravel Road* made it to #65 on the *Billboard* chart and won a Grammy award for Best Contemporary Folk Album. "That's the category they put us in," Williams said, "me, Steve Earle, Tom Waits— the ones who don't have hits on the radio." It may not have been the cover of *Rolling Stone*, but nevertheless Williams was a well-kept secret no more.[24]

~

Roots music—based on country, folk, and blues—experienced a revival at the tail end of the twentieth century. This time, instead of being confined to folk festivals, the music was part of the mainstream, an alternative to the avalanche of pop product flooding the market courtesy of boy bands and Britney Spears. Musicians from the 1960s and 1970s, such as Bob Dylan, Johnny Cash, Bonnie Raitt, and Emmylou Harris, found a new generation of fans in the so-called alt-country scene, and they embraced Lucinda Williams, too. A generation raised on the synthetic rhythms of New Wave seemed drawn to the organic, analog sound of early American music. But it wasn't just a nostalgia trip. Williams's songs, like those of Bonnie Raitt and Emmylou Harris, were specifically about modern women and their lives. "It's something I learned from Bob Dylan," Williams explained. "His lyrics were very contemporary, but he based everything musically on all the old traditional idioms, all folk and country and blues, which is what my stuff musically has been based on, too. When I listen to blues it doesn't make me feel bad, necessarily; I don't experience music that way."

The success of *Car Wheels on a Gravel Road* didn't change Williams's sound. If anything, it validated her longtime songwriting goals. Her subsequent album, *Essence* (2001), was stripped down to the bare sound of Williams's raw voice and lyrics, as if reaffirming her blues roots. "You can count your blessings," she sang, "I'll just count on blue." Recognition as a contemporary blueswoman brought with it the stereotypes long associated with the genre, however. Critics focused on her lovelorn themes, speculating that she was some kind of self-punishing martyr to romance, (supposedly) like the blueswomen who came before her. "It's been hard to dispel that image. . . . I've always identified with blues singers in that way, and I've always considered Billie Holiday a feminist in her own right and Janis Joplin, too. Just because she's singing about her man—that's personal pain, that has nothing to do with feminist politics!" Now that Williams's celebrity had increased, so had the scrutiny of her private life. Having admitted that her songs were mostly autobiographical, she saw her love life scrutinized like an open book. Williams didn't shy away from the stickiest subjects, either; sex, jealousy, and regret were all fodder for her music, and her stormy personal relationships with various musicians were fairly well known. Journalists loved to focus on Williams's so-called love affair with loss. But while the sad songs of Billie Holiday and Janis Joplin often seemed to define them, Williams the songwriter was able to use her songs to her own advantage, sometimes skewering ex-boyfriends in the process. "One guy I wrote several songs about, I think he felt a little self-conscious about it and he said, 'Well, that will teach me to go out with a songwriter.' I guess it's a little hard on that end," she said. As the songwriter, she always had the last word.[25]

Williams shrugged off the criticism and in 2003 released *World Without Tears*, one of her strongest albums, which climbed to #18 on the *Billboard* chart. Williams brought the blues into the mainstream, with the first single, a sexy groove called "Righteously," going to #36. At age fifty, and after three decades of paying her dues, Lucinda Williams proved that the blues were still relevant and there was still an audience for the "modern day blues songs" she wanted to write. "A lot of us have experienced a little bit of trouble in our backgrounds," Williams pointed out. "It's no different than Bessie Smith or Billie Holiday singing about how her man treated her badly. I'm just taking it a step further and making it a little more intellectual I guess, but it's still coming from the same place."[26]

Many of the songs on *World Without Tears* reflect the themes of the earliest blues—love, pain, and the eternal need for connection with another person. But the title song is about the importance of emotion itself. What kind of life would it be, Williams wonders, without the exquisite touch of deep sadness? Would life be worth living at all? Without the blues, how would we share our human pain? In a world without tears, she asks, "How would sorrow find a home?"[27]

Dig Me If You Dare

The human voice is the most basic musical instrument, and surely the first song ever sung was one about love. What makes the songs of twentieth-century blueswomen any different?

The twentieth century itself was different, especially in the United States. American women not only gained radically new political and social freedoms but also managed to make the issues that mattered to them the subject of a hundred years of public debate. Some of this was a result of political activism. And some of it was the result of women who made their opinions heard in another way: through song.

Whether it was the booming voice of Ma Rainey working her way through the tent shows of the American South, or the rich sound of Bessie Smith rolling out of the big black horn of the Victrola, the power of the early blueswomen was the first sign that black culture was going to shape the look and sound of the American Century. Billie Holiday carried the truth-telling edge of the blues into the sophisticated nightclub world of jazz, and Etta James drew on it to give her rhythm even more blues. Aretha Franklin linked the holy roll of gospel to the aching roar of the blues—the only possible soundtrack to the civil rights movement. Tina Turner was born with a blues voice and eventually found a blues attitude that set her free, but for Janis Joplin it was the reverse. And they all learned from each other, each taking strength from the fact that some other woman sang her joys and her sorrows and it was okay, people needed that, keep singing.

The women who came after knew that the blues was too great a resource to ignore. They tapped the blues in the same way they delved into their own memories to write their songs, finding a depth of emotion there that simply couldn't be faked. Musicians such as Joni Mitchell and Patti Smith wrote the stories of their emotional lives in a state of faith, trusting that their own particular experiences—as a folk-singing Canadian art student, as a Rimbaud-loving factory worker in New Jersey—were universal enough for someone else to understand. They captured the emotional essence of the blues—in a way that later singers with their technically perfect, octave-scaling, melismatic voices, never could. Bessie Smith had started her career on street-corners with nothing more than talent and attitude, and a hundred years later, attitude remains the blueswomen's greatest legacy.

The story of American blueswomen is a story about hard work and bad luck, about happiness and sexual satisfaction and the way it feels when you've been sweet and tried your best to be good and you're still all alone at midnight and it's raining. It's a story about African-Americans emerging from slavery, hoping for a future that is truly free, and it's the tale of a white woman who hears the music and knows that it speaks to her, too. It's the story of a good woman feeling bad and a bad woman feeling good, because no woman's all good or all bad, in the end. Most of all, the blueswomen's story is about feeling. "It seems simple to me, but for some people, I guess feelin' takes courage," Aretha Franklin said. "When I sing, I'm saying: 'Dig it, go on and try. Ain't nobody goin' make ya. Yeah, baby, dig me—dig me if you dare.'"[28]

It does take courage. No one wants to feel sad, frustrated, and angry. It takes courage to love, and sometimes it's even hard to admit we're happy. All right, Aretha: We dare.

NOTES

All page citations refer to the most recent edition, unless otherwise stated.

Introduction

1. Janis Joplin, in David Dalton, *Piece of My Heart: A Portrait of Janis Joplin* (New York: Da Capo, 1991), 116. Thomas Dorsey, in Giles Oakley, *The Devil's Music: A History of the Blues* (New York: Taplinger Publishing Co., 1976), 116.

Chapter 1

1. Darius Milhaud, "The Jazz Band and Negro Music," *The Living Age* 323 (October 18, 1924): 173.
2. Danny Barker, in Nat Shapiro and Nat Hentoff, *Hear Me Talkin' to Ya: The Story of Jazz as Told by the Men Who Made It* (New York: Dover, 1966), 3.
3. On early African-American music, see Harold Courlander, *Negro Folk Music, U.S.A.* (New York: Dover, 1992).
4. On the integration of music and everyday African life, see Olly W. Wilson, "Black Music as an Art Form," *Black Music Research Journal*, Vol. 3 (1983), 7. On the role of music in African religion, see Olly W. Wilson, "The Association of Movement and Music as a Manifestation of a Black Conceptual Approach to Music-Making," in Irene V. Jackson, ed., *More Than Dancing: Essays on Afro-American Music and Musicians*

(Westport, CT: Greenwood Press, 1985), 13–17, and LeRoi Jones, *Blues People: The Negro Experience in White America and the Music That Developed from It* (New York: Morrow/Quill, 1963), 32–49.

5. John Jacob Niles, "Shout Coon Shout," *The Musical Quarterly* 16 (October 1930): 519–21.

6. Jelly Roll Morton, in Alan Lomax, *Mister Jelly Roll: The Fortunes of Jelly Roll Morton, New Orleans Creole and "Inventor of Jazz"* (Berkeley: University of California Press, 1973), 29. Bunk Johnson, in Shapiro and Hentoff, 8.

7. Jelly Roll Morton, in Shapiro and Hentoff, 6. A "crib" was a small, barely furnished room, usually rented nightly by a prostitute as a temporary place to work.

8. Johnson, in Shapiro and Hentoff, 7.

9. Clarence Williams, in Shapiro and Hentoff, 11–13.

10. Danny Barker, Alphonse Picou, and "Advertisement, New Orleans Blue Book: Countess Willie Piazza," in Shapiro and Hentoff, 5, 10.

11. T-Bone Walker, in Shapiro and Hentoff, 249.

12. On the relationship between labor and music, see Wilson, "The Association of Movement," 17–18. Jones, 61. On heterogeneous sound in African music, see Wilson, "Black Music as an Art Form," 3.

13. W. C. Handy, in Shapiro and Hentoff, 252. Sippie Wallace, in Daphne Duval Harrison, *Black Pearls: Blues Queens of the 1920s* (New Brunswick, NJ: Rutgers University Press, 1988), 6.

14. Murray, 45–50.

15. Wilson, "The Association of Movement," 13–14.

16. Frederick Douglass, *My Bondage and My Freedom* (Urbana: University of Illinois Press, 1987), 170.

17. W. E. B. Du Bois, *The Souls of Black Folk* (New York: Penguin Books, 1903/1989), 3. William H. Holtzclaw, *The Black Man's Burden* (New York: 1915), 156–57, quoted in Leon F. Litwack, *Trouble in Mind: Black Southerners in the Age of Jim Crow* (New York: Alfred A. Knopf, 1998), 278.

18. T-Bone Walker and Alberta Hunter, in Shapiro and Hentoff, 251, 246–47.

19. Koko Taylor, interviewed in *Wild Women Don't Have the Blues*, Dir. Carol Doyle Van Valkenburgh and Christine Dall. Video. California Newsreel, 1989.

20. Ma Rainey, interviewed in 1930 by John Wesley Work, Jr., in *American Negro Songs and Spirituals: A Comprehensive Collection of 230 Folk Songs, Religious and Secular* (New York: Crown, 1940), 32–33.

21. Sandra R. Lieb, *Mother of the Blues: A Study of Ma Rainey* (Amherst: University of Massachusetts Press, 1981), 4–7.

22. Danny Barker, in *Wild Women Don't Have the Blues*.

23. Little Brother Montgomery, in Giles Oakley, *The Devil's Music: A History of the Blues* (New York: Taplinger Publishing Co., 1976), 99. Clyde Bernhardt, in Lieb, 8.

"Little Low Mama Blues," advertisement, Paramount Records, in *Chicago Defender*, January 14, 1927.

24. Gertrude "Ma" Rainey, "Hear Me Talkin' to You," *Heroes of the Blues: The Very Best of Ma Rainey*. Shout Factory 30252.

25. Gertrude "Ma" Rainey, "Memphis Bound Blues," *Ma Rainey: The Essential*. Classic Blues CBL 200020.

26. Sterling Brown, "Ma Rainey," from *The Collected Poems of Sterling A. Brown* (New York: Harper & Row, 1980), 62.

27. Mary Lou Williams, in Shapiro and Hentoff, 248.

28. Lieb, 17.

29. "Like a mother": Maud Smith, in Chris Albertson, *Bessie: Empress of the Blues* (London: Abacus, 1975), 26. Chatmon in Lieb, 18. Gertrude "Ma" Rainey, "Prove It on Me Blues," *Ma Rainey: The Essential*.

30. On "lesbian chic" and a fuller discussion of lesbianism in the 1920s, see Lillian Faderman, *Odd Girls and Twilight Lovers: A History of Lesbian Life in Twentieth-Century America* (New York: Columbia University Press, 1991), 62–92.

31. George Chauncey, *Gay New York: Gender, Urban Culture, and the Making of the Gay Male World, 1890–1940* (New York: Basic Books, 1994), 228.

32. Eric Garber, "A Spectacle in Color: The Lesbian and Gay Subculture of Jazz Age Harlem," in Martin Bauml Duberman, Martha Vicinus, and George Chauncey, *Hidden from History: Reclaiming the Gay and Lesbian Past* (New York: New American Library, 1989), 318–31.

33. On Rainey's blend of country and vaudeville traditions, including "hokum" and Clyde Bernhardt, see Lieb, 79, 13.

34. William Barlow, "'Fattening Frogs for Snakes': Blues and the Music Industry," *Popular Music and Society* 14 (Summer 1990): 8–9.

35. Ruby Walker's experience is described in Chris Albertson, *Bessie: Empress of the Blues* (London: Abacus, 1975/2003), 85. Note: All citations for *Bessie* are to the 1975 edition unless otherwise noted). Thomas Dorsey, quoted in Hans R. Rookmaaker, liner notes, *Ma Rainey, Mother of the Blues*. Riverside RM 8807.

36. "She brought the house down": Tony Langston, "The Whitney's [sic] and Ma Rainey at the Grand," *Chicago Defender*, May 23, 1925. Al Wynn, in Paul Oliver, *Conversation with the Blues* (Cambridge, UK/New York: Cambridge University Press, 1997), 138.

37. The first black-owned record label, W. C. Handy's Black Swan Records, was founded in 1921 and sold to Paramount three years later. Perry Bradford, *Born with the Blues: Perry Bradford's Own Story, The true story of the pioneering blues singers and musicians in the early days of Jazz* (New York: Oak Publications, 1965), 115.

38. Sophie Tucker, *Some of These Days* (New York: Garden City Publishing, 1945), 35, 40, 60.

39. Hunter quoted in Harrison, 210.

40. Unidentified Columbia executive, quoted in Bradford, 115.

41. On Mamie Smith's first recordings, see Robert M. W. Dixon and John Godrich, "Recording the Blues," in Paul Oliver, Tony Russell, Robert M. W. Dixon, John Godrich, and Howard Rye, Yonder Come the Blues: The Evolution of a Genre (Cambridge, UK: Cambridge University Press, 1970/2001), 250–53, and Duval Harrison, 45–47.

42. Bradford, 117.

43. Jerry Wexler, in Jerry Wexler and David Ritz, Rhythm and the Blues: A Life in American Music (New York: St. Martin's Press, 1993), 62.

44. "If not . . . boycotted": Bradford, 117–20. Stories about Tucker's failure to record the songs differ among sources. Bradford claims that a contract with Vocalion Records prevented her, others say she was ill; see Bradford, 118. From 1949 to 1955, singer Ruth Brown's string of #1 singles on Atlantic Records saved the company from bankruptcy and earned the label the title "The House that Ruth Built." For more on Ruth Brown, see Ruth Brown and Andrew Yule, Miss Rhythm: The Autobiography of Ruth Brown, Rhythm and Blues Legend (New York: D. I. Fine Books, 1996).

45. Burke interviewed in Wild Women Don't Have the Blues.

46. John Hammond with Irving Townsend, John Hammond on Record: An Autobiography (New York: Penguin Books, 1977/1981), 29.

47. Bradford, 116.

48. Hammond, 68. Bessie Smith, "Florida Bound Blues," written by Clarence Williams, The Complete Recordings, Vol. 2. Columbia 47473.

49. Memphis Slim and Bradford's royalties estimate in Barlow, 20–21. Bradford, 129. Mamie Smith's fee is an estimate based on typical fees for blues singers in the 1920s.

50. Memphis Slim, quoted in Barlow, 29.

51. Elizabeth Ross Haynes, "Two Million Negro Women at Work," The Southern Workman 51 (February 1922): 64–72.

52. Bessie Smith, "Washwoman's Blues," Bessie Smith: The Complete Recordings, Vol. 4. Sony 52838.

53. "Reclaim them": Mary Church Terrell, "The Duty of the National Association of Colored Women," A.M.E. Church Review (January 1900), quoted in Evelyn Brooks Higginbotham, Righteous Discontent: The Women's Movement in the Black Baptist Church, 1880–1920 (Cambridge: Harvard University Press, 1993), 207. Higginbotham provides a full treatment of the NACW and other church-based black women's organizations. "Experiences of the Race Problem. By a Southern White Woman," Independent 56 (March 17, 1904), quoted in Higginbotham, 190.

54. Ida Goodson, in Wild Women Don't Have the Blues.

55. Dave Peyton, "Things in General" and "The Influence of Music," in the Chicago Defender, June 26, 1926, and May 8, 1926. Langston Hughes, "The Negro Artist and the Racial Mountain," The Nation, June 23, 1926, 693.

56. Hughes, 693–94.

57. On the end of Ma Rainey's life, see Lieb, 43–48.

Chapter 2

1. Bessie Smith, "Preachin' the Blues," *Empress of the Blues: The Complete Recordings, Vol. 3*. Columbia C2K 47474.

2. Bessie Smith, in Chris Albertson, *Bessie: Empress of the Blues* (London: Abacus, 1975/2003), 24. Note: All citations for *Bessie* are to the 1975 edition unless otherwise noted. For more on Smith's childhood, see the indispensable and indefatigable Chris Albertson, *Bessie*, 23–27.

3. Chris Albertson, liner notes, *Bessie Smith: The Collection*. CBS Records CK 44441.

4. Early blues musician Danny Barker, in Nat Shapiro and Nat Hentoff, *Hear Me Talkin' to Ya: The Story of Jazz as Told by the Men Who Made It* (New York: Dover, 1966), 243.

5. Carl Holliday, "The Young Southerner and the Negro," *South Atlantic Quarterly* 8 (1909): 17–31. Quoted in Leon F. Litwack, *Trouble in Mind: Black Southerners in the Age of Jim Crow* (New York: Alfred A. Knopf, 1998), 181–83.

6. Irvin C. Miller, in Albertson, *Bessie*, 26. Smith briefly performed as a chorus girl in a show produced by Miller in 1912. "She was just a teenager": Leigh Whipper, in Albertson, *Bessie*, 26. Whipper was remembering her performance at Atlanta's 81 Theater in Atlanta in 1913.

7. Maud Smith, in Albertson, *Bessie*, 26.

8. Albertson, *Bessie*, 27, 48.

9. Janis Joplin, in David Dalton, *Piece of My Heart: A Portrait of Janis Joplin* (New York: Da Capo, 1971/1991), 116.

10. "Bessie Smith Here Next Week," *Pittsburgh Courier*, March 15, 1924, 10.

11. Zutty Singleton, "I Remember the Queen," in Art Hodes and Chadwick Hansen, eds., *Selections from the Gutter: Jazz Portraits from "The Jazz Record"* (Berkeley: 1977), 65.

12. Benjamin E. Mays, *Born to Rebel* (New York: Scribner, 1971), 9, in Litwack, 321. Lynching statistics: Tuskegee Archives on Lynching (the Tuskegee statistics are generally thought to be more conservative than other sources) (www.law.umkc.edu/faculty/projects/ftrials/shipp/lynchingsstate.html), and Litwack, 538.

13. "New Star," *Chicago Defender*, February 12, 1921, and advertisement for the Standard Theatre, *Chicago Defender*, May 14, 1921.

14. "Sweeping the Country: 3 Big Hits on Black Swan Records." Advertisement, *Chicago Defender*, December 23, 1922.

15. Shapiro and Hentoff, 239, 241.

16. Albertson, *Bessie*, 34–36.

17. On Bessie Smith's first recording session, see Albertson, *Bessie*, 37–38.

18. Bessie Smith, "Downhearted Blues," written by Alberta Hunter and Lovie Austin, *Empress of the Blues: The Complete Recordings, Vol. 1*. Columbia CK 47091.

19. Lawrence Levine, *Black Culture and Black Consciousness: Afro-American Folk Thought from Slavery to Freedom* (New York: Oxford University Press, 1978), 226.

20. A 1924 Paramount Records advertisement offered phonographs and "race records" through its mail-order service. The phonograph was $9.95. "Send No Money, Latest and Best Paramount Records," *Chicago Defender*, May 17, 1924. "Bessie is making": "Sorrowful Blues," *Chicago Defender*, May 24, 1924. "Of course": Gang Jines, "Bessie Smith," *Chicago Defender*, March 3, 1924.

21. Buster Bailey, in Shapiro and Hentoff, 244. "When it comes to fighting": Ruby Walker, in Albertson, *Bessie (Revised)*, 57.

22. Carl Van Vechten, "Bessie Smith," in Bruce Kellner, ed., *"Keep A-Inchin' Along": Selected Writings of Carl Van Vechten about Black Art and Letters* (Westport, CT: Greenwood Press, 1979), 164.

23. Bessie Smith, "Washwoman's Blues," *Empress of the Blues: The Complete Recordings, Vol. 4*. Columbia CK 52838.

24. Bessie Smith, "One and Two Blues," written by G. Brooks, *Empress of the Blues: The Complete Recordings, Vol. 3*. Columbia C2K 47474.

25. Bessie Smith, "Keeps On A-Rainin' (Papa, He Can't Make No Time)," written by Spencer Williams and M. Kortlander, *Empress of the Blues: The Complete Recordings, Vol. 1*. Columbia CK 47091.

26. Bessie Smith, "Louisiana Low Down Blues," *Empress of the Blues: The Complete Recordings, Vol. 2*. Columbia CK 47471.

27. Frank H. Crockett, "Bessie Hits 'Em," *Chicago Defender*, August 4, 1923.

28. "Entertain at Midnight Show: Bessie Smith and Charlie White Perform Before Atlanta Audience," *Pittsburgh Courier*, February 16, 1924.

29. John Hammond with Irving Townsend, *John Hammond on Record: An Autobiography* (New York: Penguin Books, 1977/1981), 15.

30. Hammond, 32–33.

31. Hammond, 46.

32. For a fuller discussion of Harlem's nightlife, see Lewis A. Erenberg, *Steppin' Out: New York Nightlife and the Transformation of American Culture, 1890–1930* (Westport, CT: Greenwood Press, 1981), 255–58.

33. Carl Van Vechten, "The Black Blues," *"Keep A-Inchin' Along"*, 52. "Rough Ethiopian voice": Carl Van Vechten, "Bessie Smith," *"Keep A-Inchin' Along"*, 162.

34. Van Vechten, "Bessie Smith," 161–64.

35. Ruby Walker, in Albertson, *Bessie*, 55.

36. Ruby Walker's recollection in Albertson, *Bessie*, 126.

37. Van Vechten, "Bessie Smith," 164. "Let's get her out of here": Albertson, *Bessie*, 126–27.

38. Albertson, *Bessie*, 128, 125.

39. Albertson, *Bessie*, 126–27.

40. Albertson, *Bessie*, 115–16; "Baby, take this thing out of me": Ruby Walker, in Albertson, *Bessie*, 70–72.

41. Ruby Walker, in Albertson, *Bessie*, 67.

42. I. Telonyou, "Town Tattle," *Interstate Tattler*, February 27, 1925, cited in Albertson, *Bessie*, 98–99.

43. Ruby Walker, in Albertson, *Bessie*, 105. Bessie Smith, "Soft Pedal Blues," *Empress of the Blues: The Complete Recordings, Vol. 2*. Columbia C2K 47471.

44. Three of Smith's recordings, "Cold in Hand Blues," "Dying Gambler's Blues," and "Woman's Trouble Blues," are credited to Jack Gee but are thought to be Smith's own compositions. See Edward Brooks, *The Bessie Smith Companion: A Critical and Detailed Appreciation of the Recordings* (New York: Cassell, 1982), 201, 200, 199.

45. Bessie Smith, "Put It Right Here (Or Keep It Out There)," *Empress of the Blues: The Complete Recordings, Vol. 4*.

46. Bessie Smith, "I Used to Be Your Sweet Mama," *Empress of the Blues: The Complete Recordings*. Bessie Smith, "I Ain't Goin' to Play No Second Fiddle," *Empress of the Blues: The Complete Recordings, Vol. 2*.

47. For more on the dual meaning of lyrics in traditional African-American music, see Levine, *Black Culture and Black Consciousness*, Chapter One, "The Sacred World of Black Slaves," 3–80.

48. Bessie Smith, "I'm Wild About That Thing," *Empress of the Blues: The Complete Recordings, Vol. 4*.

49. Art Hodes, "Bessie Smith," in Art Hodes and Chadwick Hansen, eds., *Selections from the Gutter: Jazz Portraits from "The Jazz Record"* (Berkeley: University of California Press, 1977), 63–64.

50. Hodes, "Bessie Smith," 63.

51. Bessie Smith, "Young Woman's Blues," *Bessie Smith: The Collection*.

52. Hammond, 121.

53. Bessie Smith, "Gimme a Pigfoot," *Empress of the Blues: The Complete Recordings, Vol. 5*. Columbia CK 57546.

54. Lionel Hampton, in Albertson, *Bessie*, 181.

55. Mezz Mezzrow, in Shapiro and Hentoff, 246.

56. Edward Albee, *Three Plays: The Zoo Story; The Death of Bessie Smith; The Sandbox* (New York: Coward-McCann, 1960), 25.

57. Ralph Ellison, "Blues People," *Shadow and Act* (New York: Vintage Books, 1972), 257.

58. Dr. Hugh Smith, in Albertson, *Bessie*, 196, and "Southern Whites Did Not Turn Dying Bessie Away," *Down Beat*, December 1937, 1.

59. Jack Gee, Jr., in Albertson, *Bessie*, 198.

60. John Hammond, "Did Bessie Smith Bleed to Death While Waiting for Medical Aid?" *Down Beat*, October 1937.

61. Lillian Johnson, "Entertainers Find Perils Along the Road," *Baltimore Afro-American*, December 11, 1937, 10.

62. [Unattributed author] "Denies Neglect Killed Singer," *Baltimore Afro-American*, January 8, 1939, 5.

63. LeRoi Jones, *Blues People: The Negro Experience in White America and the Music that Developed from It* (New York: Morrow/Quill, 1963), 94.

64. A 1972 lawsuit brought by Smith's adopted son, Jack Gee, Jr., claimed that during her lifetime, Smith's royalties were criminally diverted to Columbia Records. Columbia Records subsequently claimed to be holding Smith's royalties in a "scholarship fund" for needy black children but no such monies have yet been paid. See Chris Albertson's noble effort to track Smith's missing royalties in Albertson, *Bessie (Revised)*, 284–88.

65. August Wilson, in John Lahr, "Been Here and Gone," *The New Yorker*, April 16, 2001, 58.

66. August Wilson in Lahr, 59. Ralph Ellison, "Living with Music," *Shadow and Act*, 196.

67. James Baldwin, "An Interview with James Baldwin" (1961) in Fred L. Standley and Louis H. Pratt, eds., *Conversations with James Baldwin* (Jackson: University Press of Mississippi, 1989), 4.

68. Baldwin, 19–20.

69. Jae Whitaker, in Alice Echols, *Scars of Sweet Paradise: The Life and Times of Janis Joplin* (New York: Metropolitan Books, 1999), 75. Joplin told an interviewer, "When I first started singing, I was copping Bessie Smith records," in Dalton, 160.

70. Dalton, 191–92.

71. Danny Barker, in Shapiro and Hentoff, 243. Janis Joplin, in Ann Douglas, *Terrible Honesty: Mongrel Manhattan in the 1920s* (New York: Farrar, Straus and Giroux, 1995), 414.

Chapter 3

1. Billie Holiday, in Donald Clarke, *Wishing on the Moon: The Life and Times of Billie Holiday* (New York: Viking, 1994), 48.

2. John Hammond with Irving Townsend, *John Hammond on Record* (New York: Penguin Books, 1977/1981), 89–91.

3. Hammond, 91–92.

4. Hammond, 116–19.

5. "Billie's appeal": in Hammond, 119. Ralph Cooper, in Clarke, 82–83.

6. Mary "Pony" Kane, 1971 interview with Linda Kuehl, in Clarke, 27. Kane was a childhood friend of Eleanora Fagan/Billie Holiday.

7. "A real hip kitty": Billie Holiday and William Dufty, *Lady Sings the Blues* (London: Penguin Books, 1956/1992), 23. Pony Kane, in Clarke, 34–35.

8. "The only joints": Holiday, 11. Kane, in Clarke, 36.

9. Ellington and Turner, in Nat Shapiro and Nat Hentoff, *Hear Me Talkin' to Ya: The Story of Jazz as Told by the Men Who Made It* (New York: Dover, 1966), 168, 174. Note: Shapiro and Hentoff reported that Turner took the "L" train to Harlem, but no such train line then existed. He may have meant the "El" train, meaning the Ninth Avenue Elevated train, which ran along the West Side of Manhattan from 1873 to 1958.

10. Holiday, 21, 36.

11. Lillian Johnson, "What Does Billie Holiday Wear? New Swing Sensation Tells About Her Wardrobe for Afro Readers," *Baltimore Afro-American*, October 23, 1937, 8.

12. On the effect of the Voting Rights Act, see Bernard Grofman, Lisa Handley, and Richard G. Niemi, *Minority Representation and the Quest for Voting Equality* (New York: Cambridge University Press, 1992), 23–24.

13. Dorothy Mackaill, in Mick LaSalle, *Complicated Women: Sex and Power in Pre-Code Hollywood* (New York: St. Martin's Press, 2000), 76.

14. Hammond, 92.

15. LaSalle, 48.

16. LaSalle, 6–7, 85.

17. *Inspiration*. Dir. Clarence Brown, starring Greta Garbo, Robert Montgomery. Film. MGM, 1931.

18. "Trying to kick . . .": Holiday and Dufty, 42. Hammond, 92.

19. Ted Toll, "The Gal Yippers Have No Place in Our Jazz Bands," *Down Beat*, October 15, 1939. Quoted in Linda Dahl, *Stormy Weather: The Music and Lives of a Century of Jazzwomen* (New York: Pantheon Books, 1984), 124. Bobby Tucker, in Shapiro and Hentoff, 200.

20. Larry Newman, "Lady Day's Comeback," condensed from *American Weekly*, in *Negro Digest*, August 1948, 43.

21. Jill Scott, "To Billie, with Love," liner notes, *Lady Day: The Best of Billie Holiday*. Sony C2K 85979.

22. [Unattributed author], "Strange Record," *Time*, June 12, 1939, 58.

23. George Frazier, "Should Shaw Tell Pluggers to Go to Hell?" *Down Beat*, May 1938, 4.

24. Bix Beiderbecke, in Milton "Mezz" Mezzrow and Bernard Wolfe, *Really the Blues* (New York: Dell Publishing Co, 1946), 85–86.

25. Mezzrow and Wolfe, 101–2; 86. Frazier, 4.

26. Hammond, 119; John Simmons on Count Basie, in Clarke, 225; Carl Drinkard, in Clarke, 345–46.

27. Hammond, 119. On pre-Stonewall gay history, see the excellent George Chauncey, *Gay New York: Gender, Urban Culture, and the Making of the Gay Male World*,

1890–1940 (New York: Basic Books, 1994), and Lillian Faderman, *Odd Girls and Twilight Lovers: A History of Lesbian Life in Twentieth-Century America* (New York: Columbia University Press, 1991), 62–92.

28. On Monroe and opium, see Clarke, 177. On manager John H. Levy, see Clarke, chapter 13 (284–305). Memry Midgett, in Clarke, 376–78.

29. Midgett, in Clarke, 378.

30. Bassist John Levy, in Clarke, 291–93.

31. Clarke, 288–94.

32. For a fuller discussion of camp and poet Frank O'Hara's tribute to Holiday, "The Day Lady Died," see Andrew Ross, "The Death of Lady Day," *Poetics Journal* 8 (June 1989), 68–77.

33. Dahl, 122.

34. Clarke, 128. Billie Holiday also commented on the poverty of the Basie Band, see Holiday and Dufty, p. 58.

35. Holiday and Dufty, 56.

36. An aircheck is a recording made of a radio broadcast but never intended for commercial release. Count Basie, in Clarke, 129.

37. Les Robinson, in Clarke, 145–46.

38. *Billboard*, October 29, 1938, 14. On Holiday and Artie Shaw in New York, see Clarke, 147–48.

39. Artie Shaw, in Vladimir Simosko, *Artie Shaw: A Musical Biography and Discography* (Lanham, MD: Scarecrow Press, 2000), 58–64.

40. Mae Weiss, in Clarke, 140.

41. Elizabeth Hardwick, *Sleepless Nights* (New York: Random House, 1979), 42.

42. Billie Holiday, "Long Gone Blues," *Lady Day: The Best of Billie Holiday*.

43. Pauline Kael, "Pop Versus Jazz," *Reeling* (Boston: Little, Brown, 1972/1976), 39. Bryan Ferry, "To Billie, with Love," liner notes, *Lady Day: The Best of Billie Holiday*.

44. On Webster's abusive behavior, see Clarke, 175. Ben Webster, *Atmosphere for Lovers and Thieves*. Black Lion. BLP 30105.

45. On Café Society, see David Margolick's exhaustive *Strange Fruit: Billie Holiday, Café Society, and an Early Cry for Civil Rights* (Philadelphia: Running Press, 2000), 37–41.

46. Margolick, 43. "I dug it right off": Holiday, 84.

47. Billie Holiday, "Strange Fruit," *Ken Burns Jazz Collection: Billie Holiday*. Polygram 594801.

48. Billie Holiday, Holiday and Dufty, 84–85. Lena Horne, in Margolick, 58.

49. Letter from Walter White to Billie Holiday (June 9, 1939), *Collected Papers of the NAACP*, Part 7, Series A, Reel 30, #57. "Strange Record," *Time*, 58.

50. Joe Springer, in Clarke, 230. Lynching statistics: Tuskegee Archives on Lynching (www.law.umkc.edu/faculty/projects/ftrials/shipp/lynchingsstate.html).

51. Ahmet Ertegun, in Margolick, 56.

52. "Strange Record," *Time*, 58.

53. Samuel Grafton, *New York Post*, October 1939, in Margolick, 73.

54. Hardwick, 34.

55. Billie Holiday, "My Man," *Lady Day: The Best of Billie Holiday.*

56. Hardwick, 35. Anne Morrow Lindbergh, private diary (1932), in John C. Spurlock and Cynthia A. Magistro, *New and Improved: The Transformation of American Women's Emotional Culture* (New York: New York University Press, 1998), 162–63.

57. Barney Josephson, in Whitney Balliett, *Barney, Bradley, and Max* (New York: Oxford University Press, 1989), 51.

58. The word *hipster* itself derived from drug culture; it referred to the practice of opium smokers, who reclined on one hip while they smoked. See Jill Jonnes, *Hep-Cats, Narcs, and Pipe Dreams: A History of America's Romance with Illegal Drugs* (Baltimore: The Johns Hopkins University Press, 1999), 125–26; Mezzrow and Wolfe, 145. Stuff Smith's "You'se a Viper" (1936) contains the "mezz" quote. It was later recorded as "The Reefer Song" (1943) by Fats Waller.

59. Armstrong recorded "Muggles," an early "reefer song" in 1928 with Earl "Fatha" Hines. Pops Foster ("We used to smoke . . .") and Honey Cole ("a little shaky . . ."), in Clarke, 79, 81.

60. Marie Bryant, in Clarke, 202.

61. Bryant, in Clarke, 203.

62. Balliett, "Bird," in *Barney, Bradley, and Max*, 184–85.

63. Harold "Big Stump" Cromer, in Clarke, 206.

64. Holiday, in Holiday and Dufty, 116.

65. Horne, in Clarke, 215. Gladys Palmer, *Interview with Gladys Palmer*. Transcript 32–33, Banc MSS 82/69C. The Bancroft Library, University of California, Berkeley.

66. Billie Holiday, "Can a Dope Addict Come Back?" *Tan*, April 1953, 32.

67. Hardwick, 38. Drinkard, in Clarke, 318.

68. "Billie Ducats Like Hotcakes," *Down Beat*, March 10, 1948, 1. Larry Newman, "Lady Day's Comeback," *The American Weekly*, June 13, 1948, reprinted in *Negro Digest*, August 1948, 43–44.

69. "Billie Back: Sans Verbiage, Plus Lbs.," *Down Beat*, April 21, 1948, 1.

70. Oscar Peterson, in Clarke, 372.

71. Mezz Mezzrow, in Mezzrow and Wolfe, 113.

72. *Rave* magazine, January 1957. Courtesy of Experience Music Project, Seattle, WA. Artifact I.D: 1998.545.22.

73. Sinclair Traill, "A Valentine for Lady Day," *Jazz Journal*, March 1954, 1. Max Jones, "Max Jones Spends a—Holiday with Billie," *Melody Maker*, February 20, 1954, 7. Henry Kahn, "Paris Report by Henry Kahn," *Melody Maker*, November 22, 1958.

74. Major Robinson ("suffering from a liver condition"), *Jet*, April 9, 1959, 64. "Billie Holiday, Jazz Great, Critically Ill in New York," *Jet*, June 11, 1959, 56–57.

75. "Billie Holiday, Jazz Great, Critically Ill in New York," *Jet.* Miriam Van Waters, private diary (August 30, 1935), in Spurlock and Magistro, 20.

76. "Billie Holiday Continues Life Struggle in N.Y. Hospital," *Jet,* June 18, 1959, 60–61. "Words of the Week: Billie Holiday," *Jet,* June 25, 1959, 30.

77. "Arrest Billie Holiday in Bed on Dope Charge," *Jet,* June 25, 1959, 61. "Singer Sam Cooke on Dick Clark Show," *Jet,* June 25, 1959, 66.

78. "Lady Day Drops Police Guard; Still Making Good Progress," *Jet,* July 2, 1959, 56–57. "Protest Hospital Arraignment of Billie Holiday," *Jet,* July 2, 1959, 62. "Billie Holiday Loses Battle, Dies in New York Hospital," *Jet,* July 30, 1959, 60–61.

79. Frank Sinatra, "The Way I Look at Race," *Ebony,* July 1958, 42.

80. Marianne Faithfull, "To Billie, with Love," liner notes; Lawrence Durrell, *Clea* (London: E. P. Dutton, 1960), 93.

Chapter 4

1. Mike Leiber, in Ted Fox, *In the Groove: The People Behind the Music* (New York: St. Martin's Press, 1986), 159. Leiber noted that "LeRoi Jones, writing about us in the sixties, said that we were the only authentic black voices in pop music. [Laughs] He changed his tune a few years later when he became Amiri Baraka."

2. Stoller, in Fox, 159.

3. Ralph Ellison, *Invisible Man* (New York: Vintage Books, 1947/1990), 4.

4. Bruce Downes, "An Off-Beat View of the U.S.A.," *Popular Photography,* May 1960, 104–6. Jack Kerouac, Introduction, in Robert Frank, *The Americans* (New York: Scalo, 1997), unpaginated.

5. Kerouac, *The Americans.*

6. *The Wild One,* Dir. Laslo Benedek. Videocassette. RCA/Columbia Home Video, 1987.

7. Dorothy Barclay, "On Becoming a Woman," *New York Times Magazine,* February 26, 1956.

8. Etta James and David Ritz, *Rage to Survive: The Etta James Story* (New York: Da Capo, 1995), 59. See James and Ritz for details of James's childhood throughout.

9. James in *The Essential Etta James,* liner notes. Chess CHD2–9321. James and Ritz, 3–4.

10. James and Ritz, 18.

11. Jerry Wexler and David Ritz, *Rhythm and the Blues: A Life in American Music* (New York: 1993/1994), 62.

12. James and Ritz, 5, 101.

13. George B. Leonard, Jr., "The Great Rock 'n' Roll Controversy," *Look,* June 26, 1956, 41, 45, 40.

14. James and Ritz, 36–44. "Answer" songs were a staple of 1950s popular music; Big

Mama Thornton's original "Hound Dog" (1953) was "answered" by Rufus Thomas's "Bear Cat" (1953). In fact, Hank Ballard answered his own song, "Work with Me, Annie," before Etta James recorded hers; his songs "Annie Had a Baby" and "Annie's Aunt Fanny" were both released in 1954.

15. Wexler and Ritz, 91. James and Ritz, 46–47.

16. Norbert Hess, "Living Blues Interview: Etta James," *Living Blues*, Autumn/Winter 1982, 13. Etta James, interviewed by Bill Millar, "Etta James: Payin' the Cost," *Melody Maker*, September 23, 1978, 35.

17. James and Ritz, 45–49.

18. Etta James and the Peaches, "Roll with Me, Henry," *Etta James: R&B Dynamite*. Modern/Virgin Records V2–86232.

19. James and Ritz, 49. Millar, 35.

20. James and Ritz, 49–50; Patrick Snyder-Scumpy, "Etta: The Classic R&B Singer Kicks Back," *Crawdaddy*, November 1974, 63; "Payin' the Cost," 35.

21. James and Ritz, 50.

22. James and Ritz, 52, 49. Etta James, *Living Blues*, 15.

23. James and Ritz, 57.

24. Muddy Waters, "Mannish Boy," *The Anthology: 1947–1972*. MCA 112649. Etta James, "W-O-M-A-N," *Etta James: R&B Dynamite*. Virgin V2–86232.

25. James and Ritz, 60.

26. James and Ritz, 63. *Living Blues*, 15. James and Ritz, 75.

27. James and Ritz, 174.

28. *Crawdaddy*, 64.

29. James and Ritz, 68, 264.

30. James and Ritz, 111.

31. James and Ritz, 70, 83.

32. Gertrude Samuels, "Why They Rock 'n' Roll—And Should They?" *New York Times Magazine*, January 12, 1958, 17. *Crawdaddy*, 61.

33. Marya Mannes, "Female Intelligence: Who Wants It?" *New York Times Magazine*, January 3, 1960, 44.

34. "The Great Rock 'n' Roll Controversy," 48. "Why They Rock 'n' Roll," 16. Phyllis Lee Levin, "The Sound of Music?" *New York Times Magazine*, March 14, 1965, 72.

35. James and Ritz, 62.

36. James and Ritz, 63, 89. Lee Hildebrand, liner notes, *Etta James: The Chess Box*. MCA 088 112 288–2.

37. James and Ritz, 152, 112.

38. James and Ritz, 132.

39. James and Ritz, 198.

40. Robert Palmer, "Etta James: Peaches" (record review), *Rolling Stone*, December 21, 1971, 66.

41. James and Ritz, 232.

42. Palmer, 66.

43. Aretha Franklin and David Ritz, *Aretha: From These Roots* (New York: Villard, 1999), 9.

44. C. L. Franklin, in Chris Holdenfield, "Baby, I Know: Reassessing Aretha," *Rolling Stone*, May 23, 1974, 64.

45. Holdenfield, 27. Suzanne E. Smith, *Dancing in the Street: Motown and the Cultural Politics of Detroit* (Cambridge: Harvard University Press, 1999), 42. Sylvia Penn, in Franklin and Ritz, 12.

46. Franklin and Ritz, 45–46.

47. Phyl Garland, "Aretha Franklin—Sister Soul," *Ebony*, October 1967, 48.

48. "Swingin' Aretha," *Ebony*, March 1964, 88. On Motown, see Franklin and Ritz, 80, 87. Regarding recording contracts for black artists, Jerry Wexler recalled a conversation between Leonard Chess and Ahmet Ertegun (founder and president of Atlantic Records) regarding the two labels' different attitudes toward paying their recording artists. "I have an agreement with Muddy Waters," Chess said. "'Muddy,' I tell him, 'when your stuff . . . stops selling, you can come over to my house and do the gardening.'" Ertegun replied, "Funny, but I got a different kind of deal with [Big Joe] Turner. . . . If his records don't sell, I can be *his* chauffeur." Wexler and Ritz, 101.

49. Pete Welding, "Focus On: Aretha Franklin," *Down Beat*, September 28, 1961, 18. James Payne, "Aretha Franklin: I Never Loved a Man," *Crawdaddy*, July/August 1967, 33.

50. Franklin and Ritz, 92, 57.

51. "Swingin' Aretha," 88.

52. Hammond, 349.

53. "Swingin' Aretha," 88.

54. Michael Lydon, *Brother Ray: Ray Charles' Own Story* (New York: Da Capo, 1992), 269. Jerry Wexler, in Fox, *In the Groove*, 127, 126. Wexler said that if Atlantic had known there were crossover possibilities, "We probably would not have gone into that business. The only reason we could survive was because we were specialists. . . . we could do it better than Columbia or Victor. . . . The salesmen had to carry [the records] in a briefcase down to a shoeshine parlor someplace in Biloxi that also had some records in it. . . . You had to stigmatize the music, and call it what it was [rhythm and blues, as opposed to rock 'n' roll or pop], otherwise it would never have seen the daylight." Chess Records, in contrast, did not go after the same Southern network.

55. Burt Korall, "The ABC's of Aretha," *Saturday Review*, March 16, 1968, 54.

56. Wexler and Ritz, 205–6.

57. Franklin and Ritz, 108–9.

58. Wexler and Ritz, 207. Franklin and Ritz, 108–9.

59. Peter Guralnick, *Sweet Soul Music: Rhythm and Blues and the Southern Dream of Freedom* (New York: Harper & Row, 1986), 212. Franklin and Ritz, 109.

60. Guralnick, 339–40.

61. Jerry Wexler, interviewed by Timothy White, "Jerry Wexler: The Godfather of Rhythm and Blues," *Rolling Stone*, November 27, 1980, 74.

62. Wexler and Ritz, 208.

63. Wexler, in Fox, *In the Groove*, 149. "New Negro national anthem": in Phyl Garland, "Aretha Franklin—Sister Soul," *Ebony*, October 1967, 47.

64. For a lengthier discussion of the cultural politics of "Respect," see Smith, *Dancing in the Streets*, 210–15; Franklin and Ritz, 112.

65. Patricia Coffin, "Memo to the American Woman," *Look*, January 11, 1966, 16.

66. C. Gerald Fraser, "Aretha Franklin 'Soul' Ignites Apollo," *New York Times*, June 4, 1971, 22.

67. James and Ritz, 172. Unidentified fan, "Baby, I Know," 64.

68. Michael Lydon, "Soul Kaleidoscope: Aretha at the Fillmore," *Ramparts*, October 1971, 39.

69. Etta James, interviewed by Katherine Dieckmann, "Etta James," *Rolling Stone*, November 13, 1997, 152.

70. Lena Horne, quoted in "Baby, I Know," 65.

Chapter 5

1. Tina Turner, anonymous interviewer, "Ike and Tina Turner," *Ebony*, May 1971, 96.

2. Janis Joplin, in David Dalton, *Piece of My Heart: A Portrait of Janis Joplin* (New York: Da Capo, 1971/1991), 144.

3. Dalton, 227.

4. Dalton, 185

5. Dalton, 227–40.

6. Bonnie Bramlett, in Tina Turner and Kurt Loder, *I, Tina: My Life Story* (New York: Morrow, 1986), 88–89, 62–63.

7. Janis Joplin, interviewed by Karl Dallas, "Lock Up Your Sons—Here Comes Janis, Big Brother's Rock 'n' Roll Woman," *Melody Maker*, August 17, 1968, 11.

8. Paul Nelson, "Janis: The Judy Garland of Rock 'n' roll?" *Rolling Stone*, March 15, 1969, 6–8.

9. On childhood, see Turner and Loder, 1–47.

10. Turner and Loder, 45–46.

11. Tina Turner, in Ben Fong-Torres, "The World's Greatest Heartbreaker," *Rolling Stone*, October 14, 1971, 39.

12. Dara Abubakari (Virginia E. Y. Collins), taped interview with Gerda Lerner, New Orleans, Louisiana, October 11, 1970, and Renee Ferguson, *The Washington Post*, October 3, 1970, in Gerda Lerner, ed., *Black Women in White America: A Documentary History* (New York: Vintage Books, 1972/1992), 586, 591. Education statistics, U.S. Department of Education, National Center for Education Statistics (www.nces.ed.gov).

13. Turner and Loder, 57, 55. Tina Turner, Ren Grevatt, "Ike and Tina—and the Spirit of St. Louis," *Melody Maker*, July 9, 1966, 1.

14. Turner and Loder, 56.

15. Turner and Loder, 57.

16. Turner and Loder, 64.

17. Ike and Tina Turner, "A Fool in Love," written by Ike Turner. BMI Master SR-979, Sue 730.

18. Turner and Loder, 76, 86.

19. Ike and Tina Turner, "Poor Fool," written by Ike Turner. BMI Master SR-1034, Sue 753.

20. "It's Gonna Work Out Fine" was written by J. Seneca and J. Lee. The talking lead-up to the song was actually Mickey's voice, while the guitar part was performed by Sylvia, rather than Ike. See Al Quaglieri, *Proud Mary: The Best of Ike and Tina Turner*, liner notes, Sue Records/EMI CD 795846-2.

21. Ann Cain, in Turner and Loder, 96.

22. Fong-Torres, 37, 38.

23. [Anonymous author], "In the Press: Action and Excitement," *BMI*, January 1970, 18. Sally Stevenson, "Tina Turner: Ike Only Loved Stallions," *Crawdaddy*, October 1972, 46.

24. George R. Bach, Ph.D., "Her Amazing Sexual Freedom," *Ladies Home Journal*, July 1967, 63.

25. Ellen Sander, "The Life-Style That Rock Unleashed," *Vogue*, August 1969, 127, 168.

26. Ernest Dunbar, "Ike and Tina: They're Too Much" *Look*, September 3, 1970, 62. Richard Williams, "Is Tina All Sex and No Soul?" *Melody Maker*, February 20, 1971, 18. Mike Jahn, "The Turners Shift to a New Category Called Porno Soul," *New York Times*, April 4, 1971, 65.

27. Fong-Torres, 36.

28. Don Heckman, "Tina Turner Sizzles at Beacon Theater in Shift of Mood," *New York Times*, November 30, 1971, 59.

29. Turner and Loder, 104–5.

30. Bob Krasnow, in Turner and Loder, 107–8.

31. On Ronnie Spector, see Gillian G. Gaar, *She's A Rebel: The History of Women in Rock & Roll*, 2nd ed. (New York: Seal Press, 2002), 45–46.

32. Nick Jones, "Ike and Tina Show Comes to Town—All Nineteen of Them," *Melody Maker*, October 1, 1966, 3.

33. Mick Jagger, in Turner and Loder, 113. Fong-Torres, 36.

34. Fong-Torres, 37.

35. Tina Turner, "In the Press," 18.

36. Mary Karr, *Cherry: A Memoir* (New York: Viking, 2000), 125–26.

37. Karr, 126.

38. On Port Arthur, see Alice Echols, *Scars of Sweet Paradise: The Life and Times of Janis Joplin* (New York: Metropolitan Books, 1999), 6–8. Dave Moriaty, in Julie Smith, "Chick From Port Arthur," *San Francisco Chronicle*, May 27, 1970, 18.

39. *Janis*. Dir. Howard Alk. Videocassette. Universal/MCA, 1974. Karr, *Cherry*, 125.

40. Chet Flippo, "Janis Reunes at Jefferson High," *Rolling Stone*, September 17, 1970, 8.

41. Laura Joplin, interview with the Author (March 24, 2004).

42. Echols, 18–21; Janis Joplin, in Dalton, 175.

43. Big Brother and the Holding Company, featuring Janis Joplin, "Turtle Blues," written by Janis Joplin. *Cheap Thrills*. Sony 65784.

44. Janis Joplin, interviewer unknown, "Janis Joplin," *Rolling Stone*, October 29, 1970, 9.

45. [Anonymous interviewer], "Singers," *Time*, August 9, 1968, 71. Karl Dallas, "Lock Up Your Sons," 11. Joplin, "Janis Joplin," 9.

46. Janis Joplin, letter to family (August 13, 1966), reprinted in Laura Joplin, *Love, Janis* (New York: Villard, 1992), 158–59.

47. Joplin, 145–46.

48. Joan Didion, *Slouching Towards Bethlehem* (New York: Dell, 1968), 104.

49. "Singers," 71. *Janis* (videocassette).

50. Norman Mailer, *The White Negro: Superficial Reflections on the Hipster* (San Francisco: City Lights, 1957), unpaginated.

51. Janis Joplin, in Julie Smith, "What Makes Janis Sing—Ol' Kozmic Blues?" *San Francisco Chronicle*, May 26, 1970, 16.

52. See Echols, 91–132, for a longer discussion of the San Francisco Scene.

53. Echols, 137–38.

54. Dalton, 199. Janis Joplin, letter to family, in Joplin, 158.

55. Janis Joplin, letter to family. Letter to mother (March 1967), in Joplin, 158, 188.

56. Janis Joplin, letter to family, in Joplin, 157.

57. "Pogo," in John Burks, Jerry Hopkins, Paul Nelson, "Groupies," *Rolling Stone*, special issue, February 15, 1969, 13.

58. John Burks, Jerry Hopkins, Paul Nelson, "Groupies." The special issue contained a short piece on male groupies, referring to them as "fools," "vaginal substitutes," and "homosexuals," 13.

59. On Joplin's relationship with Peggy Caserta, see Echols, 251–58.

60. Dalton, 240.

61. Radcliffe Joe, "Janis Joplin Taunts, Audience Flaunts," *Billboard*, January 3, 1970, 14. Richard Goldstein, "Janis Joplin, New Shout," *Vogue*, May 1968, 214.

62. Art Hodes, "Bessie Smith," in Art Hodes and Chadwick Hansen, eds., *Selections from the Gutter: Jazz Portraits from "The Jazz Record"* (Berkeley: University of California Press, 1977), 77. Janis Joplin, letter to family (April 1967), in Joplin, 193. Mike Jahn, untitled story, Bell-McClure Syndicate, excerpted in Joplin, 219–20.

63. Alfred G. Aronowitz, "Singer with a Bordello Voice," *Life*, September 20, 1968, 20.

64. Neil Louison, "Priming the Pump," and Lillian Roxon, "A Moment Too Soon," in Robert Somma, ed., *No One Waved Good-Bye: A Casualty Report on Rock and Roll* (Outerbridge & Dienstfrey, New York: 1971), 39, 94.

65. *Monterey Pop*. Dir. D. A. Pennebaker. Videocassette. WEA/Rhino Home Video, 1967.

66. *Janis* (videocassette).

67. Janis Joplin, in Dalton, 160–61.

68. Tony Wilson, "Straight-talking, Hard-drinking and Sexy—That's Miss Janis Joplin," *Melody Maker*, April 12, 1969, 19. Mark Wolf, "The Uninhibited Janis Joplin: An Interview," *Down Beat*, November 14, 1968, 18–19.

69. Nelson, "Janis: The Judy Garland," 6.

70. Philip Elwood, "Monterey Pop Festival," *Jazz and Pop*, August 1967, 20. Wolf, 19. [Uncredited author], "Of Apollo and Dionysus," *The Christian Century*, November 4, 1970, 1309. Ellen Willis, "But Now I'm Gonna Move," *The New Yorker*, October 23, 1971, 171.

71. Wolf, 18–19. Dalton, 164. John Poppy, "Janis Joplin: Big Brother's White Soul," *Look*, September 3, 1968, 61.

72. Dalton, 163–64. *Janis* (videocassette). Dalton, 100.

73. Joplin, 164.

74. Geoffrey Cannon, "The Agony of Janis," *Melody Maker*, October 10, 1970, 25. Joplin, 164.

75. Seth Joplin, in Chet Flippo, "An Interview with Janis' Father," *Rolling Stone*, November 12, 1970, 18. *Janis* (videocassette). Dalton, 184

76. Janis Joplin, in Dalton, 199. Ironically, Ron "Pigpen" McKernan, a founding member of the Grateful Dead, claimed he had introduced Joplin to Southern Comfort. See Ben Fong-Torres, "The Saddest Story in the World," *Rolling Stone*, October 29, 1970, 14.

77. Nelson, 6. Seth Joplin, in Flippo, 18. "You'd be surprised at the number of obscene phone calls," Seth Joplin said.

78. *Janis* (videocassette).

79. Ronnie Cutrone, in Legs McNeil and Gillian McKain, *Please Kill Me: The Uncensored Oral History of Punk* (London: Abacus, 1997), 17. Roxon, 93.

80. *Janis* (videocassette).

81. Dorothy Joplin, in Joplin, 303.

82. Ralph J. Gleason, "Tina, B. B. and Mick—The Unbeatables," *San Francisco Chronicle*, November 12, 1969, 41. On Tina's relationship with Ike, see Turner and Loder, 133–36.

83. Joplin, 300.

84. B. B. King, in Dalton, 38.

85. Janis Joplin, in Dalton, 183–85, and Smith, "What Makes Janis Sing," 17.

86. Janis Joplin, in Dalton, 182–83.

87. Langston Hughes, letter to Carl Van Vechten (May 17, 1925), in Emily Bernard, ed., *Remember Me to Harlem: The Letters of Langston Hughes and Carl Van Vechten, 1925–1964* (New York: Knopf, 2001), 12. Joplin, in Dalton, 182–83.

88. Bob Gruen, in Turner and Loder, 164. Gruen was a photographer and filmmaker.

89. Turner and Loder, 168.

90. Jerry Garcia and Bob Weir, in Charles Perry, "The News Reaches San Francisco," *Rolling Stone*, October 29, 1970, 14.

91. Pamela Kane, letter to *Rolling Stone*, November 12, 1970, 3. Lester Bangs, "Try (Just a Little Bit Harder)" (record review), *Rolling Stone*, June 8, 1972, 62. Peter Gudekunst, letter to *Rolling Stone*, November 12, 1970, 46.

92. Anonymous "gospel singer," in Chris Albertson, *Bessie: Empress of the Blues* (London: Abacus, 1975/2003), 186. Note: all citations for *Bessie* are to the 1975 edition unless otherwise noted. Robert Gordon, in "Janis Joplin" (uncredited author), *Rolling Stone*, October 29, 1970, 6.

93. Ritchie Yorke, "Janis & Jimi: The Rock & Roll Way of Death," *Jazz and Pop*, December 1970, 41. Kane, letter to *Rolling Stone*, 3. Mary Furman, letter to *Rolling Stone*, November 12, 1970, 46.

94. Turner and Loder, 185–86.

95. Turner and Loder, 187.

96. Laura Joplin, interview with the Author. Turner and Loder, 224.

Chapter 6

1. Lucinda Williams, interview with the Author (February 16, 2004).

2. Joni Mitchell, "Blue," *Blue*. Reprise 2038–2.

3. Malka, "Joni Mitchell: Self-Portrait of a Superstar," *Macleans*, June 1974, 18.

4. Joni Mitchell, in Timothy White, *Rock Lives: Profiles and Interviews* (New York: Henry Holt, 1990), 334.

5. Patti Smith, "Oath," in *Early Work: 1970–1979* (New York: W. W. Norton, 1994), 7.

6. Ed Friedman, in Legs McNeil and Gillian McCain, *Please Kill Me: The Uncensored Oral History of Punk* (London: Abacus, 1997), 141. Patti Smith in Sharon Delano, "The Torch Singer," *The New Yorker*, March 11, 2002, 58.

7. Lucinda Williams, in John Morthland, "Lucinda Williams, Ramblin,'" liner notes, *Ramblin.'* (Smithsonian/Folkways SF 40042).

8. Lucinda Williams, "Maria," *Happy Woman's Blues*. Smithsonian/Folkways SF 40003.

9. Morthland, "Lucinda Williams, Ramblin.'"

10. Houston lost her title to Alanis Morissette in 1995, when Morissette's debut album, *Jagged Little Pill*, sold sixteen million copies.

11. Queen Latifah, in Veronica Webb, "The Lady Won't Be Restricted," *Interview*, November 1996, 23.

12. Erykah Badu, "Tyrone," *Live*. Universal 53109.

13. Lauryn Hill, "I Used to Love Him" and "Lost Ones," *The Miseducation of Lauryn Hill*. Sony 69035.

14. Alex Wrekk, *Stolen Sharpie Revolution: A DIY Zine Resource*, 2nd ed. (Portland, OR: Microcosm, 2003).

15. Kat Bjelland, in Gillian G. Gaar, *She's a Rebel: The History of Women in Rock & Roll*, Exp. 2nd ed. (New York: Seal Press, 2002), 388–89. Kathleen Hanna, in Andrea Juno, ed., *Angry Women in Rock, Vol. I* (New York: Juno Books, 1996), 94.

16. Kurt Cobain, *Journals* (New York: Riverhead Books, 2002), 237.

17. Kurt Cobain, from his suicide note. Accessed March 18, 2004, at www.rock mine.music.co.uk/Reaper/KurtNote.html.

18. Courtney Love, quoted in Michael Corcoran, "A Hole Lotta Love—Courtney Love's Second Album Shows This Bad Girl Can Rock," *Seattle Times*, April 21, 1994.

19. Courtney Love, "Courtney Love Does the Math," *Salon.com*, June 14, 2000, accessed March 18, 2004, at http://archive.salon.com/tech/feature/2000/06/14/love/print.html.

20. Lucinda Williams, "Side of the Road," *Lucinda Williams*. Koch 8005.

21. Williams, interview with the Author. Williams, in Bill Buford, "Delta Nights," *The New Yorker*, June 5, 2000, 58.

22. Williams, interview with the Author. Lucinda Williams, in Richard Silverstein, "Lucinda Williams," from Lyndon and Irwin Stambler, eds., *Folk & Blues: An Encyclopedia* (New York: St. Martin's Press, 2001), 671. Lucinda Williams, "Pineola," *Sweet Old World*. Chameleon 61351-2.

23. Stambler, 671.

24. Williams, interview with the Author.

25. Williams, interview with the Author. Buford, 50. Lucinda Williams, in Katherine Turman, "Songs of Experience," *Mother Jones*, May/June 2003, 84.

26. Williams, interview with the Author.

27. Lucinda Williams, "World Without Tears," *World Without Tears*. Lost Highway 170355-2.

28. Aretha Franklin, in Nat Shapiro, *An Encyclopedia of Quotations About Music* (New York: Da Capo, 1977), 163.

CREDITS

INDEX

Page numbers in *italics* refer to illustrations.

Abraham Lincoln Brigade, 113
Abubakari, Dara, 187
"advances," 148
African-Americans:
  as "Blues People," 242
  "double consciousness" and, 10–11
  Frank's photos of, 137–38
  hiding of ambition by, 46–47
  lynching of, 11, 47, 115, 136–37, 281
  mainstreaming of culture of, 136
  middle class, 53
  movie stereotypes of, 70
  northern migration of, 31, 55
  post–World War I conditions for, 91
  post–World War II conditions for,
    135–39, 142
  as record-buying market, 28
  record labels owned by, *see* Black Swan
    Records; Motown Records
  social role in South of, 40–41
  white artists' "covering" of songs by, 24
  whites' romanticizing of, 99–100,
    120–21, 135–36
  see also church, black; Harlem; racism;
    segregation; slavery; women,
    African-American
African music:
  blues retentions of, 3
  cultural role of, 3, 277–78
  in New Orleans, 4
"Aggravatin' Papa," 46
Aguilera, Christina, 255
airchecks, 107, 286
Albee, Edward, 75, 79
Albert Hall, 129–30
Albertson, Chris, 284
Albin, Peter, 213
Allan, Lewis, *see* Meeropol, Abel
All Hail the Queen, 158
"All I Want," 244
alt-country music, 272
alternative (indie) rock, 261
Alvarez, Marguerite d', 62
Amazing Grace, 176
American Idol, 256
Americans, The (Frank), 137–38, 139, 176

American Weekly, 127

Anderson Theater, 217

Andrew, Sam, 213

Andy's bar, 239

"answer" songs, 145, 257, 288–89

Apollo Theater, 89, 107, 158

"Aretha Franklin Day," 174

Arista Records, 253

Armstrong, Louis, 5–6, 16, 49, 68, 85–86, 90, 91, 100, 116, 121, 122

art, Renaissance European vs. African concepts of, 3

Astaire, Adele, 62

Astaire, Fred, 62

Atlanta, Ga., 22, 57

Atlantic Records:

   Brown's financial rescue of, 280

   Franklin's contract with, 169

   Franklin's recordings for, 171–77, 202, 252

   recording studios used by, 171

   roster of, 169, 170

"At Last," 152, 252

Austin, University of Texas at, 208, 209

Avalon Ballroom, 213, 222

Avedon, Richard, 217

Babes in Toyland, 262

"Baby Love," 191

"Baby Won't You Please Come Home," 46

Back O'Town, 5–6

Back-to-Africa movement, 44

"Backwater Blues," 54

Badu, Erykah, 259–60

"bad woman feeling good," xiii, 15, 23, 275

Baez, Joan, 215, 247, 270

Bailey, Buster, 53

Bailey, Charles "Marse," 22

Baker, Ella, 176

Baker, Josephine, 59, 143

Baker, Mickey, 193, 292

Baldwin, James, 80–81, 82

Ballard, Hank, 144–45, 147, 167, 185, 289

Balliett, Whitney, 123

Baltimore, Md., 53–54, 90–92

Baltimore Afro-American, 77, 78, 79, 92

Band, The, 180

Bangs, Lester, 234

banjos, 3, 4

Bankhead, Tallulah, 73, 100

Baptist Church, 6, 36

Baraka, Amiri, *see* Jones, LeRoi

Barclay, Dorothy, 139

Barker, Danny, 7, 14

Barlow, William, 31

barrel houses, 6

Barry, Jeff, 199

Basie, Count, 30, 101, 106–7, 110, 152, 165

Beat culture, 100

Beatles, 176, 202, 264

beatniks, 108, 210–11

bebop, 100

Bechet, Sidney, 16

"Begin the Beguine," 108

Beiderbecke, Bix, 99–100

"Be My Baby," 192

Bennett, Ronnie, 200

Bernhardt, Clyde, 21

Berry, Chuck, 152

Berry, Leon "Chu," 72

Bible, 67

Big Band era, 105

Big Brother and the Holding Company, 209, 217, 253

   Joplin's joining of, 212–13, 218–19, 229

   meaning of name of, 213

   members of, 213

   at Monterey Pop Festival, 219

   recordings of, 220, 226

Big Brother and the Holding Company, 226

Big Song moments, 254–55

Bihari brothers, 148, 149, 152, 157

Bikini Kill, 262

Billboard, 28, 108, 142–43, 146, 272, 274
"Billie's Blues," 125, 175
Birmingham, Ala., 22–23
Birth of a Nation, 70
Birth of the Cool, 139
Bishop, Valerie, 232
"Bitch Is a Bitch, A," 257
Bitch Manifesto, The (Joreen), 245
Bjelland, Kat, 262
"Black Alfalfa's Jailhouse Shouting Blues," 4
"Black and Blue," 116
blackface, 14, 24–25
"Black Mountain Blues," 82
Black Muslims, 158, 160
Black Power, 139, 160
black pride, Holiday as icon of, 109
Black Reign, 258
Black Swan Records, 48–49, 279
Blige, Mary J., 256, 259
Blondie, 251
Blow, Kurtis, 257
Blue, 243–44
"Blue," 244
Blue Books, 7
blues:
    African-American cultural source of, 3, 8–9
    as attitude, 240, 242–43, 245, 261, 275
    country, 8, 20
    dancing and, 9–10
    decline of popularity of, 70, 71, 73
    demimonde environment and, 1–2, 6
    disseminated by recordings, 29–30
    Dorsey's definition of, xiii, 15
    earliest references to, 4
    effect on American music of, 11–12
    European contributions to, 3
    evolution and institutionalization of, 240–41
    first million-selling recording of, 24
    first recordings of, 24–32
    Franklin and, 167–68

Handy's definition of, 9
    Holiday and, 88–89, 99, 109, 111, 117, 123, 133
    Hughes on sadness of, 231
    Hunter's definition of, 11
    individuality and, 9
    James and, 160
    jazz and, 6
    Joplin's view of, 231–32
    Lucinda Williams and, 239–40, 249–50, 270–71, 273–74
    musical structure of, 8
    Rainey's first hearing of, 12
    respectability and, 7, 34–35
    rock 'n' roll and, 180, 240–42
    undefinability of, 8
    vaudeville, 20
    white audience for, 240–42
Blues Brothers, The, 176
Blues Existentialism, 230
blues lyrics:
    biblical references in, 67
    black daily life described in, 54–55
    "Downhearted Blues," 50–52
    dual meanings in, 10–11
    female sexuality and, 15
    "Fine and Mellow," 117–18
    racism addressed in, 11, 17, 116
    Rainey's broadening of, 20
    topics addressed by Smith in, 50–52, 54–56, 62, 66–68, 72–73, 116, 175, 192
blueswomen:
    blues heritage passed on by, 8
    earliest references to, 4
    emotional exposure and, 180–81
    first generation of, xii, 1–36, 149, 175, 177
    first records by, 29
    human story and, 274–76
    interaction between white artists and, 25–26
    legacy of, 241–43
    Rainey as archetype for, 16, 20

record labels supported by, 29, 280
  women's life paths and, 179–80
  women's social roles and, xi–xiii
Bolden, Buddy, 6
Boogie Down Productions, 257
Booker T. and the MG's, 171
"Borderline," 251
Born with the Blues (Bradford), 279
"Bo-Weevil Blues," 54
Bradford, Perry, 24, 27, 28, 29, 30, 31–32,
    49, 170, 279, 280
Bramlett, Bonnie, 180–82
Brando, Marlon, 138–39
Bratmobile, 262
Brenston, Jackie, 185
Broadway musicals, 71
Brooks, Shelton, 25
Broughton, Henry, 76
Brown, James, 158, 160, 202, 242
Brown, Ruth, 29, 160, 162, 169
Brown, Sterling, 16
Bryant, Marie, 122
"buffet flats," 66, 72
Burke, Blue Lu, 29–30
Bush, Kate, 252

cabaret cards, 126
Café Society, 59, 113–14, 120, 122
Cain, Ann, 194
California, 196–97
"California," 244
Calloway, Blanche, 78
Calloway, Cab, 78
"camp," 104
Canada, 180
"canaries," 105–6, 253
Carey, Mariah, 252, 255, 256
Carmichael, Hoagy, 24
Carnegie Hall, 118, 126–28
Caruso, Enrico, 27
Car Wheels on a Gravel Road, 271–73
"Case of You, A," 244
Caserta, Peggy, 216
Cash, Johnny, 201, 272

Cavett, Dick, 226
CBS Records, 79, 253
"Cell Bound Blues," 15
"Chain Gang Blues," 11, 15
"Change the Locks," 268
Chapin-Carpenter, Mary, 268
Charles, Ray, 144, 162, 169, 170
Chatmon, Sam, 18
Chattanooga, Tenn., 38–42, 64–65
Cheap Thrills, 220, 226
Checker, Chubby, 146
Chelsea Hotel, 165
Chenier, Clifton, 154
Cherry (Karr), 203
Chess, Leonard, 152, 157, 175, 290
Chess, Phil, 152, 157
Chess Records, 155, 160, 161, 164
  James's recordings for, 152, 158, 172,
      175
  James's royalties and, 157
  roster of, 152
Chicago, 259
Chicago, Ill., 18, 55, 136, 152
  South Side of, 57, 70
Chicago Defender, 28, 34, 48, 53
chorus girls, 59
Christianity, 10, 33
Christy, June, 143
Chuck D, 257
church, black:
  importance of, 40
  musical influence of, 142
  women's movement and, 33–34
  see also gospel music
City Lights Books, 210
civil rights movement, 28, 30, 86, 116,
      136–37, 139, 161, 167, 168,
      173–76, 177, 191, 245
Civil War, U.S., 40
Clapton, Eric, 181, 240
Clark, Dick, 132
Cleveland, James, 162
Club Manhattan, 186
Cobain, Kurt, 264, 265, 267

Cohen, Leonard, 270
college radio, 261
Collins, Judy, 247
Coltrane, John, 100
Columbia Records, 88, 93, 125, 216, 272
    black artists and, 24
    corporate owners of, 79
    Franklin's recordings for, 166–70,
        171–72
    headquarters and studios of, 50, 85
    phonographs sold by, 26–27
    Smith and, 48–49, 50, 65, 71–72, 79,
        284
    "Strange Fruit" and, 115
Columbus, Ga., 12
Colvin, Shawn, 271
"Come Together," 202
Commodore Records, 115, 125
Communist Party, 113
Congress, U.S., 113
Connie's Inn, 58, 73
Cooke, Sam, 132, 155, 157, 158, 162,
        165, 166, 167
"cool," Holiday and, 89, 95, 109, 111,
        118–19, 153
Cooper, Ralph, 89
Cotton Club, 58–59, 72, 92, 113
country blues, 8, 20
country music, 255
"covering," of black songs by white
        artists, 24, 147, 152
Cox, Ida, 68, 258
Crawdaddy, 152
"Crazy Blues," 29, 30, 31–32, 170
Creedence Clearwater Revival, 202
Creolettes, 144–46
"cribs," 5, 278
Cromer, Harold, 123–24
crossover hits, 170, 290
Crystals, 192, 199
Cunard, Nancy, 94
Cutrone, Ronnie, 227

Dallas, Tex., 8

dance music, 251
"Dance with Me, Henry," 147
dancing, 9–10
"Dancing in the Streets," 192
Davies, Roger, 236
Davis, Bette, 104
Davis, Clive, 253
Davis, Miles, 139
Dean, James, 129
Death of Bessie Smith, The (Albee), 75, 79
Decca Records, 125, 128
demimonde, 1–2, 6
Denton, Sandy "Pepa," 258
Desdoumes, Mamie, xii, 4–6, 12, 92, 239
desegregation, 28, 136, 154, 206
Detroit, Mich., 166, 167
    "Aretha Franklin Day" in, 174
    Franklin's childhood in, 162–65
Dick Cavett Show, 226
Diddley, Bo, 152, 154
Didion, Joan, 209
Dion, Celine, 252, 255, 256
disco, 241, 242, 247
divas, 176–77, 256
"Divas Live," 256
"Doll Parts," 266
Donegan, Dorothy, 162
"Do Right Woman—Do Right Man,"
        173, 252
Dorsey, Thomas "Georgia Tom," xiii, 15,
        23
"double consciousness," 10–11
"Double V" campaign, 136
Douglass, Frederick, 10
Dove, Billie, 92, 94, 95, 96, 130
Down Beat, 77, 97, 100, 127, 166, 167,
        220
"Downhearted Blues," 50–52
"Do Your Duty," 128
"Dr. Feelgood," 173
Drinkard, Carl, 101, 126
drums, African, 4
Du Bois, W. E. B., 10, 44
Dufty, William, 90

Durrell, Lawrence, 133
Dylan, Bob, 30, 165, 246, 250, 257, 270,
    272–73

Earle, Steve, 269, 272
Echoes of Eden choir, 142, 144, 151
economy, U.S.:
    post–World War II boom in, 136
    see also Great Depression
Ed Sullivan Show, The, 147, 160
81 Theater, 22
Ellington, Duke, 91
Elliott, Cass, 219
Elliott, Missy, 259
Ellison, Ralph, 75, 80–81, 137
Emancipation, 10, 17, 37
Emerson Records, 48
entertainment industry:
    in early twentieth century, 21–22
    white ownership in, 21
    see also recording industry
Ertegun, Ahmet, 116, 171, 290
Esquire, 125
Essence, 273
Estefan, Gloria, 256
"Everybody's Somebody's Fool," 190–91
existentialism, 211, 230

Fagan, Sadie, 90, 92
Faithfull, Marianne, 133
Fame Studio, 171–72, 175
Family Dog, The, 213
Feminine Mystique, The (Friedan),
    179–80
feminism, 150, 161, 179–80, 183, 233,
    244–45
Ferguson, Gladys, 66
Ferry, Bryan, 112
Festival Express, 180
Fetchit, Stepin (Lincoln Theodore Mon-
    roe Perry), 70
Fillmore Auditorium, 213, 221, 240
Fillmore West, 59
film noir, 112, 119

Film Production Code Administration
    (Hays Code), 95, 96
"Findum, Fuckum & Flee," 257
"Fine and Mellow," 115, 117–18
Fitzgerald, Ella, 91, 104, 106, 120, 128
Fitzgerald, Zelda, 94
Flack, Roberta, 259, 260
Fleetwood Mac, 252
"Florida Bound Blues," 31
Folkways Records, 249–50, 268
"Fool in Love, A," 189–91, 193
Forrest, Helen, 109
Foster, Billy, 158
Fountain, The (Morgan), 119, 122
France, 130
Francis, Connie, 190
Frank, Robert, 137–38, 176
Franklin, Aretha, xii, 30, 45, 59, 67, 69,
    72, 112, 139, 143, 146, 160, 161,
    162–77, 163, 183, 202, 223, 224,
    226, 247, 252, 253, 254, 255, 259,
    275–76
    awards won by, 166, 177
    blues and, 167–68
    childhood of, 162–65
    children of, 164, 167, 168
    civil rights movement's "anthem"
        recorded by, 173–75, 177
    as diva, 176–77
    gospel music background of, xii,
        162–65
    James influenced by, 175
    men's relationships with, 164, 167, 168
    physical appearance of, 164
    piano playing of, 168, 171–72
    record labels of, see Atlantic Records;
        Columbia Records
    singing style of, 167–68
Franklin, Barbara, 164
Franklin, "Big Mama," 165, 167
Franklin, Carolyn, 162, 171, 173
Franklin, C. L., 162–65, 166, 167, 168,
    174
Franklin, Erma, 162, 165, 171

Frazier, George, 99, 100
Friedan, Betty, 179–80
Friedman, Ed, 246
Frightwig, 266
Frolic Theatre, 22–23
Fugees, The, 260
Full Tilt Boogie Band, 229
funk, 241, 242
Fuqua, Harvey, 155, 167

Garbo, Greta, 95, 96–97
Garcia, Jerry, 214, 225, 234
Garland, Judy, 104, 183, 221
Garvey, Amy-Jacques, 32
Garvey, Marcus, 44
Gaye, Marvin, 155
Gaynor, Gloria, 247
Gee, Jack, Jr., 77, 78, 79, 284
Gee, John "Jack," 49–50, 65–66, 71, 73, 148
Geffen Records, 265
Gershwin, George, 62
Geto Boys, 257
Getz, Dave, 212, 213
Gibbs, Georgia, 147
"Gimme a Pigfoot," 72–73, 128
Gimme Shelter, 197, 228
"girl groups," 191–92, 197, 199
Gleason, Ralph, 228
"Gloria," 245
Goffin, Jerry, 192
Go-Gos, 251
Goodman, Benny, 72, 73, 88, 93
"Good Rockin' Daddy," 149
Goodson, Ida, 34
"good woman feeling bad," xiii, 15, 275
Gordon, Kim, 261
Gordy, Berry, 21
gospel music, 10, 15, 29, 252
    Franklin and, xii, 162–65, 176, 253
    Houston and, 253
    James and, 142, 144, 151, 161
Grafton, Samuel, 116–17
Grainger, Porter, 62

Grammy Awards:
    for Carey, 255
    for Franklin, 177
    for Hill, 260
    for Houston, 255
    for James, 153, 161
    for Latifah, 259
    for Raitt, 240
    for Turner, 237
    for Williams, 272
Graphophones and Grafonolas, 27, 30
Grateful Dead, 180, 213, 225, 234, 294
Great Awakenings, 10
Great Britain, Holiday in, 87, 129–30
Great Depression, 36, 71, 86, 91, 93–94, 96, 105
"Greatest Love of All, The," 252–53, 254
Great Migration, 31, 55
Great Saturday Night Swindle, 231, 233–34
Green, Juanita, 81
Greenwich, Ellie, 199
Griffith, D. W., 70
groupies, 216
Gruen, Bob, 233
grunge rock, 241
Guitar Slim, 144
"Gulf Coast Blues," 46
Gurley, James, 213
Guthrie, Woody, 247
Guy, Buddy, 180

Hagen, Nina, 252
Hager, Fred, 28, 29
Hall, Rick, 172
Hamer, Fannie Lou, 176
Hammond, Emily Vanderbilt Sloane, 57–58
Hammond, John, 93, 145, 241, 253, 272
    family background of, 30, 57
    Franklin and, 165–66, 169, 170
    Holiday and, 72, 86–89, 95–96, 97, 100, 102, 105, 106, 120, 165–66
    introduction to blues of, 30

Hammond, John (*continued*)
  musicians signed by, 30, 72, 165
  Smith and, 58, 72–73, 77, 78, 99,
    165–66
Hampton, Lionel, 73, 78
Handy, W. C., 9, 24, 25, 54, 279
Hanna, Kathleen, 262
Happy Woman's Blues, 250, 268
Hardwick, Elizabeth, 110, 117, 126
Harlem, 26, 55, 64, 66, 158, 241
  as capital of Black America, 44–45
  Hammond in, 58
  Holiday's arrival in, 90–92
  homosexual subculture in, 19–20, 101
  nightclubs of, 44, 54, 58–59, 72, 88,
    105, 113
  post–World War I description of, 91
  segregation in, 54, 58–59, 113
  Smith in, 44–45, 50, 57
  whites drawn to, 45, 58–59
Harlem Renaissance, 24, 44, 56
Harlow, Jean, 95
Harris, Emmylou, 269, 271, 272
Harrison, Daphne Duval, 25
Hawkins, Cozetta, 141, 143
Hawkins, Dorothy, 141, 143, 144, 146,
    150, 151, 153, 164
Hayes, Isaac, 170
Hays Code (Film Production Code
    Administration), 95, 96
"Hear Me Talkin' to You," 15
"He Hit Me (It Felt Like a Kiss)," 192,
    193
Helms, Chet, 208, 209, 212–13
Henderson, Fletcher, 30, 31
Hendrix, Jimi, 202, 215, 219, 242
Henry, John, 8
heroin, 210
  Holiday and, 121–26, 152–53, 225
  James and, 152–53, 155–57, 161
  jazz scene and, 123
  Joplin and, 213, 225, 234, 235
  Love and, 265
"He's Funny That Way," 125

Highway 61, 74–76
Highway 61 Revisited, 270
Hill, Faith, 255, 256
Hill, Lauryn, xii, 259, 260
Hines, James Earle, 142
hip-hop, 242, 256–60
hippies, 210, 212, 213
hipsters, 100, 120, 127, 137, 139, 211,
    242, 287
Hitler, Adolf, 136
Hodes, Art, 69–70
"hokum," 20
Hole, 262, 265
Holiday, Billie, xii, 9, 30, 43, 53, 59, 72,
    78, 85–133, 141, 142, 143, 148,
    151, 157, 159, 162, 165, 169, 175,
    183, 192, 211, 222, 223, 224, 244,
    246, 262, 266, 273, 274, 275
  arrival in Harlem of, 90–92
  autobiography of, 90, 106, 133
  as big band singer, 106–10
  bisexuality of, 100–102, 214–15
  blues and, 88–89, 99, 109, 111, 117,
    123, 133
  cabaret card revoked from, 126
  childhood of, 89–91, 124
  "cool" and, 89, 95, 109, 111, 118–19,
    153
  death of, 130–33
  descriptions of performances by, 88,
    109, 118, 123–24, 126–27
  drug arrests of, 125–26, 132
  drug use by, 102, 104, 120–28, 225
  "film noir" style of, 112
  first recordings of, 85–89, 105
  in Great Britain, 87, 129–30
  hit recordings of, 125
  as icon of black pride, 109, 115
  influence of, 98
  James's meeting of, 152–53
  jazz poll won by, 125
  later recordings of, 129
  men's relationships with, 65, 90,
    102–4, 117–18, 158

musicianship of, 97–98, 110–11,
122–23
name change of, 93
nickname of, 107
other artists' versions of songs recorded
by, 132, 153, 161
outsider and gay appeal of, 88–89, 100,
102, 104–5
personality and persona of, 89, 93,
95–97, 99, 102, 104, 121–24, 129,
133, 220
pet dog of, 125
physical appearance of, 90, 92–93,
129, 153
singing style and voice of, 97–99,
110–11, 117–19, 127, 129, 167
Smith as influence on, 85–86, 130,
167
Smith songs recorded by, 128
"Strange Fruit" and, 112–17, 123
Young and, 107, 172
Holiday, Clarence, 90
Hollywood, see movies
homosexuals, 18–20
Holiday and, 89, 100–102, 104–5
James and, 151, 155
subcultures of, 19–20, 101
women as icons for, 104–5
"Honky Tonk Train Blues," 143
"Honky Tonk Women," 202, 228,
237
Hooker, John Lee, 200
Hopkins, Lightnin', 240
Horne, Lena, 114–15, 177
Horses, 245
Hotchkiss School, 58
"Hot Legs," 236
"Hound Dog," 135, 289
House, Son, 240, 247
Houston, Cissy, 253
Houston, Whitney, 252–55, 256, 257,
295
Howlin' Wolf, 152, 200, 271
Hughes, Langston, 35, 56, 60, 231

Hunter, Alberta, 11, 25–26, 68, 240
Hurston, Zora Neale, 94

"I Ain't Goin' to Play No Second
Fiddle," 67, 175
"I Am Woman," 247
"I Cover the Waterfront," 125
"I'd Rather Go Blind," 152, 160, 175
I Got Dem Ol' Kozmic Blues Again
Mama!, 226
"I Idolize You," 193
Ike and Tina Turner Revue, 181–82, 191
recordings of, 189–91, 193
on tour with Rolling Stones, 200–201,
228–29
white artists's songs covered by, 201–2,
228
"Ikettes," 181–82
"I'm Jealous," 193
"I'm Wild About That Thing," 150
indie (alternative) rock, 261
individuality, musical, 9
"I Never Loved a Man (The Way That I
Love You)," 69, 172–73, 202
Inspiration, 97
integration, 28, 136, 154, 206
Interstate Tattler, 66
"Into the Groove," 251
Invisible Man (Ellison), 137
"I Think It's Gonna Work Out Fine,"
193, 292
"I Thought About You," 129
"I Used to Be Your Sweet Mama," 67
"I Used to Love Him," 260
"I've Been Loving You Too Long," 197
"I Will Always Love You," 255
"I Will Survive," 247

Jackson, Janet, 251
Jackson, Mahalia, 162
Jagged Little Pill, 295
Jagger, Mick, 161, 200–201, 216, 228–29,
246
Jahn, Mike, 198

Jamal, Ahmad, 152
James, Cheryl "Salt," 258
James, Etta, xii, 43, 68, 139–61, *140*, 164,
    165, 166, 167, 172, 177, 182, 185,
    197, 200, 208, 224, 247, 253, 255,
    257, 266, 275, 289
  album of Holiday's songs recorded by,
    153, 161
  awards won by, 153, 161
  backup singers of, *see* Creolettes;
    Peaches
  birth and original name of, 141
  black audience of, 152, 158, 160, 169
  Black Muslims and, 158, 160
  blues and, 160
  character of, 159–60
  crossover success of, 161
  first singing group of, 144–45
  first radio appearance of, 152
  Franklin's influence on, 175
  gay men and, 151, 155
  in gospel choir, 142, 144, 151
  heroin addiction of, 152–53, 155–57,
    161
  hit records of, 146–48, 149, 152, 175,
    252
  Holiday's meeting of, 152–53
  men's relationships with, 155, 158–59
  mixed racial identity of, 141, 154–55
  music listened to by, 143–44
  name change of, 146
  Otis and, 145–49
  physical appearance of, 150–51,
    154–55
  prison stints of, 158
  record companies' control of earnings
    of, 148–49, 157
  royalties partially paid to, 147–49, 157
  self-image of, 159
  sexuality in songs of, 149–50
  singing voice of, 146–47, 149–50, 160,
    256
  southern touring of, 154–55, 158
  teen delinquent years of, 139–41, 144

James, Skip, 240, 247
jazz, 29, 35, 60, 162
  Big Band era of, 105
  blues and, 6
  early recordings of, 24
  Franklin and, 166, 167
  heroin and, 123
  in Los Angeles, 143
  racism and, 31
  whites' romanticizing of, 99–100
Jazz Age, 43, 82
Jazz and Pop, 221
jazz catalyst, 88
"Jazz Plus Blues Equals Soul," 152
Jefferson Airplane, 213
Jet, 130–32
Jim Crow segregation, 5, 17, 28, 31, 55,
    56–57, 76–79, 107–8, 136, 154,
    183, 205
Johnson, Bunk, 4, 5, 6
Johnson, James P., 91
Johnson, Robert, 240, 270
Jolson, Al, 24
Jones, Jo, 107
Jones, LeRoi (Amiri Baraka), 9, 79, 242,
    288
Jones, Max, 130
Joplin, Dorothy, 228
Joplin, Janis, xii, xiii, 45, 68, 152,
    179–80, 203–37, *204*, 240, 246,
    253, 262, 266, 275
  alcohol use of, 213, 225, 235, 294
  bands of, *see* Big Brother and the
    Holding Company; Full Tilt
    Boogie Band
  bisexuality of, 214–16
  blues as viewed by, 231–32
  childhood of, 203–7, 224
  clothing styles worn by, 213–14,
    227
  death of, 183, 234–35
  drug use by, 209, 213, 225, 234–35
  effect on audience and fans of, 215,
    222, 234–35

family's letters from, 208, 217, 223, 230–31

first California trip of, 208, 209

personality of, 205, 214, 220–22, 224

personal philosophy of, 210–12

physical appearance of, 71, 205, 217–18

post-Big Brother recordings of, 226, 229, 234

Rainey's influence on, 43

return visits to Port Arthur by, 207, 209, 226–28, 231

singing voice and style of, 205, 221

Smith copied by, 81–82, 83, 206–7, 220, 284

Smith's grave marker and, 81, 83, 230

stage performances and persona of, 215–17, 219–20

Turner on stage with, 230

Turner's influence on, 182

Joplin, Laura, 206, 222, 226, 227, 237

Joplin, Seth, 224, 230–31

Joreen (Jo Freedman), 245

Josephson, Barney, 113–14, 120

Kael, Pauline, 112

Kane, Mary "Pony," 89, 90

Kane, Pamela, 234

Karr, Mary, 203, 205

Kaye, Lenny, 245

"Keeps On A-Rainin' (Papa, He Can't Make No Time)," 55

Kennedy Center, 177

Kenton, Stan, 143

Kerouac, Jack, 137–38, 212

Khan, Chaka, 247

"Killing Me Softly," 260

Kind of Blue, 139

King, B. B., 148, 202, 228, 230

King, Carole, 192, 253, 256

King, Martin Luther, Jr., 168, 174

Kings of Rhythm, 185–89

Knowles, Beyoncé, 255

Kozmic Blues, 230, 232, 233

Krasnow, Bob, 199

Kristofferson, Kris, 215, 229

Ku Klux Klan, 64, 83, 108

"Ladies First," 258

Lady Sings the Blues (film), 133

Lady Sings the Blues (Holiday and Dufty), 90, 106, 133

Latifah, Queen, 258–59

"Leader of the Pack," 192

Ledbetter, Huddie "Leadbelly," 206, 249

Led Zeppelin, 240

Lee, Brenda, 190

Lee, Peggy, 106

Lee, Stagger, 64

Leiber, Mike, 135, 138, 145, 171, 288

Lennon, John, 233, 264–65

Lennon, Sean, 265

Lenya, Lotte, 246

"lesbian chic," 19, 279

"Let's Talk About Sex," 258

Levy, John (bass player), 103

Levy, John H. (Holiday's manager), 102–3

Lewis, Jerry Lee, 185

Lewis, Meade Lux, 143

Life, 217

Lifetime Achievement Award, 177

Like a Virgin, 251

Lincoln Hotel, 108

Lindberg, Anne Morrow, 119

"Little Angel, Little Brother," 269

Little Richard, 154

Live, 259

Live at Fillmore West, 176

"Livery Stable Blues," 24

Live Through This, 266

LL Cool J, 257

Locke, Alain, 44

Loma Records, 199

"Long Gone Blues," 111

Look, 144, 174, 197

Los Angeles, Calif., 196, 269
 jazz scene in, 143
 South Central neighborhood of, 142
 View Park Hills neighborhood of, 194
 Watts neighborhood of, 141, 147
"Louisiana Low Down Blues," 55
Love, Courtney, xii, 262–67, 263, 272
 drug use of, 265, 266
 early career of, 262–64
 physical appearance of, 264, 266
 recording industry sued by, 267
 "Yoko Ono" phase of, 264–65
Love, Frances, 265
Love, Monie, 257, 258
"Love in Vain," 240
"Love Is Strange," 193
"Lover Man," 125
Loy, Myrna, 73
LSD, 210, 213, 225
Lucinda Williams, 268
Lydon, Michael, 176
lynching, 11
 statistics on, 47, 115, 281
 "Strange Fruit" and, 112–17
 of Till, 136–37

McDonald, Joe, 215
Mackaill, Dorothy, 95
McKay, Louis, 102, 132
McKernan, Ron "Pigpen," 294
McPhatter, Clyde, 162
McRae, Carmen, 106
Madison Square Garden, 230
Madonna, 53, 251
Madonna, 251
Mailer, Norman, 211
"Mama," meaning of term, 14
Mamas and the Papas, The, 219
"Man I Love, The," 43
"Mannish Boy," 149
Mansfield, Jayne, 129
Mapplethorpe, Robert, 246
"Ma Rainey," 16
"Maria," 250

Mariah Carey, 255
Marihuana Tax Act (1937), 121
marijuana, 120–21, 122, 210, 225
Marin County, 213
Marinoff, Fania, 62–63, 64
Martha and the Vandellas, 191–92
Marvelettes, 191
"Material Girl," 251
Mays, Benjamin, 47
MC Lyte, 257, 258
"Me and Bobby McGee," 229
"Me and My Chauffeur Blues," 250
medicine shows, 4
Meeropol, Abel (Lewis Allan), 113–14,
 116
Meeropol, Anne, 113
Melody Maker, 130, 220
Memphis, Tenn., 171, 185
"Memphis Bound Blues," 15
Memphis Minnie, 240, 250
Memphis Slim, 31–32
"Mercedes Benz," 229
Mercury Records, 272
Merry Pranksters, 212
methamphetamines, 209
"mezz," 121
Mezzrow, Milton "Mezz," 74, 99–100,
 120–21, 135, 171
Micky and Sylvia, 193, 292
microphones, singing changed by, 98
Midgett, Memry, 102–3
Milburn, Amos, 143
Milhaud, Darius, 1
military, desegregation of, 136
Miller, Willie George, 77, 78
Millet, Kate, 245
Miltown, 155
Minnesota Fats, 141
minstrel shows, 25
 Bessie Smith in, 18, 42–43, 68
 black stereotypes in, 44
 history and description of, 12–14
 Rainey in, 12–14, 16, 42
 T.O.B.A and, 21–22, 36, 42, 68

Miseducation of Lauryn Hill, The, 260
Miseducation of the Negro (Woodson), 260
Mississippi:
  Smith's death in, 74–79
  Till's lynching in, 136–37
Mississippi Delta, 242
"Mississippi Goddam," 116
Mississippi Valley Flood, 54
Missouri, 12
"Miss World," 266
Mitchell, Jean and Abye, *140*, 144–46, 147, 149
Mitchell, Joni, 243–44, 246, 247, 270, 276
Modern Records, 145, 147, 148, 149, 152, 185
Monroe, Jimmy, 102
Monroe, Marilyn, 122
Monterey Pop Festival, 196, 202, 219, 226
Moonglows, 155
"Moonshine Blues," 23
Moore, Monette, 88
Morgan, Charles, 119
Morgan, Richard, 73, 76
Morissette, Alanis, 295
Morrison, Jim, 215
Morrison, Van, 240, 245
Morton, Jelly Roll, 4, 5, 12
Moses Stokes Company, 42
"Mother's Little Helper," 155
Motown Records, 21, 155, 160, 166, 171, 191, 192, 202
Mount Lawn Cemetery, 81
movies:
  film noir, 112, 119
  Holiday's style influenced by, 95, 112, 130
  modern images of women in, 95–97
  production code for, 26, 95, 96
  racial stereotypes in, 70
  white teen rebellion as portrayed in, 138–39

Ms., 245
Muldow, Barbara, 81
Murray, Albert, 10
Muscle Shoals, Ala., 171–73, 175, 202
"My Heart Will Go On (Love Theme from *Titanic*)," 255
"My Man," 118, 192
Mystery Lady, 153, 161

Namath, Joe, 215
National Association for the Advancement of Colored People (NAACP), 113, 115, 136–37
National Association of Colored Women (NACW), 33
"Natural Woman," 146
NBC, 152
Nelson, Paul, 221
"Nessun dorma," 177
"Never Let the Same Dog Bite You Twice," 25
Nevermind, 264
Newark, N.J., 60
"New Negro," 44, 138
New Orleans, La., 12, 16, 45, 46, 47, 48, 138, 242
  as cultural crossroads, 4
  Lucinda Williams in, 239–40
  racial varieties in, 5, 7
  see also Storyville
New Orleans Jazz and Heritage Festival, 248
New South, 38
Newsweek, 226
New Temple Missionary Baptist Church, 162
New Wave music, 241, 251, 272
New York, N.Y., 49, 56, 108, 110, 217, 245, 247
  cabaret cards required for nightclub performers in, 126
  Franklin in, 165–67
  in Great Depression, 105

New York, N.Y. (*continued*)
  Greenwich Village neighborhood of,
    19, 45, 250–51
  racism in music scene in, 31
  segregation in, 57
  see also Harlem
New York City Police Department
    (NYPD), Holiday targeted by,
    125–26, 132
New Yorker, 112, 221–22
New York Post, 116–17
New York Times, 59, 139, 198
Nichiren Shoshu Buddhism, 232–33
Nicks, Stevie, 252
Nigger Heaven (Van Vechten), 59
Niles, John Jacob, 4
1984 (Orwell), 213
Nirvana, 264, 265
"Nobody in Town Can Bake a Sweet
    Jelly Roll Like Mine," 80
North, 28, 29
  black migration to, 31, 55
  post-migration generation of blacks in,
    136–37
  racism in, 31, 55–56, 108
N.W.A., 257

"Oath," 245
O'Connor, Flannery, 250, 269
Okeh Records, 27–28, 29, 30, 31
Old Gold cigarettes, 108
Oldham, Spooner, 172
"On Becoming a Woman" (Barclay), 139
"One and Two Blues," 55
Ono, Yoko, 233, 264–65
Original Dixieland Jazz Band, 24
Orpheum Theatre, 60
Orwell, George, 213
Otis, Johnny, 145–49, 185
  James as singer with, 145–46, 149
  James's royalties split with, 147–49
Otis, Phyllis, 147

Page, Patti, 190

Page, Walter, 107
Palmer, Robert, 160, 161
Paramount Records, 15, 35–36, 279
Paramount Theatre, 105
Parental Advisory stickers, 258
Paris, 130
Parker, Charlie, 9, 123, 131
Parks, Rosa, 176, 177
"passing," 48
"Passionate Kisses," 268
Paul Butterfield Blues Band,
    240
Pavarotti, Luciano, 177
Peaches, *140*, 146, 149, 165, 167
Pearl, 229, 230, 234
Perdido Street, 5
Perkins, Carl, 185
Peterson, Oscar, 128
Peyton, Dave, 34–35
Philadelphia, Pa., 43, 48, 49–50, 56, 79,
    81, 90, 126, 230
Philadelphia Inquirer, 81
Phoenix Theatre, 131
phonographs, 23, 26–29, 30, 53
"Physical Attraction," 251
Piazza, Countess Willie, 7
Pickett, Wilson, 143, 170, 171
Picou, Alphonse, 7
"pig-meat," 15, 21
"Pineola," 269
"Piss Factory," 246
Pittsburgh Courier, 45
"Please, Mr. Postman," 191
"Pogo," 215
Poly Styrene, 252
"Poor Fool," 192, 193
"Poor Man's Blues," 116
popular music:
  African-American music's affect on,
    69
  gospel music infused into, 161
  in 1980s, 251–56
  political protest in, 112–17
  rock 'n' roll revolution in, 142

sinister aspects of love addressed in, 192–93
in Smith's repertoire, 71
Popular Photography, 137
Port Arthur, Tex., 203–7, 208, 209, 210, 224, 225, 226–28, 230–31
Powell, Adam Clayton, 168
"Preachin' the Blues," 37, 41
Presley, Elvis, 53, 129, 154, 170, 177, 185, 201
Pretty on the Inside, 264
Primaline Ballroom, 145
Private Dancer, 237
Prohibition, 43–44
prostitution:
  Holiday and, 90–92, 124, 127
  in Storyville, 2, 5–7
protest songs, 114, 116, 117, 257
  see also "Strange Fruit"
"Proud Mary," 202
"Prove It on Me Blues," 18, 66
Public Enemy, 257
publishing companies, royalties and, 148
Puccini, Giacomo, 176–77
punk rock, 241, 251, 252, 261–62
"Push It," 258
"Put It Right Here (Or Keep It Out There)," 67

Quicksilver Messenger Service, 213

Rabbit Foot Minstrels, 12–14, 16
"race man," 142–43
"race records," 28, 142–43
race riots, 44, 192, 202
"race woman," Holiday as, 115
racism, 44, 78, 86
  addressed in blues lyrics, 11, 116
  faced by Holiday, 106, 107–8, 115
  Joplin's awareness of, 206, 207, 212
  northern vs. southern, 31, 55–56
  in recording industry, 24, 26–29
  sex and, 154
  see also lynching; segregation

Radical Chic, 62
radio, 23, 70, 110, 247, 257, 261, 269
Rainey, Gertrude "Ma," xii, xiii, 12–23, 13, 52, 119, 149, 151, 177, 209, 243, 258, 266, 274
  as archetypal blueswoman, 16, 20
  bisexuality of, 17–20, 66, 100–101, 214
  childhood of, 12
  descriptions of performances by, 14, 16, 21, 22–23, 46
  final years of, 35–36
  first blues heard by, 12, 30
  influence of, 43
  meaning of stage name of, 14
  in minstrel shows, 12–14, 16, 42
  musical influence of, 20
  physical appearance of, 14–15, 20, 46
  recording success of, 24
  singing voice of, 15, 43, 46
  Smith compared with, 46
  Smith's relationship with, 18, 42, 43
  themes addressed in songs sung by, 11, 15, 17, 18, 20
Rainey, William "Pa," 12, 18
"Rainy Night House," 243
Raitt, Bonnie, 157, 240, 251, 271, 272
Ramblin', 249–50
rap music, 256–60
Rave, 129
RCA, 269
Reagan, Ronald, 255
Rebel Without a Cause, 138
Reconstruction, 5, 10, 57, 154
recording contracts, 169, 290
recording fees, 32
recording industry:
  blueswomen's role in, xii, 29, 280
  first black-owned company in, 48–49, 279
  in Great Depression, 71, 93
  music compartmentalization in, 249
  race and business and, 24, 26–29
  rise of, 23

recording industry (*continued*)
  "star" system and, 27
  sued by Love, 267
  white ownership of, 24
  Williams's troubles with, 267–72
  see also royalties
Recording Industry Association of America (RIAA), 267
recording technology, 50
record players, 23, 26–29, 30, 53
records:
  flat fees paid to artists for, 105
  as publicity for artists' live performances, 105
  white audiences exposed to black artists through, 59
record sales, by Bessie Smith, 52, 70
Redding, Otis, 143, 158, 160, 170, 173, 175, 202, 219
Reddy, Helen, 247
religious revivals, 10
R.E.M., 261
Reparata and the Delrons, 192–93
"Respect," 67, 139, 173–75, 177
rhythm and blues (R&B), 144, 150, 160, 162, 166, 169, 201, 242, 247
  coining of term, 28–29, 142–43
  early 1960s groups in, 191
  marketing of, 290
  musical growth of, 170
  1980s balladry in, 252–56
Rhythm and Blues Foundation, 157
RIAA (Recording Industry Association of America), 267
Richards, Keith, 161, 200, 216, 229, 246
"Righteously," 274
Rimbaud, Arthur, 246
Riot Grrl, 261–62, 264, 266
Ritz nightclub, 236
"River Deep, Mountain High," 199–200, 254
Robinson, Bill "Bojangles," 22, 68
Robinson, Les, 107–8
Robinson, Smokey, 162

Robinson, Sylvia, 193, 292
Rock and Roll Hall of Fame, 161
"Rocket 88," 185
rock 'n' roll, xii
  alternative, 261–62
  appeal of, 155–56
  blues and, 180, 240–42
  in California, 196–97
  first recording of, 185
  musical challenges to, 241
  race and, 170, 201–2
  rise of, 142, 143–44
  sex and, 149–50
"Rockstar," 266
Rogers, Lula and Jesse, 141, 144
Rolling Stone, 160, 182, 183, 216, 234–35, 249
Rolling Stones, xii, 161, 197, 200–201, 202, 221, 228–29, 230, 237, 240
"Roll with Me, Henry," 43, 145, 146–48, 150, 152, 167
Rome, Ga., 36
Ronettes, 160, 192, 197, 199, 200
Ronstadt, Linda, 247
roots music, 272–73
Roper, Dee Dee "Spinderella," 258
Rosenberg, Ethel and Julius, 113
Ross, Diana, 133, 160
Rough Trade Records, 268, 269
"Roxanne," 257
"Roxanne's Revenge," 257
royalties, 166
  denied to Smith, 68, 284
  flat fees given instead of, 105
  importance of, 147
  James's partial receiving of, 147–49, 157
  Rhythm and Blues Foundation's collecting of, 157
  splitting of, 147–48
  withholding of, 31–32
Russell, Rosalind, 123

Safe in Hell, 95

"St. Louis Blues," 24, 25–26, 27, 54
St. Louis Blues (film), 26
St. Mark's Poetry Project, 245
St. Paul Baptist Church, 142, 161
Salt 'n' Pepa, 258
Sander, Ellen, 196
San Francisco, Calif., 144, 196, 225, 234,
    240, 262
  beatnik culture in, 210
  Haight-Ashbury district of, 210,
    212–13, 217
  hippie culture in, 210, 212, 213
  Joplin's first visit to, 208, 209
  rock music scene in, 213
San Francisco Chronicle, 228
Saturday Night Live, 236
Saturday Review, 170
Savoy Ballroom, 105
Scott, Jill, 98
"secret angels," 151
Seeger, Pete, 270
segregation:
  ending of, 136, 154
  in Harlem, 54, 58–59, 113
  Jim Crow, 5, 17, 28, 31, 55, 56–57,
    76–79, 107–8, 136, 154, 183, 205
  in New York, 57
Seidemann, Bob, 217
Sensation Seekers, 94
"separate but equal," 78
Sexual Politics (Millet), 245
Shangri-Las, 192, 197
Shanté, Roxanne, 257
sharecropping, 8, 32, 74
Shaw, Artie, 93, 107–10, 115
Shearer, Norma, 95
"Side of the Road," 268, 270
"sides," 50
Simon and Garfunkel, 176
Simone, Nina, 116, 253, 259
Simpson, Ophelia, 4
Sinatra, Frank, 132–33
singers, for big bands, 105–6, 253
singing:

  microphones and, 98
  technique vs. emotion in, 254–56
Singleton, Zutty, 45–46
Sioux, Siouxsie, 252
Siouxsie and the Banshees, 251, 252
"Sissy Blues," 18
"Skylark," 168
slavery, 3, 4, 10, 12, 40, 56, 67, 74, 175
Slick, Grace, 213, 215
Slouching Towards Bethlehem (Didion),
    209
Small's Paradise, 58
"Smells Like Teen Spirit," 264
Smith, Andrew, 38, 42
Smith, Bessie, xii, 6, 16, 20, 22, 23, 30,
    31, 33, 37–83, 39, 90, 92, 94, 98,
    99, 108, 120, 127, 129, 131, 142,
    143, 144, 149, 150, 151, 157, 159,
    162, 177, 183, 209, 211, 224, 225,
    235, 244, 245, 258, 259, 261, 266,
    270, 274
  background and early career of, 37–45
  bisexuality of, 19, 65, 66, 100–101,
    214
  black writers' appreciations of, 35, 56,
    79–81
  death of, 74–79, 82, 133
  descriptions of performances by, 46,
    60–63, 69–70
  film performance of, 26
  final recording session of, 72–73, 85,
    86, 88
  first recordings of, 48–52
  grave marker of, 81, 83, 230
  Holiday influenced by, 85–86, 130,
    167
  Holiday's recordings of songs by, 128
  as icon and image, 49, 53, 64, 81–83
  Joplin's copying of, 81–82, 83, 206–7,
    220, 284
  men's relationships with, 49–50, 52,
    65–66
  money earned by, 62, 68, 71
  number of recordings made by, 68

Smith, Bessie (*continued*)
  personality and character of, 38,
      41–42, 47–48, 53–54, 63–64, 68
  physical appearance of, 46, 60–61,
      70–71, 217
  popular songs in repertoire of, 71
  public persona of, 68–69, 73, 89
  Rainey compared with, 46
  Rainey's relationship with, 18, 42, 43
  record sales of, 52, 70
  reissue of recordings of, 79
  royalties denied to, 68, 284
  singing style and voice of, 43, 51–52,
      72–73, 80, 110–12, 119, 128
  stabbing of, 64–65
  topics in lyrics of songs of, 50–52,
      54–56, 62, 66–68, 72–73, 116,
      175, 192
  Van Vechten and, 54, 59–64
  white audiences and, 55–56, 60,
      62–64, 73
  writer's credit on songs of, 49, 66–67,
      148
Smith, Clara, 27, 49
Smith, Clarence, 42
Smith, Hugh, 76–79
Smith, Mamie, 27–29, 30, 31, 170
Smith, Maud, 42
Smith, Patti, xii, 245–46, 253, 261, 275
Smith, Trixie, 27
"Smoke Gets in Your Eyes," 71
"Soft Pedal Blues," 66
"Some of These Days," 25
songwriting credits, 49, 66–67, 147–48
Sonic Youth, 261
Sony, 79
soul, in singing, 47–48
Soul music, 143, 152, 160, 170, 241, 242,
      247, 252
"Soul Serenade," 173
"Soulville," 168
South, 29
  black church in, 40
  blacks' social role in, 40–41

crossover hits in, 170
James's touring of, 154–55, 158
Jim Crow segregation in, 5, 17, 28, 31,
    55, 56–57, 76–79, 107–8, 136,
    154, 183, 205
New, 38
Smith's white fans in, 56–57
Southern Comfort, 225, 294
Southwestern Presbyterian College, 40
Spears, Britney, 272
Spector, Phil, 192, 198–200, 254
spirituals, 10, 60, 231
Spivey, Victoria, 16, 68, 149
"sporting houses," 6–7
Springer, Joe, 115
Springsteen, Bruce, 30, 165
"Stand By Me," 135
"Star-Spangled Banner, The," 254–55
Stax recording studio, 171
Steinem, Gloria, 177
Stewart, Rod, 152, 236
Stokes, Moses, 18
"Stolen Sharpie Revolution," 261
Stoller, Jerry, 135–36, 138, 145, 171
Storyville, 239
  black district of, 5–6
  description of, 2, 5–7
  Desdoumes in, 4–6, 92
Straight Outta Compton, 257
"Strange Fruit," 112–17, 123
Streisand, Barbra, 247
Sue Records, 189
Sugar Baby Doll, 262
Sun Studios, 185, 201
Supremes, 191
"Swanee River," 12
Sweet Inspirations, 253
"Sweet Mistreater," 192
Sweet Old World, 269, 271

"'Tain't Nobody's Business if I Do," 128,
    261
Tan, 125
Tatum, Art, 162

Taylor, Billy, 72
Taylor, Koko, 12, 258
"Tea for Two," 71
Teagarden, Jack, 72
teen rebellion, 138–39
"Tell Mama," 43, 152, 175
Tennessee, 183
tent shows, see minstrel shows
Terrell, Mary Church, 33
"That Thing Called Love," 27–28, 29
Theater Owners' Booking Association
    (T.O.B.A.), 21–22, 36, 42, 68
Them, 245
"There Goes My Baby," 135
"Think," 176
Thomas, Carla, 247
Throwing Muses, 261
Till, Emmett, 136–37
Time, 99, 115, 116
Tin Pan Alley, 69
Titanic, 255
"Tommy," 192
"tough-girl" groups, 192, 197, 199
"Town Tattle" gossip column, 66
Traffic, 180
"Traveling Blues," xiii
"Tribute to a Lady," 132
"Trouble in Mind," 166
Tucker, Bobby, 98
Tucker, Sophie, 24–26, 27, 29, 280
Turner, Ike, xii, 103–4, 237
    abuse of Tina by, 103–4, 182–83, 191,
        194–95, 229, 232–34
    career of, 185–86
    character and reputation of, 185–88
    manager and record label of, 199
    relationship with Tina of, 188–90, 194,
        197–98, 202, 232–34
    see also Ike and Tina Turner Revue
Turner, Joe, 91
Turner, Tina, xii, 67, 179–80, 183–202,
        184, 215, 247, 256, 275
    awards won by, 237
    Buddhism and, 232–33

childhood of, 183–85
children of, 188, 194, 232, 236
divorce of, 234, 236
film based on life of, 237
Ike Turner's abuse of, 103–4, 182–83,
        191, 194–95, 229, 232–34
influence of, 182, 201
Joplin on stage with, 230
Los Angeles home of Ike Turner and,
        194
memoir planned by, 195
mixed racial heritage of, 185
name change of, 189–90
physical appearance of, 185, 188, 197
post-Ike rebirth of, 236–37
"River Deep, Mountain High" and,
        199–200, 254
as singer with Kings of Rhythm,
        187–89
singing voice and style of, 190, 192,
        198
stage persona of, 197–98, 220, 228
see also Ike and Tina Turner Revue
"Turtle Blues," 207
Twain, Shania, 255, 256
twelve-bar blues form, 8
"Twist, The," 146
2 Live Crew, 257
"Tyrone," 259–60

U2, 261
"U.N.I.T.Y.," 259
U.T.F.O., 257

Vanderbilt, Cornelius, 57
Vanderbilt family, 30
Vanity Fair, 60
Van Vechten, Carl, 19, 54, 135
    as patron of black artists, 59–60
    Smith and, 59–64, 79
    writings of, 59–60
vaudeville, 25
    blues style, 20
    see also minstrel shows

Vaughan, Sarah, 98, 104
VH1, 256
Victor Records, 24, 26–27, 30
Victrolas, 23, 27
Village Vanguard, 166
Vogue, 217, 253
voting rights, for women, 33, 82, 94, 193
Voting Rights Act (1965), 94, 193

Waits, Tom, 272
Walker, Frank, 49
Walker, Ruby, 23, 53–54, 61, 63–64, 65, 66
Walker, T-Bone, 8, 11, 143
Wallace, Sippie, 9, 16, 240, 258
Waller, Fats, 31
"Wallflower, The," 147
Wall of Sound, 199
Ward, Clara, 162
Warhol, Andy, 227
Warwick, Dionne, 247, 253
Washington, Dinah, 168, 270
"Washwoman's Blues," 33, 54
Waters, Ethel, 68
Waters, Muddy, 149, 152, 200, 240, 290
Watley, Jody, 251
Webb, Chick, 77
Webster, Ben, 112
"Weeping Willow Blues," 60
Weir, Bob, 234
Weiss, Mae, 109
Weiss, Sid, 109
"We Shall Overcome," 10
West, Mae, 104
Wexler, Jerry, 145, 253, 290
    Franklin and, 169–73
    term "rhythm and blues" coined by, 143
What's Love Got to Do With It, 237
"What's New," 129
"When the Levee Breaks," 240
White, Ted, 168, 169, 173
White, Walter, 115
white audiences:

blues and, 240–42
Chess Records' failure to reach, 152, 290
exposure of black artists to, 59, 202
in Harlem nightclubs, 58–59
James and, 152, 161
jazz romanticized by, 99–100
R&B and, 170
Smith and, 55–56, 60, 62–64, 73
at T.O.B.A. shows, 22
Whiteman, Paul, 24
white musicians:
    black songs "covered" by, 24, 147, 152
    as first to make jazz and blues recordings, 24
White Negro, The (Mailer), 211
Whitman, Walt, 246
Whitney Houston, 252–53, 295
Wild One, The, 138–39
Wiley, Lee, 106
Williams, Bert, 22, 27
Williams, Clarence, 6–7, 49, 50
Williams, Hank, 270
Williams, Lucinda, xiii, 247–51, 248
    blues and, 239–40, 249–50, 270–71, 273–74
    early career of, 239–40, 247, 249–51
    recent recordings of, 272–74
    recording industry troubles of, 267–72
    singing voice of, 247–49
Williams, Mary Lou, 17–18, 91
Williams, Miller, 270
Willis, Ellen, 221–22
Wilson, August, 79–80
Wilson, Jackie, 166, 167
Wilson, Teddy, 111
Wilson, Tony, 220
"Without the One You Love," 166
"W-O-M-A-N," 149, 175
"Woman of Heart and Mind," 243
women:
    blues lyrics' treatment of sexuality of, 15, 149–50
    California's new style of, 196

as "canaries" for big bands, 105–6
    drugs and, 155
    emotional coolness and, 119
    as gay icons, 104
    labeled "hysterical," 94, 119
    in labor force, 186–87
    modern movie images of, 95–97
    in 1980s music, 251–56
    in popular culture, 73
    in post–World War I era, 94
    race and sex and, 154
    standards of beauty and, 70–71,
        217–18, 253–54
    typical entertainment career trajectory
        for, 26
    voting rights for, 33, 82, 94, 193
    World War II era images of, 96
    see also blueswomen; feminism
women, African-American:
    chorus girls as ideal type of, 59
    hypersexualization of, 150
    job options for, 32, 33, 91, 186–87
    rap music and, 256–60
    social struggles of, 32–36, 64, 82–83
    standard of beauty for, 188
    voting rights for, 193
    see also blueswomen
Wonder, Stevie, 191
Woodson, Carter G., 260

Woodstock festival, 204, 219, 226, 241
"Work House Blues," 62
work songs, 8–9
"Work with Me, Annie," 144–45, 146,
    167
    Ballard's "answer" songs to, 289
    James's "answer" song to, see "Roll
        with Me, Henry"
World Without Tears, 273–74
Wyeth Laboratories, 155

X-Ray Spex, 252

Yippies, 212
"You Can't Keep a Good Man Down," 29
"You Give Good Love," 252
"You Know I Love You," 188
Young, Lester, 107, 118, 123, 172
"Your Hit Parade," 28
"Your Mother's Son-in-Law," 88
"You Should'a Treated Me Right," 67,
    193
youth culture, 43–44
"You've Got to See Your Mama Ev'ry
    Night," 25
Yo-Yo, 258

Zaidins, Earle W., 132
Zydeco music, 154